To Edward Bacon

with best wishes & many thanks for his help.

Yours sincerely,

[signature]

Oct. 1970

The Destruction of Knossos

THE DESTRUCTION
OF KNOSSOS

The Rise and Fall of
Minoan Crete

BY

H. E. L. MELLERSH

HAMISH HAMILTON
LONDON

First published in Great Britain 1970
by Hamish Hamilton Ltd
90 Great Russell Street, London W.C.1

Copyright © 1970 by H. E. L. Mellersh

SBN 241 01816 1

Printed in Great Britain by
Western Printing Services Ltd, Bristol

CONTENTS

ILLUSTRATIONS

between pages 88 *and* 89

Endpapers

Maps and Plans
(maps drawn by Patrick Leeson)

ACKNOWLEDGEMENTS

I should like to express my great indebtedness to Mr. Edward Bacon for his assistance and encouragement, as also to Professors S. Marinatos and A. G. Galanopoulos for their help and information: none of these is of course responsible for my views.

I would also like to thank:

Lord William Taylour for supplying prints of his photographs of the 'idols' referred to at the end of Chapter XV, and for allowing me to reproduce one of them;

the Librarian of the Institute of Archaeology, London, for help given;

the Keeper of the Ashmolean Museum, Oxford, for permission to reproduce the photograph of the replicas of the Mycenaean shaft-graves finds;

the producers and publishers of my *Minoan Crete* for permission to reproduce from that book the plan of the Palace of Knossos.

I am also greatly indebted to the translators of various classics from which I have quoted, particularly E. V. Rieu and his translations of Homer's *Iliad* and *Odyssey*; and to Penguin Books for permission to quote from these editions of Homer and from H. D. F. Kitto's *The Greeks*, and to Cambridge University Press for a passage from *Documents in Mycenaean Greek* by M. Ventris and J. Chadwick.

H.E.L.M.

Chapter I

Introductory: the Minoan–Mycenaean Synthesis

A KNOWLEDGE OF Knossos burst suddenly upon the world. When, in the first year of this century, Sir Arthur Evans began to dig on the site of Knossos near to Crete's capital city of Heraklion (then called Candia), the idea that the ancient civilization of the island should have any great historical significance was held by virtually no one.

Now it is very different. Evans unearthed at Knossos a civilization that had been almost entirely forgotten and not in the least suspected. This he called the Minoan. He had been preceded by the German Heinrich Schliemann, who, digging at Troy and at Mycenae in the Peloponnese, had proved that the Homeric heroes were a reality and not a myth and had brought to light another ancient civilization, which came to be called the Mycenaean.

The Minoans and Mycenaeans, and their interaction, have been the subject of study ever since—archaeological, philological, literary, theoretical. At times the discussion has broken out into acrimony; and opinions and beliefs have varied and changed. Put shortly, the steadfastly held opinion of Evans himself was that at all times the Mycenaeans were a comparatively unimportant and uncivilized people who owed practically everything to the tutelage of their powerful and highly sophisticated neighbours, the Minoans. Then in the early 1950's a slow reaction was brought to a head by the discovery that the 'Linear B' script found at Knossos and also on the Greek mainland was written in an archaic form of Greek. The boot, it was now declared, was on the other foot: it was the Mycenaean Greeks who were the powerful ones, and, though they may have learnt from the Minoans initially, they had soon overtaken them.

That reaction has lost its impetus; it is possible now to discern an intermediate interpretation that can command respect.

It is this middle-course interpretation that will be followed in this book. Undoubtedly the Mycenaean Greeks have been proved to have produced a greater and richer civilization than was until recently believed. But undoubtedly too the Mycenaeans owed a very great deal to the unique Minoan civilization that Arthur Evans unearthed. It is the inter-relationship of these two peoples and cultures that matters.

An effort will be made to unravel the tangled, or seemingly tangled, course of that inter-relationship. The theme will be that it was a highly fruitful one: it will talk in fact of a 'Minoan-Mycenaean synthesis'.

Such a synthesis is highly important historically. As a result of it there came, after the interval of a dark age, that amazing world experience, the flowering of classical Greece. This is an event that will always seem miraculous, and we are never likely to understand fully how it came about. We can, however, at least try to understand and go on trying. Generally, of course, it came about as a result of the previous history of the Aegean and Middle Eastern world. But it came about also—it must have come about—as a legacy from the Minoan-Mycenaean synthesis. It may not necessarily have been a wholly good legacy, though the result was good. But it must indeed have been a powerful one and one potentially beneficial.

Now the decline and destruction of Knossos and the Minoan civilization is likely to have been due largely to the Greeks, first and most importantly the Mycenaeans and finally the Dorian Greeks, though Nature, in the way of earthquake and volcanic eruption, clearly helped considerably. The Greeks, then, must have bitten back at the hand that fed them. That is true: there is not necessarily any justice in history. But what also seems true is that it was never a very vindictive bite; if more than a friendly and importunate nip it was not an amputation—which was very fortunate for the world.

What must always be remembered, nevertheless, is that the Minoans and the Mycenaeans were two very different peoples. The Minoan was of Mediterranean stock; the Mycenaean, for all he may have ruled over a similarly indigenous population, was an Indo-European. The two must have been as different as are arab pony and cart-horse, as greyhound and bull terrier, as gazelle and lion—all such similes are inaccurate but each perhaps holds a grain of truth.

The very difference itself may have been a fertilizing agent, more so than between similar types. The Mycenaean must have been a very forceful person. He was at one and the same time the bronze-clad hero of the *Iliad* and the *Odyssey* and also the rich merchant prince of the archaeological record (it will be one of the tasks of this book incidentally to show that the two images are not in fact irreconcilable). This Mycenaean, however, is a very different person from the artistic, hedonistic, vital but peaceable Minoan that the discoveries of Arthur Evans seem to show. The Minoan of the kiss-curl and bare bosom and flounced skirt of the court lady, of the romantic bravery of the bull-leaping toreador, of the subtle sensitivity of the ceramic artist, of the naïve but unfanatical religiosity of the upraised-armed worshipper—the Minoan is a unique creature, as surprising to us as it was to Arthur Evans and his helpers when they first demonstrated him to an astonished world. And yet, however different he may be from the Greek of the times of Pericles or Socrates or Aristotle, there is a traceable connection between the two. Perhaps it lies a little in the Spartans who so surprised the Persians when they combed their long locks before the battle; or in the athletes at the Games; or in the emotional participants in the Dionysian mysteries; even in that same Aristotle who sought with his young wife for biological specimens on the shores of Lesbos, since if he was scientist rather than artist he was, like the Minoan, displaying an impassioned interest in the beauties and patterns of nature. If Knossos had not risen in the time of the childhood of the Mediterranean peoples, had not survived through many vicissitudes and catastrophes, and had not finally fallen to a second wave of uncivilized Greeks who yet also possessed the Greek capacity to learn and benefit even from what they destroyed—if none of that happened, then later, classical Greece would never have become the Western world's most brilliant and unforgettable memory.

*

One final word by way of introduction, and by way of plea.

The evidence for the history of the Minoan–Mycenaean synthesis is fundamentally no more than the ancient legend and the dug-up artefact, and the reader is requested to bear that in mind. It is not easy always to be definite, indeed it is dangerous to be too definite. The evidence is inadequate, constantly being added to, and constantly being argued over. Any writer's interpretations will depend, finally, on his predilections—what appeals to him and his particular nature as the likely truth. The reader must hope that the present writer's predilections are sound and reasonable.

Chapter II

The Distant Past

IT SEEMS, on consideration, inevitable that the Mediterranean should have become the cradle of civilization, should be destined to be known as the Middle of the World. It lies on either side of thirty-five degrees of latitude, in a truly temperate zone; and it does not suffer, as do most other lands in that latitude, north or south, from the extremes of climate that are the lot of all solid land masses untempered by the presence of the sea. Here the sun shines but it does not scorch, at least not unduly, either the plants that are sun-lovers or the human beings who too are sun-lovers because their pigmentation is just sufficient to receive benefit and not harm. Throughout history—or it may be truer to say throughout most of history, and there may be significance in that 'most'—there has been enough rainfall for food-giving plants to thrive.

Yet the Mediterranean does not begin the human story. It would be truer to say that this role is taken by the Ice Ages. The Mediterranean, as it were, waits in the wings. It may even have been waiting for its own beauty and its own blossoming, separate from man's occupation, in that its climate was bleaker and wetter than in historical times. It is not unscientific or fanciful to think of it indeed as a Paradise or Garden of Eden, but with man led to it rather than created there—led by his own initiative and inquisitiveness, God-given no doubt, after a long and harsh period of apprenticeship.

The probationary period for the difficult task of earning a living upon this planet was the Palaeolithic or Old Stone Age, a long stretch of time to which we have given those alternative names but which would be better called simply the 'Hunting Age'. All men are heirs to that age; but the early civilizations are self-evidently a great deal nearer, with fewer subsequent accretions to the sum of culture and tradition to dull the memory. The overwhelming impression thus carried over to his successors by Hunting Man must surely have been

4

this: an intimacy with the rest of animal life. Indeed, he must have regarded it as precisely that, 'the rest of animal life', with no Christian or any other dogma to confuse or deny the simple issue. He, the 'naked ape' who, unaccountably, had lost his taste for a vegetarian diet along with most of his body hair, knapped his flint weapons not only with mouth-watering anticipation but with some solemnity and even awe at his temerity in seeking to kill these creatures so much larger, more potent, even more noble than himself. We talk with happy generalization of the 'Nature worship' of early human societies. But this is surely a later idea. For the hunter it is animal worship, or rather animal *regard*, a deep, puzzled, intimate regard, half proprietary, half humbly and hopefully companionable, such as a dog may feel for the kitten it has adopted, or a lonely king for his clumsy, half-witted jester. From this in general stems all totemism, so difficult for us to understand. And from it in particular must come the Cretan regard for the bull. That is something no easier to grasp; but, by inspecting its tremendous skull in some museum, we can at least conjure up in the mind's eye *Bos primigenius*, the huge aurochs. Palaeolithic man had truly some impressive beasts as his companions.

This necessarily brief outline of man's early history has already leaped forward to the times of the cave paintings, Lascaux and Altamira and the rest, which exemplify, as nothing else can, the strange deep intimacy just referred to; and, in passing, it may be noted that cattle are already the favourite animals for depiction, often as fierce and potent, but sometimes as—there is no other word for it—lovable and loving. These paintings are thought to date from about 20,000 B.C. By then *Homo sapiens* was a skilled and organized hunter, having existed as a species perhaps a hundred thousand years, and being the product, as three-quarter man, as half-man, as ape-man, and man-ape, of many more thousands of years, perhaps a million, perhaps two. There is only one significance in those vast aeons of time, and that is their vastness: change and development move with the slowness of organic evolution and not of history; the human intellect as a speeder-up of processes can be equated in its scope with the computer as a speeder-up of the abacus. At least we may believe that *something* out of all those aeons, some subconscious inheritance from the life that was being led, must have remained with the men of the early civilizations which for ourselves is now almost entirely lost.

If Old Stone Age man lived in a world of large and imposing animals that constituted at any rate a potentially full larder and a not over-difficult existence, he also lived, it must be remembered, in a harsh world of still existing ice reluctant to disappear. What is para-doxical, and significant, is that not only did he seem to flourish under those conditions but that he thrived particularly where they were most apparent. This was so, no doubt, chiefly because the animals most easily hunted shared his predilection for those conditions: the reindeer and the mammoth, for instance, in the tundra lands next to the ice-belt, and the horse and the bull and the bison in the adjacent territories, the open steppes. But it may also be that, strangely but encouragingly for our self-esteem as a species, man succeeds most dramatically where his environment is difficult and a challenge to him; certainly it is under such conditions that he is stimulated to invention and progress.

The New Stone Age or the Neolithic was certainly a time of challenge and progress. It was also a time when man, perforce, began to think in terms not of vast plains over which his animals roamed but in terms of sea-shores and forests and growing plants. With the final retreat of the ice the earth's smooth plains became as it were hirsute, growing on themselves the hair of forest, while the naked ape, having turned carnivore, very nearly had to revert to being a vegetarian. The times of the island-dweller, the age of the Cretans for instance, had not yet come. But the time when he was a possibility was fast arriving.

With the climatic change at the end of the Ice Ages and the natural geographical changes accompanying it, man was met with the sort of challenge that has spelt doom and extinction to many a more special-ized and less intelligent species. He was faced inexorably with a dreadful choice between three modes of action. He could remain and try to go on existing as before. That way lay extinction; for his quarry, the browsing and grazing animals, would largely trek north to follow the near-to-ice conditions of tundra and open steppe in which they also only could survive, leaving behind the unfamiliar and difficult forest. Or man could follow his prey. That was the choice that many took, and it was the more conservative one: leave one's home but not change one's way of life. And this trek of the last of the palaeolithic hunters, northwards until they became (to make a wide generalization) the Esquimaux, has been traced. The third choice was the hard one, the revolutionary decision. The heirs of those who took it were the founders of our world's early civilizations. They discovered, and followed, a new and fruitful way of life.*

The word 'fruitful' has here a quite material as well as a meta-phoric meaning. The men who took the third choice became the first partners with Nature as opposed to the mere rapers of her fecundity, predators upon her animate life. They became the first farmers.

That is the significance of the New Stone or Neolithic Age. It has been called the Neolithic Revolution, which indeed it was. But 'neo-lithic' is describing simply a result, not a cause. Man changed the shape and form of his flint tool because he used it in a new way. No longer did he only stab and tear and gouge, and scrape the skin of the animal killed. He put his flint on the end of a stick, and hacked the earth and hoed, so that the seeds he planted and tended might be encouraged to grow; he made an axe-head and hafted it, and hewed down the forest so that he might sow his seed. And in either process the flint became polished, so that he found it a good idea to polish it beforehand. In this way was born the tool which later archaeological discoverers were to consider as typical and consequently to give its users a name, *neo-lithic*, rather as if we were to call the motor age the spanner age or the smithy-turned-into-garage age.

No one will ever know which came first, the New Farmer or the New Husbandman, the man who has learnt to grow and tend crops or the man who has learnt to tame and tend animals. In either instance, it might well, for that matter, have been a woman, for such is the convention that a long palaeolithic past has implanted, that men do the 'manly' things, that is to say hunt and fight, while women take an interest in and perform the less heroic. As to priority, one may argue that standing crops would attract the wild animal and make him ripe for taming; or one may think of man's long-standing intimacy with animals and argue that domestication would be sure to come first. What seems to be a fact, and really rather a surprising fact, is that the two great inventions came at approximately the same time, give or take, that is to say, some hundreds of years, perhaps a thousand or so: one must be as vague as that.

But there is no need to be vague about the tremendous poten-tialities of the Neolithic Revolution, potentialities that were slowly but surely being realized. Gone were the changeless times, gone was

* See, for instance, *The Testimony of the Spade* (1957), a fine review of North and Middle European Stone and early Bronze Ages, by Geoffrey Bibby.

the happy hunting ground upon earth, where beasts—with a little magic encouragement, no doubt—proliferated obligingly, and there was scant need to trouble one's head with thought. Now, life was uncertain. There was the chance of starvation. There was also the chance of such a bumper harvest that time would be available to think of other, stranger, things.

One result of all this, and again surprisingly, was the movement of man about the face of the earth. This was not the beginning of total movement—the seas, even the inland seas, were still inviolate— but man's quartering of the land's surface in palaeolithic times was considerable. Again the ice helped him, by locking up so much water in frozen masses around the poles that land bridges existed that have long since vanished, across the Mediterranean for instance, down through the East Indies to Australia, probably across from Siberia to Alaska. So, beginning in the early times before *Homo sapiens*, the world had become populated, very sparsely but widely, and probably from one or two centres in East Africa and South-east Asia. And, following the beasts they hunted, or from sheer curiosity, men wandered, 'home' being where they found themselves.

Now, in neolithic times, travelling was continued, a little more sophisticatedly, less extensively perhaps but more purposefully. The herdsman guided his flocks to new pastures, or fluctuatingly to seasonal ones, or optimistically to where rumour had it better grazing land existed. The farmer, rapidly exhausting his soil, because he knew no effective way of replenishing its fertility, moved on similarly in a hopeful or a grimly essential search for fresh fields. Such treks were certainly not rapid affairs by any standard. They might last over generations, only stopping when the sea barred further progress or when such high fertility was found as necessitated no more than a shuttle service, back and forth within a defined area. That such treks could have been, for a tribe, extremely serious and quite total affairs is suggested by Caesar's experience at the beginning of his Gallic wars. The Helvetii were living very much a neolithic existence. Hearing rumours of better land in Cisalpine Gaul, they elected to move in entirety; and, so that there should be no hesitation among the less enterprising and no turning back, they burnt their villages before they set out.

With neolithic adventurousness went neolithic inventions. For the farmers, these included the cultivation of fruits as well as grains: the olive and the vine for instance. The fermented drink, in all seriousness, was a supremely important invention, and it must have been an old one. Both Homer and the Old Testament—the ancient laws of Deuteronomy, for instance—talk of wine with established familiarity; and one likes to think, surely not without reason, that Britain's Beaker People, because they produced such magnificent beakers, must have had something significant to put in them, finding a substitute in a colder climate for the grape they had left behind and producing beer instead.

And then there was the pressing need of containers, both for drink and for other products. So pottery was invented, the baked clay that takes on a new consistency and that, though certainly not unbreakable, is indestructible. The first inventor of the pot not only conveyed an invaluable boon on his fellows, and on the archaeologist of later ages. He bequeathed also opportunity, the opportunity for artistic expression, in shaping the pot and in decorating it. And he gave, curiously enough, great scope for man to display his conservatism as well as his artistry and inventiveness, the conservatism which caused the first pots often to be copies of other forms of container, the basket and the leather bag, and which displays itself in the persistence throughout a culture of a method of making or of decorating.

The next great field of neolithic invention centred round clothing. It is a long way from the scraped animal pelt to the rustling or gossamer dresses of the belles of Minoan Crete or New Kingdom Egypt, but the neolithic age took the first step in that journey, and more than the first step. It was convenient that many natural fibres would submit themselves, by their constitution, to be twisted into a continuous thread. It was clever of man to discover the convenience. And it was clever of him, also, to extend the principle of withy-weaving or basket-making to the new entity he had created.

Finally we come to that invention which had particular significance for Crete since it enabled the island to be discovered and populated: the ship.

No doubt many a palaeolithic man bestraddled a tree-trunk that lay half rotting in the river, rolled off it again, but managed to use it to reach the river's further bank. Very likely it was a palaeolithic man who succeeded in making an animal skin more or less airtight, and blew it up and used it to help himself swim the river. The conquest of the globe's most ubiquitous element had begun. But it was a pretty feeble beginning. To hew out from the tree-trunk a reasonably seaworthy boat would surely need the *neolithic* man's smooth axe. As for an even passably efficient sail, that would require the art of spinning and weaving. It would also demand considerable intelligence and inventiveness to realize the possibilities, not to mention courage to make use of them. The Nile, we are told, has this advantage for the would-be sailor, the stream will carry him down whereas the prevailing wind will carry him up. It seems very likely, therefore, that the first really successful sailors were early inhabitants of that civilization which the Nile alone made possible, the Egyptian.

Inventions are spread by man, and with surprising rapidity. One may therefore safely envisage the New Stone Age man, wherever he is, using the sailing boat for his daily business. And what a godsend this was, what a saving of effort. No more did he need to make his way through thicket and forest, no more up craggy mountain and over boggy depression. Now he glided easily over the smooth and shining water. Of course it was not always smooth, the gods below were even more moody and unpredictable than those above. But there was always propitiation. And hope. And courage.

The really courageous person is he who, like Tennyson's Ulysses, explores 'beyond the utmost bounds of human thought' or at least of average human imagination, and has the temerity to venture beyond this straight clear line of the horizon over which one fell to—what? Coast-hugging in a ship is one thing, though heaven knows that can be dangerous enough; island-hopping, where the next landfall can be seen, is one thing. But to sail out into the unknown, hopefully and bravely beyond the horizon, is very much another. No doubt the first men to do it did so by mistake, blown or carried by currents off their course. Some of these must have had tales to tell, of unknown islands glimpsed. Finally, some anonymous pioneering hero must have set out on purpose to sail beyond the horizon, and others must have followed. They were not palaeolithic people; no island that was obviously out of sight of other land in those times shows any trace of palaeolithic occupation. But the neolithic revolution, it has been safely established, started around the Eastern Mediterranean; and so it may seem likely that that sea's out-of-sight islands would be amongst the first in the world to receive human visitation, and colonization.

Crete lies in the middle of the Eastern Mediterranean, where the sea is narrowest, less than two hundred miles from either the African or the Anatolian coasts, out of sight of the Greek islands, but with the fingers of the Peloponnese insistently pointing towards her.

Indeed Crete was asking for, waiting for, human occupation. In neolithic times it received it.

The temptation to imagine that first landing should perhaps be resisted, for it can lead to no increase of knowledge. But Crete is beautiful and at that time it may well have been more beautiful still. It would smell of thyme and the sun's warmth, a scent that would come to those adventurers before ever they landed. The mountains were noble, and the valleys fertile. Perhaps they landed in the south where later King Rhadamanthus would have his summer palace, and they would see the twin peaks near Mount Ida, where their descendants would believe the god Zeus was born. Perhaps they would see a fine specimen of the wild aurochs grazing—and leave him severely alone.

The date? Strict chronology is the bugbear of the archaeologist, but he has to face it. Probably, then, around 6,000 B.C.

The people? Here also there can be no very definite answer. But the fact has no great significance. For the people are sufficiently far back in time for the island itself to shape them. They would be followed by others, by waves of others perhaps, and from different places. But they are all likely to have been of the prevailing Mediterranean type, 'dark whites' as they have been called, dolicho-cephalic or long and narrow headed, little and lithe and slender and graceful. That is enough for us to know.

Chapter III

Neighbours and Educators

THE OTHER early civilizations differ from the Minoan. For one thing they arrive rather earlier. But that is not the main difference.

They are great-river civilizations. Here seems to emerge a sort of necessary phase in the evolution of human society. With the Yantgse and the Indus Valley civilizations we need not be concerned: the latter in any case does not seem to have been wholly original. It is the two great civilizations, of the Twin Rivers, Tigris and Euphrates, and of the Nile respectively, that are important for Western history in general and for the history of Crete in particular.

They were, in a way, civilization-made-easy. Mention has been made of the early farmers' need to move on after exhausting the soil. In the Tigris-Euphrates delta and in the Nile Valley there was no need to move on. Those who had the initiative to go there—and the prospect may not have looked altogether inviting—found in the first of these two instances waters that were over the years slowly receding to leave rich fertile silt, and in the second instance a river that obligingly produced the same results by a yearly inundation. In both countries the inhabitants rapidly learnt to make better use of these phenomena by skilful irrigational control.

Here in fact lay the secret of progress. There was prosperity to be had, but not with complete ease, as on a Polynesian island. *Dolce far niente* would not be possible. But, more than ever before, there would be sufficient ease to stimulate thought and inventiveness.

Before favourably and admiringly sketching these two pioneer civilizations, Egyptian and Sumerian, it is justifiable to make a point of contrast with the forthcoming Minoan. It is the contrast, to put it at its extreme, between mud and sparkling water, between dull flatness and exhilarating mountains—no wonder the Hebrews, and no doubt others, sang, 'I will lift up mine eyes unto the hills'! Too much could easily be made of this. But if a country shapes a people, then

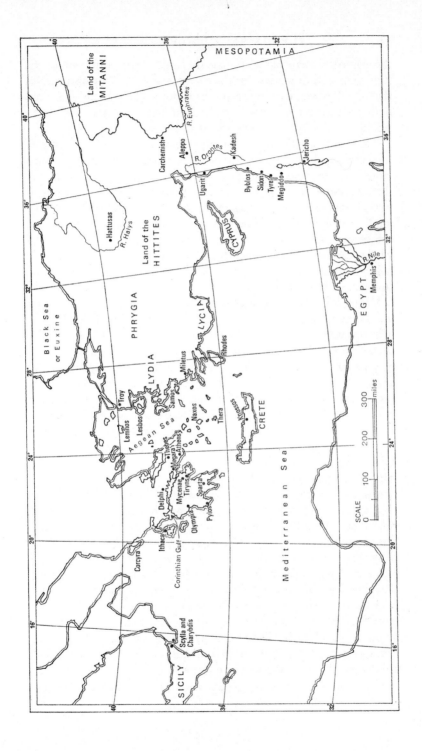

the Minoans were likely, to say the least, to be different to the Egyptians and Sumerians or their successors the Babylonians. Not that the Egyptians or the Sumerians were likely to develop into dullards, that would be going too far. But they were more likely to be placid and to acquiesce in regimentation.*

That they would need regimentation was certain. Laws and human control would be necessary. If Nature is to be harnessed on a large scale, then such control is something that cannot be done by the individual. Irrigation is a communal affair, wherein if one man were to implement his wishes unchecked they would be likely to be totally detrimental to his neighbour. The same fact applies to the use of the harvest: however prolific it may be, it will not last the whole year round, nor enough be left for next year's sowing, if there is lacking some over-riding authority that will impose a system of storage and check the improvident.

Hence, it may be said, priests and kings. This is not the place for a philosophical dissertation on the growth of civilization. But the Minoans were certainly both heirs to and, in a later way, contributors to the process. That the word 'priest' should be coupled with 'king' may perhaps seem surprising. But one must always remember the absolutely fundamental, one might say the incurable, religiosity of early man. The priest is the man with 'know-how'. And he receives it, beyond anyone's doubt, from God, from the gods, from the power and the spirit, the *mana* behind all material things. He is given that power, or he achieves it; and he is set apart from the rest of mankind by the possession of it. The yearly life-giving inundation of the Nile happened to coincide with the appearance over the horizon of the firmament's brightest fixed star, Sirius. The Egyptian priests learnt this; and it was not chicanery on their part but common sense that they should keep the knowledge to themselves and acquire priestly power from the knowledge. After all, it might not happen next time, if by their magics they did not ensure that it did. Such is but one example of how priestly power was achieved, and regarded. As for the king, he was the embodiment of *mana*, the mouthpiece and instrument of divine power. He might be priest-king himself, or figurehead or even puppet of the priests, in an infinite variety and gradation of roles: that in Crete he never seems to have become this last, whereas in Egypt sometimes he did, is no doubt the reflection of a difference between the two civilizations.

* The Indus Valley civilization appears to have been most highly regimented.

One other aspect of the early river-supported civilizations, to which Crete was also inevitably heir, was of paramount importance. A division of labour developed rapidly. Food production was so easy that everyone need not be a farmer; on the other hand some other types of production were so difficult that everyone could not be a farmer. The mud-flat river valley, however desirable in one way, was less so in another. It was a very special habitat, in fact a specialized one. There existed for instance no stone for tool-making: it had to be fetched. Thus the traveller and the merchant came into being; trade was born. And trade soon spread to other things besides necessities. The great and important men—and their wives—needed things of significance and beauty, or if they did not need them they wanted them. The craftsman was born. Also, since what comes from outside tends to seem more significant and more beautiful, the merchant found himself another job.

And so on. There is no need to particularize further. There was growing up in the world that first elaborate entity, first nucleus of civilization, the city-state. This was a paternal, as well as a theocratic, affair. The king, the priest-king, the 'Tenant Farmer of God' (as he was called in Sumeria), had his palace, and the palace was everything. It was administrative centre, central storehouse, temple, seat of the sole employer. No one questioned the arrangement. It was a system that would be copied and have great powers of persistence, as will be seen when considering the palace-citadels of Crete and Mycenaean Greece.

As the Fourth Millennium B.C. gave way to the Third and as the Bronze Age in the Near East approached, Egypt and Sumeria went their parallel and not dissimilar ways, still well ahead of any other civilizations. Both developed writing, the Egyptian hieroglyphics having the advantage over the Sumerian cuneiform in that it could be painted on papyrus as well as incised on stone, an advantage the Minoan script must have inherited, though whether it was ever made use of we do not know. Both are somewhat inefficient tools of expression compared with the Phoenician alphabet, though brilliant inventions in all conscience. The written word gave added power to the ruler. His messengers could carry his orders to the utmost limits of his domain. His clerks could keep tally of his possessions, both inanimate and animate. He could set up his edicts for all to see, and perpetuate his boasts.

The large domain, the empire, was in fact in process of formation.

With it comes another invention, war. One need not subscribe to the myths of a Golden Age or the Noble Savage to believe that warfare was a comparatively late occupation of man. Territorial ambition is the great begetter of war; and when men are scarce upon the face of the earth and there is territory to spare there is little need to fight. Here is something from which the Minoans, safe in their self-contained island, for a long time did not suffer, though in the end they did not escape.

Personal ambition also engenders war, as it does an empire. There enters into history the 'famous name', the name that comes down to us of the conquering hero, the founder of a nation. In Egypt it is Narmer, in Sumeria it is Sargon. Narmer amalgamated Egypt of the delta with Egypt of the river, to form the combined Upper and Lower Kingdom (in his famous palette one can see him doing it symbolically, seizing an unfortunate native of the watery lands by his top-knot); and ever after the pharaohs would wear a double crown. Sargon, supported by a favourable myth that also was to bolster up Moses, that of being saved by providence from watery death in his cradle, overthrew one of the Sumerian city kings who was a tyrant and, moving further north, away from the enervating swamps, founded his new centre of empire, Akkad or Agade, and in the process injected a new element, a Semitic one, into the possibly over-pacific blood of the Sumerians.

The middle of the Third Millennium, the time of the use of copper and very soon the inception of the Bronze Age, of which in their different ways the Minoans and the Mycenaeans were such brilliant exemplars, has been reached. Most of the rest of the world would live on for some centuries in a neolithic age; much of it, including Britain, had not yet emerged from the palaeolithic age. But in and around the Eastern Mediterranean much prosperity and sophistication had been achieved. Palestine had its cities though all around the more primitive-living pastoral people roamed. In the heights of Anatolia and of upper Mesopotamia two virile nations were forming, the Hittite and the Assyrian. But Sumeria and Egypt, the two great pioneers, still led the advance, each quietly developing its skills and its ideas, both of which were exportable. Egypt was building its pyramids. Sumeria had already learnt to stage its spectacular funerals.

Before closing the chapter it may be useful to look at these two last-mentioned facts. For they embody not only ideas, which always have significance, but religious ideas that mattered particularly to the

Bronze Age world and so therefore to the Minoans. There is something rather pleasantly appealing about Minoan religion, so far as one can understand it. It appealed to the Greeks—so far as they could understand it. But it was not fundamentally different from the religions of the older civilizations, all having common roots in the neolithic concept.

Around 2600 B.C. people began to build pyramids; and some three hundred years earlier, outside the city of Ur, people had staged the spectacular holocaust of the funeral of Queen Shubad (unearthed by Sir Leonard Woolley in the 1920's). The pyramid is a house for the dead king whence, having joined the gods, he may spread his benign influence over the still living. As for the dead Sumerian queen, trundling down the ramp on her ox-drawn wagon into her vast grave, seventy-four of the living were sent to die beside her: here is working, in anxious, confused, hopeful minds, something of the same concept as the Egyptian, a belief not only in an after-life but in an influence upon the living by the great ones who have passed over, an influence importuned in this case by the solemnity and extent of the sacrifice.

There survives in this Sumerian instance something of the dark aspect of primitive neolithic religion, with its gruesomely practical realization that blood poured into the earth is an excellent fertilizer and the mystical belief that went with it in the cycle of life arising from death. The Minoans seem on the whole to have happily freed themselves from this darkness. The point to be made here, however, in seeking to assess the influence of the earlier civilizations upon the Minoans, is a wider one. Bronze Age man—and neolithic man too, for in this matter there was little difference—was essentially a religious man. Not economic man, not political man, not a man of any particular nation; but, more fundamentally than any of these, religious man, yet in a sense very different from any interpretation modern man would place on the word and in any case difficult to understand.

That difficulty, however, can be exaggerated. In all descriptions of primitive religion one will find much discussion as to whether it is sun worship or moon worship or earth-mother worship or animal worship. But exactly what sort of worship it was, or we think it was, matters very little—and in any event 'worship' is probably the wrong word. Neolithic and Bronze Age religion, wherever it may be, is awe, plus superstition, plus belief in magic power, plus a very practical desire to bend that magic power to one's own good. The desire could exert itself in many ways, from the bloodiest of mass sacrifices, through comparatively mild omen-seeking and omen-influencing, to that most cheerful pleasuring of the gods by spectacular ritual and ecstatic dancing which also pleased the human performers and spectators. That the Minoans were particularly fond of this last form of religious observance and apparently were not overwhelmed by superstition must have helped considerably towards that breakthrough, via the Mycenaeans, to the clear, unsuperstitious, logical thinking which the classical Greeks achieved.

*

A point half-way through the Third Millennium has been reached in this sketch of the early pre-Minoan civilizations, without the mention of more than a couple of proper names. They will begin to come soon enough, the well-documented pharaohs in their dynasties, Hammurabi, the law-giver of Babylon, and so on. But so far the names are mostly not more than semi-mythical, heroes of folk-memory that embody in their person perhaps a happening, an achievement, or the exploits of several persons rolled into one. Such is the Sumerian Gilgamesh, who with his brute-minded but faithful companion Enkidu (an earlier and more benign Minotaur?) met many adventures, sometimes defied the gods, and in the underworld had speech with the immortal Utnapishtim, whom the Hebrews were to call Noah and the Greeks Deucalion, a name also given to a Minoan king. Or there is the Egyptian Imhotep, the prototype of the clever man, the hero-inventor, who had his equivalent in Minoan Daedalus.

Unhappily it would seem that the Minoan names that have come down to us, as also the Mycenaean, must all be called mythical. Heinrich Schliemann, however, when he excavated at Troy and Mycenae, destroyed for all time our disrespect for the myth.

Chapter IV

Knossos a Name: the Myths and Stories

A MIDSUMMER NIGHT's dream, a fairy tale, a science-fiction story: Homer's *Odyssey* is all of these. The clues it gives to the truth about ancient Crete are the most tenuous of all. One may therefore begin with them.

Odysseus, that 'resourceful man' whom the Romans called Ulysses, was on the last lap of his remarkable journey home after he had done so much to bring about the fall of Troy. Shipwrecked for a second time, he was washed ashore on the island of Scheria, the land of the Phaeacians. Now Scheria will be found on no map, ancient or modern.* But then neither will one find the island of the Lotus Eaters, or of Circe or of Calypso, though Sicily, the home of the one-eyed Polyphemus, and Ithaca, the home of Odysseus himself, are real enough. At least we know that this hero, when not wafted into Cloud Cuckoo Land, was in the Mediterranean; and if that sea is made to appear a vast and limitless one, we may reflect that perhaps it would also seem so to us, were we in a not very efficient sailing boat or on a raft. By the kindness of his protecting goddess, Athene, Odysseus is washed up on this island of the Phaeacians; and the suggestion is that she could not have done better for him, since here are a great and powerful trading and seafaring people who will have the ability and the kindness to see him home. We know from archaeological evidence that the Minoans on their Mediterranean island were a great trading and seafaring people. Who else then could the

* However, one of the ancient sources does place the mythical Phaeacians on a real island, that of Corcyra (Corfu) in the southern Adriatic. This was Appolodorus, when he is recounting the story of Jason and the Argonauts, told in greater detail by his predecessor Appolonius.

Pausanias, writing in the second century A.D., says that the people of Corinth have a tradition that Scheria *was* the old name for Corcyra. But this is very tenuous evidence; and Corcyra had achieved, by the time of the writing of the *Odyssey*, no such great prosperity as could possibly have led to the tradition of the splendid and graciously living Phaeacians.

19

Phaeacians be? It is very hard to say. This is purely negative evidence; but as such it is quite powerful. Scheria is not Crete. But neither is Robinson Crusoe's island the isle of Juan Fernandez, and if Swift used fact for fictional purposes why should not have Homer?

It is indeed an idyllic picture that Homer paints. He does so of a purpose, of course, to show what luck had at last befallen his hero and how clever the man was going to be in exploiting it: we must be prepared to do some heavy discounting if we wish to take the island of Scheria as a true reflection of the island of Crete.

Yet you need only visit Mallia, one of the unearthed palaces of the Minoans, and on a day of clear autumn sunshine walk down to the bright sandy shore and bathe in its utterly pellucid waters. Then you will find it not in the least difficult to believe in Homer's idyllic story. Or at any rate in the opening of it.

Princess Nausicaa and her handmaidens also had been bathing, somewhere on the shores of Scheria. They also had come down from a king's palace, though they had had 'a smooth-running mule-cart' to take them. The thought had entered young Nausicaa's head—a thought planted there by the goddess Athene so that the crucial meeting might take place—that she might bring her washing down to the stream's mouth and the shore, and combine the useful chore with a little fun, bathing and a game of ball. Her father, King Alcinous, favoured the scheme and ordered the mule-cart to be made ready; her mother, Queen Arete, favoured it too, and had a picnic prepared.

Odysseus meanwhile, cast up naked and exhausted and having found a sheltered spot by the mouth of the stream, lay fast asleep. However, a shriek from one of the girls as the ball fell in the stream awoke him. He proceeded to behave like a perfect gentleman, and Nausicaa like a perfect little lady.

We must resist the temptation of making fun of this naïve idyll, as we must also of recounting it in detail. It is there for the reading. In short Odysseus is clothed, brought home, presented, made much of, feasted, and finally provided with a boat, manned by stalwart Phaeacians, to take him back to his native land. In the process the Phaeacians tell Odysseus a good deal about themselves and their country. It is this that is interesting.

First Princess Nausicaa boasts a little of the magnificent city to which she is about to conduct her guest. He will see the fine harbour for instance. 'It is here that the sailors attend to the rigging of the black ships, to their cables and their sails, and the smoothing of their oars. For the Phaeacians have no use for the bow and quiver, but spend their energy on masts and oars and on the graceful craft they love to sail across the foam-flecked sea.'*

Odysseus, for propriety's sake, is left to make the last part of his journey alone. When he asks the way of a girl carrying a pitcher he is speaking in reality to his patroness the bright-eyed Athene, who is certainly taking good care of her protégé. He must follow her without asking the way of any others, she warns, 'for the people here have little affection for strangers and do not welcome visitors with open arms. They pin their faith on the clippers that carry them across the far-flung seas, for Poseidon has made them a sailor folk.' An insular folk, too, in fact and in more than one sense of the word: there is a hint of a less idyllic reality here.

Odysseus follows his guide, gazing about him with admiration, at the fine buildings and fertile gardens; an admiration that increases as he reaches and enters the palace of the king. The walls are of bronze 'topped with blue enamel tiles'. Over the seats that are ranged round the great hall are 'delicately woven covers that the women have worked . . . for the Phaeacians' extraordinary skill in handling ships at sea is rivalled by the dexterity of their womenfolk at the loom'.

Already it is late in the evening, and Odysseus is not feasted that day but merely fed. He is, nevertheless, given the promise of a manned ship to carry him home. This will be, it is King Alcinous's boast, regardless of how far across the sea Odysseus's home may be: 'Nor does it matter if the spot is even more remote than Euboea, which is said to be at the world's end by those of our sailors who saw it, that time they took red-haired Rhadamanthus to visit Tityos, the son of earth.' Here is the only allusion to an actual Minoan personality; but there are so many names mentioned that we cannot legitimately make very much of this.

The next morning, after the promise to Odysseus is solemnly ratified at the marble-seated place of assembly, comes the full and proper feast. It must indeed have been a lengthy affair, for Odysseus, caught weeping when the bard's song is none other than that of his own exploits at Troy, is moved at last to reveal his own identity and in addition to tell of all his adventures after he had departed from the defeated city. There follows, in true Homeric style, games in the

* This and the following quotations are taken from E. V. Rieu's translation in the Penguin Books edition.

famous guest's honour. A little contretemps now arises. An unman-
nerly guest taunts Odysseus for not taking part himself; whereupon,
of course, Odysseus shows them what he can do. He takes the discus,
and 'the Phaeacians, lords of the sea and champions of the long oar,
cowered down as it hurtled through the air'. It far outstrips all the rest.
Odysseus follows this by a little judicious boasting: he could beat
them all at boxing and wrestling and with 'the polished bow' if he
tried. Whereupon the king makes the following reply, interesting to
us and surely more conciliatory than the old boaster deserves.
Odysseus, the king observes, is no doubt justified in his speech and
action by the boorish treatment he has received. But: 'When you are
banqueting in your own home with your wife and your children
beside you, and the talk turns on what the Phaeacians excel in, I
want you to be able to tell your noble friends that Zeus has given us
too a certain measure of success, which has held good from our fore-
fathers' time to the present day. Though our boxing and wrestling
are not beyond criticism, we can run fast and we are first-rate sea-
men. But the things in which we take a perennial delight are the
feast, the lyre, the dance, clean linen in plenty, hot baths and our
beds. So forward now, my champion dancers, and show us your
steps, so that when he gets home our guest may be able to tell his
friends how far we leave all other folk behind in seamanship, in speed
of foot, in dancing and in song.'*

All was accordingly arranged, the sacred dancing floor swept, and
Odysseus was soon being impressed by 'a band of expert dancers, all
in the first bloom of youth'.

In due course Odysseus, loaded with gifts, is making his sentimental farewells to the beautiful white-armed Nausicaa and is
stepping into the Phaeacians' lovely curved ship. These ships, King
Alcinous explains, have no steersmen and have but to be told of their
passenger's destination: 'Our ships know by instinct what their
crews are thinking and propose to do. They know every city, every
fertile land. . . .'

So, with that fairy-tale boast, this description of a fairy-tale island
that Minoan Crete may well have inspired is ended. Odysseus did
indeed reach home—to meet, significantly, a situation as anarchic

---

* By Roman times the mythical Phaeacians, perhaps because of the order in
which the king here lists their predilections, had earned the reputation of having
been gluttons, Horace using the word as synonymous with gluttony. This could
hardly be applied with any justification to the slim-waisted Minoans.

and unhappy as did some other of his companions, though by his wiliness he dealt more effectively with it.

The Minoan mythology gathers way with something less contrived and artificial. These are the stories that have survived about the legendary King of Crete, the famous King Minos, including, of course, his dealings with the Athenian Theseus, in which he comes off a very second best.

All the stories are Greek. It is not for nothing that in any collection of peoples' myths and legends those of the Greeks will fill the largest section. The Greeks had a great past and they knew it; they collected, therefore, the tales of that past and recounted them, if with a variable degree of belief, at least with care and respect. Homer was the first to write them down, in the eighth or seventh century B.C.; then the poets of the early fifth century, lyricists such as Pindar and Bacchylides, tragedians such as Euripides and Sophocles. There is Herodotus of the same century, a historian who travelled to pick up his evidence and was not above re-telling many a story, being careful to make it clear, however, that he did not necessarily believe them implicitly himself. And there are—much later—a Greek of Alexandrian times, Apollonius Rhodius, and four Greeks of Roman times, Diodorus Siculus, the better-known Plutarch, Apollodorus, mythologist, and Pausanias, voluble traveller. The Augustan Romans, Ovid and Vergil, merely borrowed, for their own purposes, the latter adding his own inventions; but no one will deny that they told their tales well, and at least they were considerably nearer to the times they wrote of than to ourselves.

The Greek legends distinguish between two kings named Minos, and it may be that the title denotes a dynasty. The first Minos was son of Europa, a nymph of Phoenicia whom Zeus took the trouble to seduce, appearing out of the sea in the shape of a bull and carrying the girl back with him to the land of his birth, which was Crete. This Minos had two brothers, Rhadamanthus and Sarpedon, and the three ruled the country jointly. They quarrelled, however, and Rhadamanthus left for Greece and Sarpedon for Asia Minor, to rule respectively over the Boeotians and the Lycians.

Minos I was above all a great law-giver, as indeed was also his brother Rhadamanthus*, both becoming after death judges in the

* There is a story that Heracles once took advantage of a Rhadamanthine Law, that of justifiable homicide in self-defence: Heracles had killed the brother of Orpheus, who had had the temerity to hit him over the head with a lyre. . . .

underworld. Like Moses and Hammurabi, Minos claimed divine authorship for his laws—'familiar friend of Zeus', Homer called him—and was also said to have inspired a later mythical law-giver, Lycurgus of Sparta. In order that his country might be protected, Minos got Hephaestus, the great god-artificer, to make for him and bring to life the giant Talos, a sort of bronze policeman or coast-guard, who patrolled the island thrice daily and threw stones at intruders—until the wicked Medea pulled out his plug and let out all his life-blood or ichor.

Minos II is a more real character and a formidable one, great in love and war. We meet him first sacrificing to the gods in the Cycladic island of Paros, over which presumably he also ruled. While doing so he hears that the Athenians have killed his son Androgeus. He at once, 'being master of the sea', sets out in revenge. He fails to capture Athens and moves on a few miles westward to Megara, where he is more successful. Success comes through the wiles of a woman, the Princess Scylla, who for love of him cuts from the head of the king, her father, the famous purple lock of hair the lack of which weakens both him and his city's power of resistance. Minos rewards the girl not as a lover but as an upholder of morality, having her towed to death in the wake of his ship after she has attempted to board it.

Returning to Athens and having no greater success, King Minos prays for help to his ancestor, the immortal Zeus. Zeus visits a plague upon the city; and to buy off the curse the Athenians agree to send an annual tribute of seven youths and seven maidens 'without weapons', as Apollodorus puts it. 'to be fodder for the Minotaur'.

So we come to the famous story of Theseus and the Minotaur, which has great significance in the interpretation of the causes of the fall of Knossos. It is the story of the besting of Minos, and if not of his end then of events that led to his end. Theseus, it must be realized, is a great man on many counts, one of the Athenians' greatest heroes.

Queen Pasiphae, having borne her husband Minos several children, proceeded to develop an unnatural passion for a bull—not a particular bull apparently but bulls in general. Minos's prize artificer, Daedalus, and an Athenian who already seems willing to do a disservice to the king to whose court he has fled, exercises his practical genius by making a wooden decoy cow into which the queen can insert herself. The unholy alliance is effected and the result is a bull-headed monster which has to be kept in the inner recesses of a maze called the Labyrinth and there fed on human flesh. This is the dreaded Minotaur (or, in Greek, 'Minos-Bull') for which the Athenians are bound to supply the 'human fodder'.

The story is taken up by Pausanias, who relates that King Minos, on the third occasion of the collection of the tribute, had come over to Athens to do his own choosing, rashly picking the Athenian king's son Theseus amongst the youths and a certain comely Periboea amongst the maidens. Minos sailed back with them and on the way he could not keep his hands off Periboea. Meeting opposition from Theseus, who had appointed himself protector of the band of intended victims, Minos taunted the proud prince, particularly on his claim to be descended from the sea-god Poseidon. Let him, declared Minos, retrieve this ring, and promptly threw one into the water. Theseus dived for it, and came up with not only the ring but for good measure a golden crown, gift of Poseidon's wife.

Some say that this episode occurred in the harbour of Knossos, where the Cretan king met the boatload, Theseus having come not at Minos's choice but of his own free will, and that the exploit led Princess Ariadne to fall in love with him. All versions agree, of course, that the king's daughter did fall in love with Theseus—but one could expect little else.

. Then there came the crucial trial of strength. Only later versions talk of anything so crude as a magic sword given to Theseus by his lover. But all agree about the clue box, containing a thread, which Theseus was to let out so that he might find his way out of the Labyrinth, the idea inevitably emanating from the ingenious Daedalus.

The Minotaur is duly slain, Theseus returns by the aid of his thread, makes good his escape with his band of victims intact, and takes with him the infatuated Ariadne as well.

Then the story takes an unexpected turn, or at least an unsentimental one. Apparently princesses who throw themselves at the heads of enemy princes must not expect handsome treatment. Ariadne's fate is better than Scylla's but that is all that can be said. She is left behind by Theseus at the first call on the way home, on the island of Naxos, where the god Dionysus takes pity on her.*

* Ovid makes Princess Scylla, inveighing against King Minos for his scorn of her, exclaim: 'Now, indeed, I am not surprised that Pasiphae preferred her bull to you: of the two you were the more savage!'—an invention of the Roman poet of no deep significance but some neatness.

As for Theseus, he goes on with his career. He commits the famous act of forgetfulness that any modern psychologist would say was subconsciously intentional, failing to change his sails from black to white as a signal of success, which omission makes his watching father dive in despair into the sea and so earns Theseus the throne. Later, he marries Ariadne's younger sister Phaedra.

Minos, abandoned and betrayed by his daughter, concentrates his need for vengeance on Daedalus, who has helped in the rebellion. He follows him to Sicily, whither the latter has, literally, flown, losing his over-ambitious son Icarus on the way. In Sicily Daedalus has to be found. He is caught by his own ingenuity. Minos carries about with him a puzzle: how to insert a thread through a spiral shell. Daedalus, shown it, hits on the idea of harnessing the thread to an ant and letting that creature do the work for him. It does so and more, for Daedalus, by his tell-tale ingenuity, is discovered, and summarily killed. Minos then meets his own fate, when he is killed in his bath by the daughter of the king of Sicily, at whose court Daedalus has been discovered.

These are the Greek legends which relate to Crete in her heyday, but what is one to make of them? It is not being irresponsible or unhelpful to say that almost anything can be made of them and that the mythologists and anthropologists in their time have done so. One needs discipline as well as imagination and erudition for the task. There will be attempts at interpretation as this book proceeds, but at this stage three points can be safely made.

The first is that the impression is given that the Minoans were, in strange ways not easily understood, obsessed with bulls. The second is that here is depicted, at the time of Greece's own early myth-ridden history, a powerful kingdom extending over the seas beyond the shores of Crete itself. The third is that Crete and Greece are considerably bound up together and that Greece, originally in a subservient position, seemed in the end to emerge triumphant.

*

Finally, in the realms of mythology, two quotations from Greek literature have a bearing upon the decline and fall, rather than the peak of power, of the Minoan civilization.

The first has the ring of authenticity. It is from Homer, not the fanciful *Odyssey* but the *Iliad*, which is full of factual detail which the archaeologists and philologists and historians later then Grote have so often proved correct.

Homer in the *Iliad* is describing a set of incidents occurring in that long siege of Troy which the alliance of Greek kings undertook in order to avenge the abduction by a Trojan prince of the daughter of one of their number, the Spartan Helen. It is written some four or five hundred years after the event, which however is a proved historical fact; it is a collection from earlier epic poems, recited by the court bards of the times; and is a strangely mixed collection of anachronisms, romantic imaginings and authentic, circumstantial detail.

An outstanding example of this circumstantial detail is the famous list of ships that comprised the Greek expedition and their provenance. It is a long catalogue full of names; but, with the beauty of those names and the poetic adjectives of description that are added, the whole passage reads with a glorious romanticism. The names are real enough, however; as time goes on and archaeologists continue their work they are being proved more and more real. Agamemnon of Mycenae, leader of the expedition, has of course the largest contingent:

> The troops that came from the great stronghold of Mycenae, from wealthy Corinth and the good town of Cleonae; the men who lived in Orneiae and in lovely Araethyrea; in Sicyon, where Adrestus reigned in early years; in Hyperesie and in steep Gonoessa: in Pellene and round Aegion: in all the length of the coast and the broad lands of Helice—these, in their hundred ships, King Agamemnon son of Atreus led.

Next in the size of his fleet of ships comes old King Nestor, from Pylos in the west of the Peloponnese, who contributes ninety. Then Diomedes commands eighty ships, manned by Achaeans from Tiryns 'of the Great Walls' and Troezen and the island of Aegina. And tying with him, also with eighty ships:

> The illustrious spearman Idomeneus led the Cretans: the men from Cnossus, from Gortyn of the Great Walls, from Lyctus, Miletus, chalky Lycastus, Phaestus and Rhytion, fine cities all of them; and the other troops that had their homes in Crete of the Hundred Towns.

'Crete of the Hundred Towns': Homer is fond of repeating this resounding phrase. And Idomeneus is depicted as one of the true brotherhood of Greek heroes at the siege of Troy. He does not do anything spectacular; but he is among the nine noble comrades who volunteer to fight the very redoubtable Hector as deputies for Helen's husband Menelaus who, everyone believes, would be beaten.

King Idomeneus is, according to Apollodorus, the grandson of Minos II. He also, significantly, encountered misfortune on his return from Troy, as did so many of the Greek heroes; he in fact met the identical situation that faced Agamemnon and Odysseus, insurrection and intrigue in his absence. In this case his rival, Leucus, 'the White', having already made himself master of ten of Crete's towns, managed to turn him out of the country altogether. There is another story of Idomeneus being banished from his country on his return from the Trojan War, because his behaviour had brought about a plague or pestilence. This pattern of events continually reappears: each hero returning from the Trojan War seems to encounter trouble, and thereafter the story abruptly ends. Of Odysseus and Achilles and Agamemnon and Nestor and the rest we know the fathers and the grandfathers, but of their sons little or nothing and of their grandsons nothing at all. It is the same with King Idomeneus of Crete.

The final clue in any search through the literature of ancient Greece for news of the Minoans is to be found in Plato's Atlantis, another dream-land, another Phaeacia, built however not for a pretty tale but as a political, a Utopian, example. Atlantis has caused more starry-eyed, lunatic-fringe re-creations of history than any other ancient myth. The geological evidence, however, makes it fairly plain that if there was ever a continent where the Atlantic waves now roll then it was in a distant past measurable in millions and not thousands of years; and that conclusion rules out, except for the wilfully blind, all question of habitation by *Homo sapiens*.

As for the possible Cretan connection, it is memories of a Utopian society we are concerned with, not an historical account of it: the positioning of the mythical island in the Atlantic may well have been no more than a convention, as the Celtic Island of the Dead is also placed in the Western Ocean.

What is interesting is that Plato describes Atlantis as disappearing in a great cataclysm. This is where to many modern minds the fact of an historical cataclysm becomes significant. Some time in the middle of the second millennium B.C. the southern cycladic island of Thera suffered a terrific volcanic explosion. The island, now called Santorin, is at the present day purely a volcanic island; and its volcanic crater is twice as big as that caused by the eruption of Krakatoa in the East Indies in 1883. That eruption killed 35,000 people and, besides raining down ashes, sent out a tidal wave fifty feet high which actually reached Cape Horn, over seven thousand miles away. There is now a growing belief that the Thera catastrophe was the cause of the greatest physical catastrophe suffered by Knossos.

This belief will be dealt with in greater detail in due course. The point to be made here concerns the added evidence this spectacular cataclysm offers in support of Plato having Knossos and the Minoans in mind when he made references to the tale of Atlantis.

These occur in the *Timaeus* and the *Critias*, discussions that purport to follow the long exposition by Socrates of a Republic or ideal state. They illustrate, as it were, the ideal state in action and embody an account of war between *two* ideal states, an earlier Athens and an 'Atlantic Island' situated outside the Pillars of Hercules. The tale is said to have been related to Solon, the founder of the Athenians' true and not mythical greatness, when he visited the priests of Egypt in their city of Sais. 'Solon, Solon,' they said, 'you Greeks are always children,' possessing no support or discipline from a body of remote tradition. They then proceeded to tell him what happened nine thousand years previously, thus neatly establishing the conception, pleasing as it would be to Plato's readers, that Athens would be easily the most ancient state in Greece.

The Atlantians, under 'a powerful league of kings', having subjected to their rule Libya and Tyrrhenia (central Italy) attacked both Egypt and Athens. Athens, however, 'surpassing all others both in magnanimity and military skill', prevailed, and thereby 'ensured likewise the most ample liberty for all of us without exception who dwell within the Pillars of Hercules'. Subsequently, however, came 'violent earthquake and deluges', which resulted both in desolation for these first early Athenians and also the total disappearance of Atlantis beneath the waves.

The second and longer reference, in the *Critias*, concerns the glories of Atlantis and not of the early Athenians. It is only fair to mention descriptions that would seem to have no connection with Minoan Crete as archaeology has revealed it to us, as well as those that do. There is a reference to elephants for instance and the island is imagined with a ring of canals. There are fortifications, and military barracks, and ten thousand war chariots. There are also buildings lined with silver, roofed with ivory and pinnacled with gold;

but that extravagance can be attributed to the sort of poetic enthusiasm that was still being indulged in when Coleridge wrote of
Xanadu.

More in line with what may be imagined of the Minoans from the
works of art they have left behind is that they built in 'variegated'
style 'by way of amusement'. They constructed temples, palaces,
docks, canals and harbours, these last 'full of vessels and merchants
coming from all parts, causing from their multitude all kinds of
shouting, tumult and din all day long and the night through'—a
likely touch. As to the king's palace, in its centre was planted the
temple 'difficult of access', and as a whole its excellence 'was proportioned to the magnitude of the government and also to the order
observed in the sacred ceremonies'. There were fountains and baths,
'the kings' baths and those of private persons being apart'. For the
rest, there were strict but human laws, and much prosperity, coming
not only from maritime trade but from the island's natural fertility,
'warmly acclimated' as it was and with its fairest of mountain-domi-
nated plains, its timber-forests and its rivers.

At the centre of the island was a column on which were inscribed
the laws, and here every five or six years was administered demo-
cratic justice. What goes before is of interest:

> And when they were about to judge, they previously gave each other
> pledges, according to the following fashion:
> As there were bulls grazing at liberty in the temple of Poseidon, ten
> men only of the whole number, after invoking the god to receive their
> sacrifice propitiously, went out to hunt swordless, with staves and
> chains, and whichever of the bulls they took, they brought it to the
> column and slaughtered it at its head under the inscription . . .

Then a goblet was filled with the blood of the bull and a solemn
libation made and a communion oath taken. No one is likely to have
invented completely such a curious and idiosyncratic custom. Later
there will be an examination of the pictures, on the Vaphio cup and
elsewhere, of the 'swordless' capture of bulls, and also the magnificent bull's-head rhyton; and we may then remember Plato and
believe that he certainly had some memories or other of Crete on
which to elaborate his theme.

Finally, Plato, through the mouth of Critias, does not fail to point
his Utopian moral. The Atlantians 'practised mildness united with
wisdom . . . and contentedly bore, as a burden, the mass of gold and

other property; nor were they deceived by the intoxication of luxury, or rendered intemperate through wealth'. Not for a time, that is to say; but there came a day when they could no longer uphold these divine and lofty virtues; and when that day came Zeus visited upon them their just retribution. . . .

The true fate of Knossos was not so neatly illustrative of poetic justice as Plato made out nor so simple. However, a considerable research has been made of late years at Santorin, and the result has been a steady strengthening of the belief that Plato did have the Minoan civilization in mind when he described his Atlantis and that he was recounting a true historical happening when he told how it came to its end.

Santorin now shows dramatically what must have happened and what a tremendous cataclysm must have taken place. Instead of being one large island as Thera once was, there are now three islands forming the best part of a circle round a small central fourth, which they face from dark volcanic cliffs across a lagoon of great depth: the island was in fact blown to pieces.

A. G. Galanopoulos, a seismologist who has been the most active in these researches, has, with the help of Edward Bacon, archaeological editor of the *Illustrated London News*, written a book on the subject (*Atlantis*, 1969). The authors first deal with all other theories as to the true origin of Atlantis and duly demolish them, to their own and probably most readers' satisfaction, including all the theories that would place Plato's mythical Utopia in the Atlantic Ocean. The suggestion is then made that Plato, in dating the catastrophe to 'nine thousand years ago', has muddled his interpretation of the Egyptian signs for *thousand* and *hundred*, so that 'nine hundred years ago' was intended (in other words 1500 B.C.), thus bringing the date to one that lines up most satisfactorily with that given by scientific evidence (carbon-14 dating of organic material from Santorin: 1410 ± 100 B.C.). The probability of this mistake is reinforced by the fact that Plato's other large numbers seem much more understandable when similarly divided by ten.

The main contribution of the book comes from a careful study of the island itself. It is shown first that considerable archaeological evidence exists of a Minoan civilization of the right date in Thera. Then the present shape of the battered island is taken into account. Plato, it is recalled, speaks both of a royal city and also of a fortified metropolis; and the latter is shown to fit remarkably closely to the present central island, whilst the former fits very well to a description of Crete. In other words, the authors are claiming that Plato's Atlantis represents a memory of a Minoan civilization which possessed an offshoot—perhaps one of many such—in the island of Thera. The volcanic explosion completely destroyed the latter and also did such damage to the former so as virtually to end its existence—a fitting punishment for having the temerity to oppose the growing might of Athens.

*

As will be seen, however, the latter deduction by Plato can by no means be wholly accepted.

Chapter V

By Way of the Archaeologists

I T IS obvious that sooner or later the Mycenaean and Minoan
sites would be explored by the archaeologists. What mattered
were the people involved and the timing.

On the whole, posterity has been fortunate. The job might have
been done earlier, in the 'forties and 'fifties of the nineteenth
century for instance, when, as in Mesopotamia, men were keen only
on tearing out from the earth spectacular 'pieces' that could add to
the prestige of their particular national museum. It might have been
carried out much nearer to our own times, when expenses would
have been enormous, funds hard to obtain, and consequent control
tight and inhibiting. In fact the job was done—the important initial
job—around the turn of the nineteenth and twentieth centuries, and
by two men who had command of their own funds and were most
certainly not inhibited. Heinrich Schliemann and Arthur Evans were
two of the most uninhibited men in the world.

Both have left their imprint so ineradicably on what they did that
it is important to know about the men and their excavations. Our
understanding of the history they helped to unearth, our mental
picture of the civilizations they discovered, are inescapably affected
and coloured by them and their interpretations. Both excavators
were a law unto themselves; but this is even truer of the Englishman
than of the German, and Evans's discoveries were in the end more
extensive and more important.

The career of Schliemann shows what can be done by the posses-
sor of a simple faith and a one-track mind. Schliemann was an extraordinary man and he must have been a pretty un-ordinary boy. At
the age of seven, he tells us*—and there is no reason to do more than
make slight allowance for romantic self-dramatization—he was
poring over a picture of Troy in flames and arguing hotly with his
father that, however fanciful the picture, something of that walled

* In *Ilios, City and Country of the Trojans* (London, 1880).

city must remain. He was also imbibing a romantic interest in the past from his father, who although only a poor parson—poor, apparently, in most senses of the word—possessed a genuine historical enthusiasm. Already the young Henry was showing a literal-mindedness and naïveté that never left him. He lived in a deep country district of northern Germany, and local legends, of which there were many, told for instance of a near-by mound where was buried a child in a golden cradle, and also of a pond from which a maiden was wont to rise holding up a silver bowl. 'My faith in the existence of these treasures was so great,' wrote Schliemann, 'that whenever I heard my father complain of his poverty, I always expressed my astonishment that he did not dig up the silver bowl or the golden cradle.'

Tragedy came to the boy's family when he was nine, the year being 1831. His mother died, and his father, convicted of adultery, was dismissed from his parsonage, Heinrich was sent to live with an uncle, received a patchy education, and at fourteen was apprenticed to a grocer, there to live out for some years a miserable, drab and overworked existence. Schliemann's passionate romanticism, however, had not left him. There followed now the second of the self-described incidents which are so much in character and which one must believe. One day a miller's apprentice, whom drunkenness had dragged down from better days, called at the shop on business. He proceeded, at what spur is not evident, to recite Homer in the original Greek 'observing the rhythmic cadences of the verses'. 'Although', continues Schliemann, 'I did not understand a syllable, the melodious sound of the words made a deep impression on me, and I wept bitter tears over my unhappy fate. Three times over did I get him to repeat to me those divine verses, rewarding his trouble with three glasses of whisky, which I bought with the few pence that made up my whole fortune. From that moment I never ceased to pray to God that by his grace I might yet have the happiness of learning Greek.'

A few years later, a pale and ardent young man prone to tuberculosis, he was learning Greek. He was learning a number of modern languages too, setting aside half his exiguous salary as a shipping clerk to pay the fees. He was beginning to exhibit a flair for business, and he had the determination to do two things, to acquire learning and to acquire wealth. He did both, the first self-taught, the second acquired in the roles of merchant and then banker. It was not until

1863, when he was forty-one years of age, that he retired from business and began his second career, of lone and amateur and self-supporting archaeologist.

One of his first acts was extraordinary but typical of the naïve, humourless directness of the man. Having divorced his first wife, he asked a friend to search out for him a Greek wife: 'She should be poor but well educated; she must be enthusiastic about Homer and about the rebirth of my beloved Greece . . . She should be of the Greek type with black hair, and, if possible, beautiful. But my main requirement is a good and loving heart.' He got all that, which was surely more than he deserved. It is not many prospective brides who have to pass an examination before their wedding day, and fewer whose examiner is their intended husband. But young Sophia, thirty years this serious German's junior, carried it all off with flying colours: 'When did Hadrian come to Athens; what passages of Homer do you know by heart?'—she gave satisfactory answers. What was more to the point, she carried off the marriage with flying colours too. She bore Schliemann a son, christened Agamemnon; she proved a loyal co-worker and a delicately skilled excavator (which was more than Schliemann was), and she and her family added guile to loyalty in helping to outwit the Turkish authorities and save from the probable fate of being melted down the golden 'treasure of Priam' which she and her husband had found at Troy. That treasure included a beaded headdress. Convinced that it had once graced the brow of Helen, Schliemann reverently placed it upon the head of his young Greek wife. That was an act of sentimentality so magnificent as to raise it to the plane of historical significance, the fact that Schliemann had got his dating wrong and that the diadem could never have been Helen's detracting little if anything from the significance.

This romantic German was seeking, it might truly be said, to unearth not history but Homer. Homer had told how the earliest of Greeks had banded together to avenge the wrong wreaked upon one of their women, the ever fair Helen, and had sailed to Troy to carry out, with some vicissitudes, their purpose. Schliemann regarded his self-appointed task as, essentially, to prove that Homer had told a true story and that Homer's Greeks were real Greeks. He went about his task therefore, and almost literally, with Homer's epics in hand. First he visited Ithaca, the reputed home of Odysseus, and then Mycenae, the home of the leader of the Greeks, Agamemnon. He did a little digging and met with no spectacular success; and then, impatient and imperiously drawn thither, he transferred himself across the Aegean and in the wake of the thousand ships to Troy itself. His real work had begun.

To date, there had been little digging at Troy but considerable search for and discussion concerning the exact site. The favourite choice was near a village called Bournabashi, eight miles from the sea, where an imposing rocky height looked as if it ought to be the scene of the great epic and where optimists thought they had discovered two springs of different temperature which tallied with Homer's description of the twin sources of the river Scamander, boiling and freezing respectively. Schliemann came along, tested thirty-four springs and found them all of the same temperature as no matter, considered the traditional site of Troy near to the village of Hissarlik and on a less imposing height, pointed out that the distance to the sea was here three miles and not eight, which tallied with more than one reference in the *Iliad*, and began to cut a slice through the site.

He came upon walls, in fact walls upon walls, and arrived at the conclusion, rightly, that there had been many cities of Troy, each built upon the ruins of its predecessor. But he was convinced, wrongly, that the Troy of the *Iliad* must be deep down, at the bottom. And the lowest walls were mean affairs, nothing like the 'topless towers of Ilium'. He was bitterly disappointed. He persevered, however; and did discover, first a paved road and then traces of a considerable towered entrance, each with accompanying signs of fire. That was enough for Schliemann. He announced to the world that he had discovered the Scaean gate, from above which captive Helen and her father-in-law Priam had surveyed the scene and before which Hector and Achilles had fought.

The power of orthodox learning in the eyes of the self-educated can be surprising. The experts, particularly those of his own nationality, poured scorn upon Schliemann's claims; and Schliemann was horribly daunted.

He decided in fact to give up, to cease his labours. Then was enacted one of those romantic occasions that sometimes do happen in real life. On the very last day before that set for the end of the dig, Schliemann found his great cache of golden rings and bracelets and goblets, his 'treasure of Priam' that included the famous 'jewels of Helen' with which he decked his wife.

The immediate result of this discovery was a violent quarrel with the Turkish authorities which followed upon his success in keeping his finds out of their hands. After a lawsuit, and in due course, Schliemann transferred his attention to Mycenae.

Here again he followed his usual practice of believing and acting upon what he read; and here again his literal-mindedness paid off. Pausanias had said that the main royal tombs at Mycenae were to be found *within* the palace walls. Antiquarians prior to Schliemann had found these walls, and also imposing tombs—unfortunately rifled and bare—that were *outside* them. Nevertheless, regarding the terrain within the walls and finding it rocky, they had announced that no one could have sunk graves there and that therefore the walls referred to by Pausanias must have been an outer ring now disappeared and that their graves were indeed the royal ones: satisfied with their explanation but empty-handed they went their way. Schliemann simply dug where Pausanias indicated he should dig, rock or no rock, and came upon unrifled graves of unexampled magnificence.

Here in all conscience was Homer's Mycenae 'rich in gold': gold toilet boxes and gold-studded dresses for the women, beautiful gold-inlaid daggers for the men, some sad little princes or princesses wrapped entirely in gold sheeting, and for the men again, 'pompous in the grave', gold breastplates and gold masks for their faces. Here Schliemann made his second magnificent sentimental gesture. Though they immediately crumbled to dust on exposure to the air, the men's faces beneath their masks were recognizable as such. Schliemann pulled off the most magnificent of the masks, and had the greatest moment of his life. 'I have', he telegraphed to the King of Greece, 'gazed upon the face of Agamemnon.'

That Schliemann was once more proved wrong is again of little significance. His gold-masked monarch was proved later to be a Mycenaean king of some three centuries earlier than the Homeric hero. Nevertheless Schliemann had shown that Agamemnon's Mycenae was, like Troy, very real, and that it had indeed been rich as Homer had said, and rich before Agamemnon's time too. He had in fact proved what he had set out to prove; he had demonstrated that the Grotes of this world were wrong when they refused to credit myths and legends with having no grains of truth embedded within them. He came to England to lecture, and was acclaimed by all, from the classically educated Prime Minister, Gladstone, downwards: 'I was received as if I had discovered a new part of the globe for England!' he wrote ecstatically, and his self-esteem and confidence were restored.

He built himself an imposing house in Athens, in which he set out his treasures and entertained the famous and the enquiring. He excavated twice more at Troy and also again at 'Homeric' sites in Greece. The chief of these was Tiryns, not far from Mycenae, to which stronghold Homer had given the truthful epithet 'of the great walls'. There he discovered frescoes of distinctive style which were to interest Arthur Evans more than their discoverer, also traces of a great hall or *megaron* that tallied strikingly with the description of the same thing in the *Odyssey* and so pleased Schliemann himself.

In 1886, seeking yet more Homeric sites, Schliemann bethought himself of Knossos, visited the site, negotiated for its purchase, but failed to achieve his purpose. There are two stories connected with this failure, each of which illustrates a significant aspect of Schliemann's character. The first is that, on being shown the site, he fell on his knees and offered up a little prayer of thanks to Zeus for safely guiding him there, an act which sadly shocked the Moslem owner. Here was Schliemann the romantic. The other story is that he checked on the number of olive trees stated to be growing on the site being offered him, and finding that he was being cheated to the extent of 1,612 trees, forthwith broke off the negotiations. Here the practical, direct-minded businessman was gaining the ascendancy, and with results that, had he lived, he would no doubt have come to regret. The next year, hurrying home to wife and Athens, he ignored, against doctors' orders, a severe ear infection and died at Naples in his sixty-sixth year.

Schliemann had always thought in terms of Homer, and had shown little interest in aspects of the civlization he had disinterred that did not have a bearing on his belief that these 'Aegeans', later to be called Mycenaeans, whose artefacts he was discovering, were indeed the people who had made the famous trip to Troy. He did in fact consider that he had proved conclusively that the two peoples, the disinterred and the storied, were one and the same. That is the assumption which coloured all his work. It could be, and indeed can still be, disputed, though it would now be very difficult to do so with any show of reasonableness.

*

In Athens in 1883 two men of very different genius had met: Heinrich Schliemann, with only four years to live, and a young man with hardly more than a third of his life behind him, Arthur Evans. This is how Evans* later described his predecessor:

> Something of the romance of his earlier years still seemed to cling to his personality, and I have myself an almost uncanny memory of the spare, slightly built man—of sallow complexion and somewhat darkly clad—wearing spectacles of foreign make, through which—so fancy took me—he had looked deep into the ground.

Was then Arthur Evans also a romantic? Perhaps so, but in a different way. His was a romanticism not childlike but sophisticated and—if this is not too much of a paradox—scientific. He was the art connoisseur who yet sought to see the human story behind the art he surveyed; he was the expert detective who yet dreamt of following clues to thrillingly successful conclusions. Evans had, in 1883, gone to visit Schliemann with his wife; and 'they laughed,' writes Evans's biographer,† 'at the odd little man and his preoccupation with Homer.' But 'Arthur,' she continues, 'found his gold work from Mycenae beautiful, exciting, and puzzling: it was not of a kind that appealed to him, because it was not classical: but how did its quasi-Assyrian and quasi-Egyptian elements come to be combined with the Aegean . . . ?' How indeed? Evans was being drawn unconsciously towards the task that was to make him famous.

The formative background of Arthur Evans was not so romantic as that of Schliemann's—unless of course it is wrong to call a struggle against poverty romantic. His father was Sir John Evans, very much an archaeologist in his own right and also a rich man, being head of the paper-making business of the Dickinsons, into which family he had married. Arthur therefore grew up in an atmosphere of affluence and of business and intellectual success, in the midst of a large, ramifying but close-knit family of much self-assurance and, it must be said, of mutual admiration: though by inherent nature humble rather than arrogant, he was never likely easily to brook criticism or accept denial.

---

* In his preface to the English edition of Emil Ludwig's *Schliemann of Troy* (1931).

† Joan Evans, his half-sister, in *Time and Chance, The Story of Arthur Evans and His Forebears* (1943). (Taken out of its context the quotation may give the wrong impression unless 'then' is inserted before 'appealed'.)

Arthur had in his early manhood drifted into, rather than entered, that activity which early brought him a modicum of fame and which in some ways coloured the rest of his life. He travelled in the Balkans, and fell in love with both the land and its peoples. Moreover, he found those peoples struggling against the effete and tyrannical rule of the Turks, and he fell in love with them all the more for their bravery in that struggle. Blessed with the power in his pen to express both his admiration and his indignation at the tyranny, he became correspondent to the *Manchester Guardian* under its newly appointed editor, C. P. Scott. Having shown himself as brave and courageous as the insurrectionaries he admired; having earned the hatred first of the Turks and then of the Austrians, whose tyranny had been exchanged by his unhappy friends for the earlier Moslem one; having alienated by his rashness the sympathy of his own government, he in due course and in the year 1882 found himself incarcerated in Ragusa (now Dubrovnik) gaol. With the help of some family wire-pulling at home and some intrigue on the spot (including the classic ruse of containing messages in loaves of bread), he was released and expelled. He came home, looked for a congenial job, and found it—or so he hoped—in the curatorship of Oxford's Ashmolean Museum.

Though Arthur Evans was not above employing the ruses of classical antiquity to help him get out of prison, he had little love for scholastic classicism in general and less for the particular brand of it favoured in the Oxford University of the time. There is no need to go into detail; but the facts have some bearing on Evans's later outlook and the attraction for him—perhaps inherent but also partly induced—of art that demonstrably was not classical. He found the Ashmolean in a miserable state and being run, or rather neglected, by a clique of dons, with the formidable Jowett at their head: they—at any rate in the estimation of Evans—had no proper conception of archaeology at all and thought of it, if they thought of it at all, as a sort of bastard, or nuisance, appendage to true classicism.

Evans won his battle to modernize and revivify the Ashmolean, but at an expense of time, intrigue and patience that left him exhausted and utterly disgusted. One of the advantages of the Keepership of the Ashmolean was that considerable absences were allowed, so that the holder of the office might the better refresh and equip himself. Perhaps the authorities rather encouraged this undeserved scourge to absent himself; in any case Evans, always anxious to shake the dry, academic dust of Oxford from his feet, was not slow in obliging.

So, as the 1880's changed to the 'nineties, Evans was acquiring a new interest. It was an interest in primitive systems of writing, one that had already attracted his father, and one that appealed to the evolutionary sense which he had always possessed, the sense of historic development and the desire to trace things back to beginnings. Already he had found traces of such early writing as far apart as Lapland and the Alpes Maritimes; and in particular there was that part of Schliemann's collection which had interested him, the hieroglyphics on some of the 'bead-seals', archaic forerunners of the signet ring. In her biography Joan Evans has this to say: 'Evans was extremely short-sighted and a reluctant wearer of glasses. Without them, he could see small things held a few inches from his eyes in extraordinary detail, while everything else was a vague blur. Consequently the details he saw with microscopic exactitude, undistracted by the outside world, had a greater significance for him than for other men; it was this cloistered vision that fostered his power of seeing and interpreting details in coins and engraved gems.' That is not at all a fanciful idea: the interests and predilections of all of us are probably more influenced by our type of eyesight than we ever imagine.

Early in 1893, and this time alone, Evans was again in Athens, examining Schliemann's collection of bead-seals and doing his best to collect more of them. Then, he was hurrying back to his wife who was gravely ill, and then holding her hand while she quietly sank to her death. Evans was overwhelmed with grief; though it has to be added, in illustration of his independent and in some ways insensitive character, that in dragging her round Europe, not always overwillingly for her own part, or in leaving her while he followed his bent and travelled alone, Arthur Evans certainly did not help his wife to achieve longevity.

So in the spring of the next year, 1894, now and for the rest of his forty-seven years of life a childless widower free to travel abroad virtually as much as he wished, and—to be fair to him—no doubt anxious to assuage his grief in activity, Evans at the age of fifty-two started a new life and began the career for which he is famous. He arrived in Crete.

He did not fall on his knees and offer up a prayer to Zeus when he arrived at the site of Knossos. He examined the tentative diggings that had been lately made and, as he confided to his diary, 'I copied the marks on the stones, some of which recall my [seal-stone] "hiero-glyphics"'. Nor when he began to negotiate for the purchase of the site did he bother about the number of olive trees on it. Nevertheless the negotiations proved as difficult as Schliemann had found them, if not more so. It was Crete now that was in the turmoils of revolt against the Turk—a fact which of course intrigued and pleased Evans, as well as possibly nearly costing him his life; he listened unmoved to a tale that fanatical Moslems had been attempting to waylay and kill him at night. It was not until the last year of the century, with Crete freed at last from any vestige of Turkish rule and quietening down under the administrations of King George of Greece, that Evans was able to start his famous excavation.

He had, naturally, not been idle in the meantime. He succeeded in buying half the Knossos site, but then met endless obstruction in negotiating for the second half. He turned aside, remembering his *Manchester Guardian* and Ragusa days, to help the victims of the recent revolt and civil war. There were long, adventurous and arduous travellings to other ancient sites on the island. There was the determined search for more of those engraved gems, which he had found in Schliemann's collection and in the dealers' shops of Athens.

It is this last activity that gives the clue, not only to Evans's reasons for tackling the excavation of Knossos but also for his basic outlook, which never changed. It was the seal-stones for which he was searching. The Athens dealers had told him that most of those that they possessed came from Crete. And in Crete he did find them, 'galopetras' or milk-stones as the peasants called them, precious artefacts that had survived for three and a half thousand years to be put to a new magic use, as talismans ensuring to their lucky owners, when they were nursing mothers, that their suckling babes would thrive.

The initial cause for Evans's interest in these bead-seals was, as has been said, his new interest in primitive hieroglyphic writing of all kinds; and it is a double irony that, first of all, he was never able to decipher the Cretan scripts which he did find and, secondly, that the final transliteration of the last of these should have been most instru-mental in upsetting his own theories and casting doubt on his own system of dating. That is, however, something that should not be stressed too much. For, whatever his initial interest, Evans had wider aims from the start. Not by any means did all the seal-stones have hieroglyphics engraved upon them. Many showed neat, stylized portrayals of animals, bulls and the like; some displayed intriguing scenes of worship and other human activities. These interested Evans almost as much as the hieroglyphics. They were so different from anything coming from that over-scrutinized source from which he was now reacting and from which nobody else seemed able to escape, the classical source. They were unique, yet they showed perhaps Egyptian, or Mesopotamian, or Syrian affinities. And then some came from Mycenae and, as Schliemann would have put it, from other 'Homeric' sources, whilst others, not recognizably different, came from Crete. Evans, the historically-minded, the evolution-minded, was stirred to his depths. As with every system of hieroglyphics, so with every culture: it had its predecessor to which it owed its development; it had its successor, to which it bequeathed development.

That was, and was to remain, Evans's unchanging outlook: how did the civilization he was about to disinter connect with what lay behind it and what lay before; how had it been influenced and how had it influenced?

Chapter VI

Knossos the Reality

ON NO account must familiarity be allowed to dull one's appreciation of the wonder that Arthur Evans performed. Under the earth, and not so very far under it, lay the material evidence of an unsuspected and almost entirely forgotten civilization. Time and weather, and the force of gravity that makes things tumble, and the fertility of nature that covers what tumbles, and the indifference of man, which causes him to leave what he has made when his interest shifts—all these potent forces, positive and negative, had covered the material evidence of the life of ancient Crete.

Here, if the legends had any basis of truth, the streets had lain with their fountains, amongst those edifices built for pleasure's sake 'in variegated style', under the shadow of the palace wherein lay the temple 'difficult of access'. Here the sailor had stridden fresh from the near-by tumultuous port of Amnisos where he had been attending to the rigging of his black ship; here the sacred bull had been led, captured by the swordless trapper; here the youths and maidens had danced and sung, proud of the peaceful reputation their land possessed.

All this—or something different, nobody was yet to know—lay waiting for the spade of the archaeologist. With luck it would be a careful spade directed by a knowledgeable archaeologist endowed with a vivid but disciplined imagination. Knossos was in fact lucky.

Arthur Evans set about his task with optimism and a lavish expenditure—amongst the stores ordered, his biographer notes with amusement, were one gross of nail brushes and an equal number of bottles of Eno's Fruit Salt, outer and inner cleanliness being equally provided for. Evans started with thirty workmen and later increased the number to a hundred. He was soon to employ a full-time architect on the site. He enlisted expert assistance but left to himself over-all direction and the decision where to dig. He started work on March 23, 1899.

He was rewarded from the start. A labyrinth of buildings was revealed. On the second day fragments of fresco were found. On the fourth day Evans was noting: 'The extraordinary phenomenon: nothing Greek—nothing Roman:' the great period of Knossos was being shown to go back beyond anything previously discovered in the Aegean. That was what he had hoped for.

A drain filled with fragments of pottery appeared, more and more walls of what Evans now believed was a palace, more pieces of fresco. Then large rings of pottery began to show in the earth: they were the mouths of the huge *pithoi* or storage jars. Then, on April 5:

> A great day! Early in the morning the gradual surface uncovering. . . revealed two large pieces of Mycenaean fresco . . . One represented the head and forehead, the other the waist and part of the skirt of a female figure [later realized to be male] holding in her hand a long Mycenaean 'rhyton' or high funnel-shaped cup . . . The figure was life-size, the flesh colour of a deep reddish hue like that of a figure in Etruscan tombs and the Keftiu of Egytian paintings. The profile of the face was of a noble type: full lips, the lower showing a slight peculiarity of curve below. The eye was dark and slightly almond shaped. In front of the ear is a kind of ornament and a necklace and bracelet are visible. The arms are beautifully modelled. The waist is of the smallest . . . It is far and away the most remarkable human figure of the Mycenaean age that has yet come to light.

Evans, it may be noted, was being modest, calling his find Mycenaean, from their similarity to some of Schliemann's; soon, however, he would take courage and name them with his own invention, Minoan. In fact he had uncovered the famous 'cup-bearer' wall-painting, the slightly epicene figure of a handsome youth walking in procession. Here for the first time lay revealed a member of the forgotten race. Evans's foreman was set as night-watchman before the fresco could be carefully borne away. 'Believed by him', Evans notes, 'to be Saint with halo. Has troubled dreams. Saint wrathful. Wakes and hears lowing and neighing. Something about, but of a ghostly kind.' Everybody in fact was in their different ways impressed.

Soon there came a different find, that of clay tablets on which were incised writing, and writing of a sophisticated type, not pure pictograms but more like the Egyptian cursive writing and so dubbed by Evans 'Linear'. This, of course, pleased Evans immensely. This was what he had come to find: such a great civilization as he hoped and believed had existed could not possibly have been wholly illiterate, and here was fast appearing not only evidence of that greatness but also of a growing literateness. It is ironical that Evans should have found so soon the largest cache of incised tablets he was ever to find, yet should never have been able to achieve more than the first rudiments of their decipherment.

Then, so early too, came one of the most significant discoveries of all, that of the Throne Room of the Palace of Knossos. Evans first called it the Bath Room but soon changed his opinion. The 'bath' was shallow and had no drain, and steps led down to it from the larger part of the room. And in this larger part there stood against the frescoed wall the remains of a stone high-backed chair or throne. The name of the room was consequently changed and the bath regarded as a 'lustral area' or place for ceremonial anointing. Evans, in his lordly way, sent for the Swiss artist and expert living in Athens, M. Gilliéron, and Gilliéron began for Evans the first of his many tasks of restoration, that of the frescoes of the Throne Room. Their chief feature comprised two imposing and curly-maned griffins whose beaks point upwards and inwards to the point where the king's head would rest when he sat upon the throne.

This throne room when first opened up was found in some confusion, a point of significance not lost upon Evans. He sent a long telegram of news to *The Times* newspaper, *The Times* published it, and Evans's father read it and sent his son a cheque for £500 towards expenses. . . .

*

Since Arthur Evans spent the next thirty years, off and on, excavating at Knossos, it would not be profitable to continue to follow the course of his discoveries chronologically. The main, definitive discoveries were made in the first few seasons, and all that followed, whether achieved by himself or others, served only to corroborate and elaborate the picture.

Perhaps the most startling of Evans's discoveries was that, so early on, he was able to show what these people of a lost civilization, these 'Minoans'* of his, had looked like. The men appeared as broad-

---

* This practice of naming the Bronze Age Cretans throughout their history after the name of one of their kings or dynasties has been called as foolish as naming all Britons subsequent to William the Conqueror 'Victorians'. But that is an accusation manifestly unfair, if only because change was much less rapid in

shouldered, slim, athletic, lightly clad. They wore only the loin cloth or pair of drawers that had already been made familiar to Evans in Mycenaean seals and the Egyptian pictures of the 'Keftiu', showing either a cod-piece or a special sort of folding to the front which sometimes ended in an elaborate tassel. This highly distinctive piece of clothing, sometimes simple, sometimes gay and elaborate, was always drawn very tightly about the waist, there being often a metal waistband, presumably never taken off until broken or sawn asunder. This dress in no way implies austerity or simplicity, however. For the hair is worn long and curled (or curly) and there is an obvious fondness for jewellery, necklaces and bracelets and the like; the young prince, or priest-king as he is alternately called, walking in beauty through, it would seem, a field of irises, is crowned with a magnificent peacock-feather headdress.

The women were even more startling and unexpected in their costumes than the men. Again there was tight-lacing. Again there were jewellery and provocative curls. But also there was the long flounced skirt, worn below either a diaphanous chemise or—in modern terms—topless. This skirt must have been something very special. It reached the ground; it was obviously heavy, and it was either flounced horizontally or pleated vertically, or both, and it seemed to cling to the legs. Such a skirt would never have been worn in a warm climate for purely utilitarian purposes; nor, one would imagine, in view of the top half of the costume or the lack of it, would it have been worn for modesty. As more examples came to light, in the way of figurines as well as frescoes, it became apparent that originally the long flounced skirt had been a priestess's wear. The priest throughout the ages seems either to have spectacularly overdressed or underdressed, and here the intention appears to have been to do both things at once.

There was nothing priestly, however, about the women Evans was discovering. Most revealing, startling, and delightful were the famous miniature frescoes found, fallen into fragments, in the maze of lower rooms in the northern part of the second Knossos palace, and which proved on being pieced together to be of only a few feet

the second millennium B.C. than it has been in the same millennium A.D. 'Ancient Cretans' is a cumbersome name; and as no one knows what these people called themselves, 'Minoan' is as good a title as any and better than most. It will be used in this book.

across. They were nevertheless full of detail, yet—being true frescoes, painted on plaster before it dried—done in a dashing style. One of them showed crowds watching some spectacle and included ladies in, as it were, the boxes and the stalls. These were indeed ladies, society ladies; they were so obviously gay, so obviously gossiping to each other. Evans, later, let himself go in his description of them: one lady 'raises her hand in amazement, "You don't say so!"' and another does the same 'in depreciation of her sharp-tongued neighbour'. And these ladies are dressed in the once priestly, once (and perhaps still) ceremonial fashion. There was, of course, nothing reprehensible in this; it was probably not the first time or the last that ceremonial or religious dress had been copied to advantage by the mundane. But it does show the Minoans, at least in the later years of their prosperity, as a highly sophisticated people; it in all probability shows them, though certainly not slighting or making fun of their religion, at least religious in an unportentous, cheerful, unfanatical way. These vivacious, fashionable ladies certainly deserved the title that the startled Frenchman gave them: '*Mais, ce sont des Parisiennes!*'—Parisiennes of the naughty nineties. When a later and larger fresco of a young girl was found, large-eyed, cherry-lipped, with a love-knot in her hair, she was named by her delighted discoverers '*La Parisienne*'.

Were they, these gossiping, sight-seeing ladies, perhaps watching the bull-games? Here was another discovery that Evans made. 'Everywhere the bull!' he wrote. Then the sentiment was focused into something specific, and again startling, by perhaps the most famous fresco of all, that of the Bull Leap. This portrays an action which was subsequently to be found represented many times and in other media, on seals, in delicate bronze or ivory statuettes, in crude votive offerings: there could be no doubt, therefore, that the Minoans had indulged in a ritual sport both strange and unique. Men, and girls too, had vaulted over the back of a charging bull, daring to use its terrible horns as no more than a sort of conveniently placed pair of parallel bars. Here was something odd and slightly sinister—did it perhaps represent in some unexpected way the reality behind the Theseus legend?

The bull-games are something to which we shall return. Nor does the significance of the bull end with this fresco. There was another found at the north entrance to the palace of Knossos and now resting there duly restored, the painting on the wall of a great bull's head.

Pendlebury in his book on Crete,* while remarking that this fresco showed signs of having lasted beyond the general destruction of the palace, refers also to the Minotaur legend: did the sudden and startling sight of this depicted guardian of the palace help to give rise to the legend? This particular portrayal could be said to have another significance. For here is not so much a dashing painting of action as a sensitive painting of a noble animal, itself sensitive. It is comparable not to a modern painting of a bull-fighting scene but to the finest and gentlest of the palaeolithic cave paintings. A subtle people the Minoans, one begins to feel, not easily understood.

An artistic people, too: that fact became abundantly clear as Arthur Evans continued to unearth ancient Knossos.

There are two forms of art in particular that stay relatively unharmed in the ground and so help the archaeologist. One is the art of the worker in precious metals, the other is that of the ceramic artist. Both were found in Crete and in the lands to which the Cretan artists penetrated, pottery in particular.

There is, without any manner of doubt, something unique about Minoan pottery, a gaiety, a swing, a natural, uninhibited exuberance. It is all too easy for the expert to enthuse over pottery finds, for he can thus display both his special knowledge and his special sensitivity. It is equally easy for the layman to be prepared to be bored by the display. But he does not have to do so in this instance. Unearthed Minoan pottery, as with all of its kind, does help the archaeologist to discern trends and changes and to get his dating right. But it does so very much more. Minoan pottery cannot help telling something of the character and feelings of the men and women who made it, because it is so outstanding and so distinctive. Look through any well-illustrated book on Minoan art, and the effect cannot help but become apparent. Occasionally the art may seem to a less uninhibited age in bad taste, certainly not always 'functional'. But it is always generous and unstilted and naturalistic with the sufficient formalism of the art that conceals art. Here is the work of a people, living in a beautiful island, with the sensitivity to appreciate that beauty and the skill to reproduce it. Harriet Boyd Hawes, one of the earliest excavators in Crete, has put it well:

* *The Archaeology of Crete* (Methuen, 1939). J. D. S. Pendlebury, protégé of Evans, was Curator at Knossos in the 1930's; he died fighting in Crete in World War II.

At the height of his power the Minoan potter went direct to nature for his inspiration. His designs are full of grace and exuberance; reeds, grasses and flowers adorn his vases; the life of the sea is represented with astonishing fidelity; but his naturalism is controlled by a rare power of selection and grouping. Some of his most charming patterns were painted on vases as thin as the egg-shell cups of Middle Minoan* style, others were executed on jars so heavy and coarse that no idea of their being decorated was at first entertained by the excavators. With a true instinct for beauty, he chose his favourite flowers, the lovely lily and iris, the wild gladiolus and crocus, all natives of the Mediterranean basin, and the last three, if not the lily, of his own soil.

He chose too, Mrs Hawes might have added, from the life of the seashore. He collected its shells, he peered down from his fishing boat through the clear water at the writhing octopus, he watched the pearly nautilus sail by like a miniature argonaut and then found its spiral shell washed up on to his shore and took it home and copied it. He delighted to see the grace of the porpoise and of the flying fish.

Arthur Evans was able eventually to uncover the whole extent of the six acres of the palace of Knossos; indeed, though it was by no means his sole task it was his main one. With its vast, sprawling extent, its multiplication of rooms and passages, its dark, underground series of storerooms, it might very well have given the Greeks a word that meant to them a maze, and perhaps a terrifying, claustrophobic one at that, either to a Mycenaean used to the rough, manly openness of his baron's-hall megaron or to a later Dorian, used to not much more than a hut and the open air. However, Evans and those who followed after him have been able to show that Knossos —as also those rather lesser palaces, of Phaistos, Mallia and Zakro, of which more later—sprawled not haphazardly but of a set intent.

The Minoans were enabled by two favourable phenomena to build outwards from a central courtyard and to extend more or less indefinitely as their pleasure or their convenience dictated. The first of these aids was their country's island position, their command of the sea, and so their conviction that fortified walls and battlements were not necessary for their palaces. The second was the bright and pellucid light that made illumination of their rooms from small inner courtyards or 'light wells' not only sufficient but most pleasant and restful. A third factor which made casual and continual building extension easier was the flat rather than the gabled roof.

* This chronological term is explained in the following chapter.

So, then, the great palaces of which Knossos is the parent and pattern. They are the centres round which the houses of the citizens —courtiers, officials, priests, scribes, merchants, artists, artisans, servants—clustered, clinging in this land not so much for protection, which did not seem necessary, as for convenience and companionship. The palace was nevertheless a true centre, royal, administrative, religious, mercantile, economic.

The central feature of the palaces is always a great rectangular courtyard measuring some fifty yards by twenty-five and with its longer axis pointing north and south; to the west of the courtyard are placed the official rooms and halls of the palace, to the east the private.

Knossos is built on a gently rising hill, the top of which has to an extent been sliced off by the original architects. It is not such a commanding site as Phaistos, which sails like a ship in a green sea of fertility and looks across to rugged and imposing mountains. It is certainly not as imposing a site as Greek Mycenae, but then the latter is not so much a palace as a fortress. It is a beautiful site; it still is and must always have been so, especially in the spring, a peaceful site, looking across country not dramatic nor spectacular but happily productive.

To the visitor who approached the palace of Knossos, on the other hand, the sight must have been dramatic, as also beautiful. Here again was no fantastic gothic pile rising to the heavens, no mythical 'topless towers'. Here was a great expanse of glistening white, long and low though rising to three storeys, made gay by wooden pillars blue and brown and red and—this is supposition but a reasonable one—by fluttering pennants along its length.* The visitor would in all probability have approached by the road that comes from the south and would have caught his first glimpse of the imposing southern propylon or gateway from across the shallow ravine which bounds the palace site on the south and east.

The visitor, by another likelihood, might well have been in a mood to be delighted and impressed. For facing the palace across the ravine, where this first view would be obtained, had been built a rest house, or caravanserai as Evans romantically called it; and if the visitor had rested, perhaps spent the night here, he would have been both pleased and prepared for beauty. This caravanserai the modern

* Egypt had long had the pennant—evolved, suggests Sir Grafton Elliott-Smith, symbolically from the human umbilical cord.

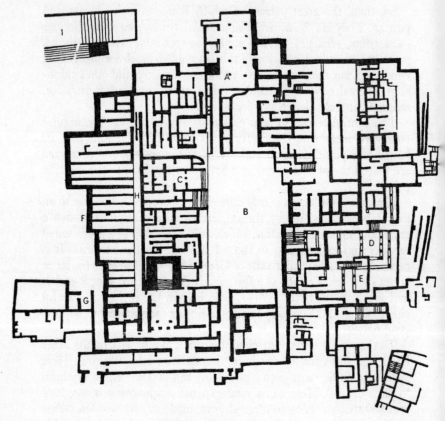

Plan of the palace of Knossos

A North Entrance
B Great Courtyard
C Throne-room
D Hall of the Double Axe
E Queen's megaron
F West Court
G South-west portico
H Corridor of the magazines
I Theatral area

visitor may also see, though there are very few that do so and the guides do not seem to include it in their itinerary. It necessitates a further walk of half a mile or so along the road from Heraklion beyond the official entrance to the palace. There, on the left of the road, duly signposted but rather lost in greenery, are the excavated ruins of the caravanserai. The main, pillared, room has been restored; and there is also restored a frescoed dado of partridges and hoopoes —the hoopoe still flies at Knossos and Heraklion. There is too, a separate small building housing an ever-bubbling spring, and above it is a niche where, it is thought, the grateful visitor was expected to leave his votive offering, a more poetic contribution than ten per cent on the bill.

So, in the sunshine of the morning—and very many Cretan mornings are filled with sunshine—the visitor would cross the ravine and the river (now untended and almost non-existent) by the great viaduct. Only some piers of this viaduct now remain, but these are enough to suggest something of the major engineering and architectural feat that it must have constituted. Over a hundred yards long, balustraded, it was wide enough to take the flocks of sheep and laden carts and pack animals that came to swell the central store, as well as the visitors, as well as the small army of artisans, slaves, clerks, storemen and workmen that streamed across to their daily employment.

In due course the visitor would have found himself in the open Western Court, which, being the general outer courtyard or waiting room for the palace, must always have shown a busy scene.

It is into this open square (Fig. F on the plan) that the modern visitor will enter, coming up through the turnstiles and along a short tree-lined walk. He may notice three large and deep refuse pits, now dry and clean but once perhaps a little smelly—unless that is to malign the Minoans, who may well have been fastidious.

At the south-east corner of this outer courtyard there stands one of the two main entrances to the palace (G). It leads to the main central courtyard (B), rather strangely by narrow passages round three sides of a square; and, as along these passages were found remains of frescoes suggesting a procession, they have been called the processional corridors and may well have been so. The more imposing entrance, however, is at the north end of the palace-complex (A); and it is here that the contemporary visitor may be imagined to enter and where the modern visitor will do well to follow suit. Both will have found themselves traversing the narrow stone way, 'the oldest road in Europe', which now ends abruptly but must once have gone on to the coast and then eastwards to the palace of Mallia. Both will also be led by this paved way to come upon something less expected by the modern visitor than the ancient, that is to say a wide, paved

platform bounded by shallow steps on two sides which is believed to
have been a 'theatrical area' (I), or what Homer more reasonably
calls a dancing floor (built, he adds, by Daedalus for Ariadne of the
lovely tresses). There is a more imposing example of the same thing
at Phaistos; and as the steps there end abruptly in a high wall it is
reasonable to suppose that in both places they were in reality seats
for the audience. Here, possibly, the king and his entourage were met
on their return to their palace and presented with some dance and
spectacle which was symbolic and religious as well as welcoming.

Now at last the ancient visitor would have found himself entering
the palace proper. Passing through the northern propylon (with
provision, it would seem, for a sentry, for the Minoans were not
idiotically averse to any military protection), leaving behind on his
left the quarters of the palace artisans and clerks, he would mount a
sloping ramp (as one still may do), to be faced with the fresco of the
guardian and noble bull already mentioned. Through a final covered
passage he would pass and then he would be out in the sunshine again
and into the central feature of the palace, the great court (B).

Here, on facing right, he would see what he might well have so far
disappointedly missed, the main façade to the palace. This, facing
inwards to the main courtyard, rose, it is believed, to something like
forty-five feet. The row of brightly painted wooden supporting
pillars would display that typical Minoan characteristic which
Arthur Evans discovered and reconstructed, the slight tapering from
top to bottom, deriving perhaps from the original use of only
roughly dressed trees put in upside down to prevent any chance of
their sprouting once more. In front of the visitor would rise a wide
stairway to the upper rooms and to his left a pillared shrine, as
pictured in one of the miniature frescoes of crowds and gossiping
ladies. (This fact has led some people to believe that the bull-games
were held in the great courtyard, though most envisage a wider arena,
probably on the gentle eastern slopes of the palace hill.) What comprised the upper rooms of the western half of the palace, to which
the wide staircase led, no one will ever know, for they have crumbled
down to unrecognizable ruin. Evans, taking an analogy from the
piano nobile or principal floor of Italian medieval palaces, has
imagined imposing halls and reception rooms, guided in his tentative
reconstruction by the varying thickness of the supporting walls.

To the right of the stairway to the *piano nobile*, that is to say as our
imaginary visitor faces it, lies the heart of the official wing of the

palace, the throne room (C) and its antechamber. To penetrate there the visitor would not only have to be important but also no doubt submit to much protocol and even some purification ceremony, for all ancient kings, even in such an exceptionally sophisticated and mundane society as the Minoan may have been, were hedged about with a great barrier of sacred symbolism.

Here in this room Evans found the throne of gypsum, a comfortable but not vastly imposing throne; and now it rests in what must be its proper position, against the walls with frescoes on each side flanking it. The main feature of these frescoes is the pair of noble, stylized griffins, those eagle-headed lions symbolizing through the animal kingdom a human puissance in the realms of both earth and air. If the king sat between the upraised heads of these beasts, wearing the sort of feathered headdress that the prince in the fresco wears, he might well have looked impressive.

This is the room that so impressed not only Evans but also Evans's later assistant, Pendlebury. The room, as has been said, was found in a state of some confusion, especially the lustral area, where it is believed ritual anointing would have taken place, with the vessels for this ceremony lying on the floor. Pendlebury has imagined some hurried frantic ritual being enacted in a vain endeavour to stave off the destruction—of fire and sword or of fire alone—that on one fatal morning in the spring 'when the wind was in the South' had befallen the palace. Dare we, he asks, imagine the king putting on the mask of the bull? In other words, Pendlebury is suggesting a more direct cause for the minotaur story than a mere general aura of bulls to impress the simple-minded and marauding Greeks, nothing less than King Minos wearing the mask of the creature that symbolized both strength and terror.*

It is an intriguing idea, this, and one that certainly need not be scornfully dismissed. In fact it will do no one any harm to think of Theseus and the legends as he wanders round the ruins of Knossos. A great deal of the west wing, the area between the throne room and western outer courtyard, is taken up with vaults and cellars, long corridors where in the huge pithoi were stored the oil and grain or where in lined cubicles lay more valuable treasure. These corridors are now mostly open to the sky. But when they were basements they must have been dark; and there are many of them and they would be

* A more recent suggestion however (by Dr. Helga Reuch) is that the throne was not that of a king but of a priestess.

very confusing. It is here if anywhere that one can legitimately imagine Theseus with his clew-box and his thread, and his sword and his beating heart.

*

To envisage the eastern or private wing of the palace of Knossos one may abandon the convenience of the imagined visitor and abandon too any feeling of the sinister. The east wing really does seem to be all sweetness and light, or perhaps, rather, comfort and light, light-wells, and warm airiness from the shaded sun, and drains and conveniences. The king, as he came out with relief into the sunlight of the central court and crossed to the eastern wing, would cease to be a peg for symbolism and become an ordinary pleasure-loving human being.

The eastern wing of Knossos is built on a falling slope. The Minoan architects utilized to the full a situation open to favourable winds and the cool morning sun, sheltered in other directions and remote from the hubbub of the entrance court and the public business of the western wing. They actually cut away part of the crown of the hill and formed a partially artificial terrace twenty-five feet below the level of the central court, up to which they built. This gave them the chance to construct the 'grand staircase' with its pillars and light-well, which is so well known and which Evans did his best to restore.

This staircase is not wide by Versailles or English country-house standards, but it is imposing enough. It has been imagined as peopled by courtiers, bronzed and slim-waisted, and by their ladies in their rustling flounced skirts, moving before their king in cere-monious procession. No doubt the famous stairway has witnessed such scenes, But since it was the private quarters down to which the stairway led, it is perhaps more reasonable to visualize a lone figure, that of Minos himself—very human, experiencing the spiritual metamorphosis of a change from the priestly figure to the family man.

There are, in particular on the eastern side of the palace, what Evans believed to be the queen's quarters; in particular there is her *megaron* or personal living room. A long and narrow room, divided in its middle by pillars, illumined by twin light-wells, it may well have been a very pleasant place indeed. Evans found considerable evidence of how it was decorated on ceiling and walls—the fresco of the dancing girl was found here—and he told his faithful artist to paint an imaginative reproduction of it.

Near by was the queen's bathroom—a hot bath, said King Alcinous, did the Phaeacians delight in—and the queen's lavatory. 'On the face of a gypsum slab to the right,' wrote Evans with technical enthusiasm, 'is a groove for a seat about 57 cm. from the floor. Outside the doorway of the latrine is a flag sloped towards a semicircular hole, forming a sink, and from this opens a small duct leading to a main drain. The aperture leading to the main drain, partly masked by a curious projection, deviates from the centre of the seat, thus leaving room on the right for some vessel used for flushing the basin. As an anticipation of scientific methods of sanitation, the system of which we have here the record has been attained by few nations at the present day.' Here perhaps speaks, rather too pessimistically, a man with memories of roughing it in the nineteenth-century Balkans. It is also a fact that here is the aspect of the site of Knossos which nowadays excites the interest of the common run of tourist more thoroughly than any other. Perhaps, however, neither Evans's praise nor the common interest is misplaced. For here is evidence both of clever architectural engineering and also a due regard, so comparatively early in history, for the comforts and decencies of civilized living.

There is also evidence at Knossos of a more subtle knowledge of the properties of running water and a more artistic use of its powers. The main drains, well supplied with ventilating shafts and manholes, were made of sections of terracotta pipe fitted into each other and made slightly tapering, so that, says Evans, they 'were admirably designed to impart a shooting motion to the flow of water so as to prevent accumulation of sediment'. A particularly neat piece of engineering work was found in excavating the steps down to the east bastion of the palace. A channel had been cut at the side of each flight of steps to take away the excess waters of the heavy autumn rains. But these flights, quite steep, were at right angles to each other, and the problem facing the Minoan architect was to slow down the flow of channelled water so that at right-angle bends it was prevented from spreading out over the landings. He solved the problem by constructing the fall of the water-channels in a series of curves natural to the fall of water, that is to say parabolic. 'Nothing in the whole building,' wrote Evans 'gives such an impression of the result of long generations of intelligent experience on the part of the

Minoan engineers.' Another of Evans's discoveries, of the fresco of a fountain,* suggests that the Minoan Daedaleans of Knossos had beauty in mind as well as utility, and knew, in this respect as in many others, how to produce it.

*

It must not be supposed that Arthur Evans was the sole excavator of Knossos, either as palace or surrounding city, nor that other sites have not been explored by other archaeologists: they have, both early and late, and they are still being explored. There is much more to tell of what has been discovered. But it may wait until the chapters which seek to establish what life was like in the heyday of Cretan Bronze Age civilization before it collapsed.

It was Evans who drew up the curtain; and very dramatic, and unexpected, has been the scene that he managed to portray. Here was the reality behind the fabled Knossos, or, more accurately, here was what was left of the reality of Knossos, the physical remains. Others have succeeded Evans, both in excavation and also in interpretation, some following the master, some rebelling against what they felt was an unjustified monopoly of ideas. Interpretation is always a dangerous as well as a fascinating business.

It would, however, be a loss if the danger frightened off the interpreter. A few aspects of the Minoan civilization are surely indisputable; and it is as well to end this chapter by stating them shortly, lest, because taken for granted, they are forgotten or ignored.

Here then, in ancient Bronze Age Crete, was a prosperous, peaceful, well-ordered society; here was a people leading, by all appearances, a happy, gay, comfortable, sophisticated but artistically sensitive existence, content to leave others alone so long as they could be left alone in their island existence.

* See *The Palace of Minos*, Vol. II, p. 460.

Chapter VII

The Uninvaded Island: Early History
Reconstructed

NEARLY A thousand years of history lie between the appearance of Crete as a Bronze Age civilization and the brief couple of centuries of brilliance which preceded her decline and fall. Here are thirty generations or more, of lives crowded with events and shocked by circumstances memorable to their owners. And yet we know no more of them than may fill a few pages. That is a sad thought. But in one particular it may well be the reverse. For happy is said to be the land that has no history; and that sort of happiness, it does seem likely, was the lot of the Minoans from the middle of the third millennium to nearly the middle of the second.

However, just as no man is an island, so no island is indefinitely inviolate. If all that was happening outside Crete, wars and movements of peoples, did not affect Crete at the time, it did so in the latter end. It is best, therefore, to see this period of the Minoans' long, slow, undisturbed development against the background of wider events—the most significant of these being the appearance of the Mycenaeans upon the Mediterranean scene.

First, it is essential to become familiar with the system of dating that Arthur Evans devised. To be strictly accurate it is a system not of dating but of changing phases of culture, based upon interpretation of changing pottery styles. The actual dates credited to the series of changes have been altered by experts following Evans (though in fact not greatly altered) and there are those who would like to do away with the system altogether and substitute a new one, as will be explained. These facts do not mean, however, that the Evans system may be ignored and forgotten. It will be found still almost impossible to do without it; and in any case nine books out of ten, and all the original definitive books, make some use of the Evans system, so that to be ignorant of it, or to allow oneself to be confused by it, is a great handicap.

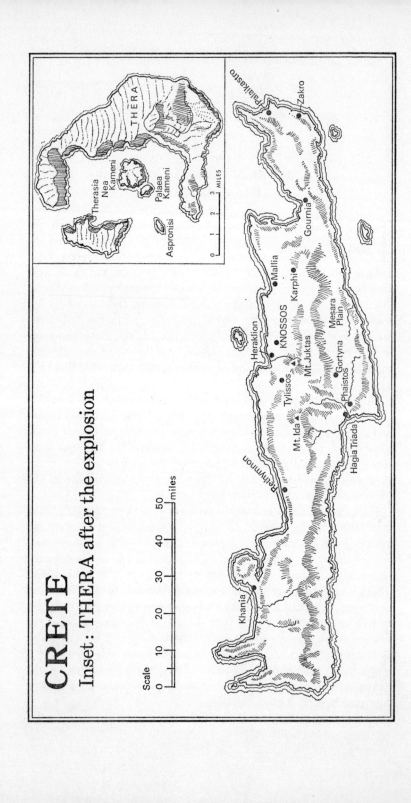

CRETE
Inset: THERA after the explosion

Scale

0   10   20   30   40   50
miles

THERA

Therasia
Nea
Kameni
Palaea
Kameni
Aspronisi

0   1   2   3
MILES

Palaikastro
Zakro
Gournia
Mallia
Karphi
KNOSSOS
Mesara
Plain
Heraklion
Mt. Juktas
Gortyna
Tylissos
Phaistos
Mt. Ida
Hagia Triada
Rethymnon
Khania

A small defence of this kind of chronological system may not come amiss. It is well known and obvious that pottery, being highly breakable (and so discardable) but also highly indestructible, will appear in quantity on any archaeological site, and that in conjunction with stratigraphy—the deeper down, other things being equal, the older—it will prove an invaluable guide to dating. It is also remarkable how tell-tale is the style, both in shape and decoration, of any piece of pottery discovered. What is done by the artist mirrors what is thought and felt by those around him; and, men being conservative, traditions in method remain inviolable, until some real shock to ways and thoughts has occurred. To date by pottery styles, therefore, is not the line of least resistance, the lazy way; it is the sensible way. It must never be forgotten, however, that it *is* a dating by pottery: Evans's E.M. IIb (for instance) does not mean the years 1800–1700 B.C.; it means the particular sub-division of the 'Late Minoan' culture that is designated by that shorthand title and which, incidentally, is thought to have lasted during the years of the eighteenth century B.C.

Evans divided the Cretan Bronze Age culture into three main divisions, to tally with the accepted divisions of ancient Egyptian history, Old or Early Kingdom, Middle Kingdom and New Kingdom. So, therefore, Early, Middle and Late Minoan, shortened for the convenience of the expert (who is not over-concerned with the non-expert) into E.M, M.M. and L.M. respectively. Egyptian history interposes between each of her three divisions an 'Intermediate Period', euphemistic phrase for a time of chaos and revolution. There is no sign that Crete so suffered. Evans did, however, think he detected three legitimate sub-divisions in each of his periods, E.M. I, II and III and so forth. These have not only been retained, but there has been found a need to sub-divide some of them into *a*'s and *b*'s. (There is a further elaboration used by most archaeologists whereby the civilizations of, respectively, mainland Greece and the Greek islands are called Helladic and Cycladic. In this way, we may also have cultures designated E.H., M.H. and L.H. and also E.C., M.C. and L.C. These will tally quite closely in date with the corresponding early, middle and late periods of Crete; but obviously they cannot be expected to tally exactly.)

A table is given in an attempt to make these matters plain; but in this book as little use as possible will be made of these Minoan abbreviations and elaborate sub-divisions (and none of the Helladic

Chronological Table of Minoan Civilization

Absolute Chronology	Arthur Evans's Chronology	'Palace' Chronology	B.C.	Approximate Egyptian Equivalent
BC	EARLY MINOAN	PRE-PALACE PERIOD		
2600–2400	Early Minoan I	Phase I	2600–2400	Old Kingdom
2400–2200	Early Minoan II	Phase II	2400–2200	(Dyns. 4 to 6)
2200–2000	Early Minoan III / MIDDLE MINOAN / Middle Minoan Ia	Phase III	2200–2000	1st Intermediate Period
2000–1900	Middle Minoan Ib	OLD-PALACE PERIOD Phase I	2000–1900	Middle Kingdom
1900–1800	Middle Minoan IIa	Phase II	1900–1800	(Dyns. 11 and 12)
1800–1700	Middle Minoan IIb	Phase III	1800–1700	
1700–1600	Middle Minoan IIIa and b	NEW PALACE PERIOD Phase I	1700–1600	2nd Intermediate Period
1600–1450	LATE MINOAN / Late Minoan Ia and b	Phase II	1600–1450	New Empire
1450–1400	Late Minoan II	Phase III	1450–1400	18th Dyn.
1400–1320	Late Minoan IIIa	POST PALACE PERIOD Phase I	1400–1320	
1320–1260	Late Minoan IIIb	Phase II	1320–1260	19th Dyn.
1260–1150		Phase III	1260–1150	20th Dyn.

or Cycladic). There is always a danger in using such aids to orderliness, and that is the unconscious tendency to treat them as too exact, too real. As J. D. S. Pendlebury once observed, some Cretan king did not wake up one morning and sternly observe to his chamberlain, 'Today we have finished with Late Minoan Ib and are embarked upon Late Minoan II.'

What he did observe, what more than one Minoan king must have observed, with either happiness or horror in his eyes, was the building of his palace at Knossos, or its destruction, or its reconstruction. Here we have the grounds for the new chronological system which has been invented in substitution for the old and which may quite possibly come to replace it. It is based on these very happenings, the building, destruction and rebuilding of the palace of Knossos, which corresponded, though not exactly, with a similar process at the other palaces of ancient Crete. The newly proposed Periods are Pre-Palace, Old Palace, New Palace and Post-Palace. Each of these, as before, is divided into I, II and III.

This system has the advantage of giving twelve instead of nine sub-periods and so eliminates—so far—the need for a's and b's. More importantly and less academically, it has the advantage of being based on crucial historic happenings and not on changes in pottery styles, which, however significant, are only reflections of events rather than events themselves. The Bronze Age Minoan people did slowly accumulate skill and knowledge and prosperity so that they could burst forth into an age of palaces; they did witness the destruction or despoliation of those palaces by earthquake, perhaps several times but certainly on one major occasion; they did set to and rebuild; they did witness a final destruction, from which cataclysm, whatever the cause, they never fully recovered.

In fact these 'palatial' divisions do give a sort of potted history of Bronze Age Crete. Before proceeding to try to clothe that skeleton as far as it can be clothed, there is one further thing necessary to say about chronological systems. How far, it may be asked, do the 'palatial' system and Evans's system, as brought up to date, tally? The answer is, pretty well, as can be seen from the comparative table. The main points of difference are two. Evans's Middle Minoan (M.M.) overlaps on both sides of its equivalent Old Palace Period. The newly invented fourth division, Post-Palace, is entirely equivalent to no more than one old sub-division, L.M. III. What it comes to is that the split between Late Minoan II and III is of much greater significance than the split between Middle and Late Minoan, M.M. and L.M., as a whole. What matters is the destruction of the palaces.

We return, after that necessary digression, to the early and formative centuries of the Minoan civilization and to the influences of the Mycenaean upon it. It is a Bronze Age story. If M.M. and L.M. and the rest are artificial divisions, so of course is the division between mankind's Stone Age and Bronze Age. It is in fact, as has been stated, nowhere near so important a break as was the change-over from Old to New Stone Age, palaeolithic to neolithic, when that 'neolithic revolution' occurred which set mankind on its course as farmer and partner with Nature rather than hunter and predator. Bronze Age men were still tillers of the soil, with the outlook which that occupation engenders.

Nevertheless, the change, the new skill, is significant. A new material, metal, had been found, and the means of handling it. It was an amazing substance that was both hard and malleable, that could be hammered and honed into shape and sharpness and that could yet be melted by great heat and then reshaped and resharpened. There was gold, which was very beautiful and never tarnished, and there was copper for utilitarian and warlike purposes, the bowl, the axe, the adze, the sword, the spear. Then came some genius—Hephaistos, the god, perhaps—and he added a modicum of tin to the copper in the molten state and produced a metal as bright and shining but also harder and with a better cutting edge.

The trouble was that the ingredients were scarce. The poor man did not have his bronze bowl; he certainly did not have his bronze sword, dagger, shining breastplate and resplendent helmet. Only the aristocracy had those; and great store indeed did they set by them.

The Bronze Age does see in fact the rise of aristocracies. The two are not necessarily cause and effect; but the fact that bronze is scarce and precious and also makes the best possible paraphernalia for a fighting man was no doubt a considerable contributory factor. The king had long since arrived, and no doubt with an aristocracy around him. But now the aristocracy itself begins to grow important. Like an amoeba under the microscope the cradle of civilization stirs. Its twitchings are the movement of an armed nobility, moving in revolt or in the invasion of countries not their own. Crete is in train to suffer from one of these movements, but by no means yet: if the Bronze Age is an age of warfare and warriors it is also an age of prosperity;

and the islanded Minoans will for a long time experience only the second and happier fate.

Slowly in the Middle East the world was forming which would later threaten Crete. Sumeria was the first to be deeply stirred. The new aristocrats were Semites, calling themselves Akkadians. Their leader was Sargon, 'King of Kings'. He was the man who came from nothing, who was the first to invent, or have invented for him, the 'babe found in the bullrushes' story, the man whom the goddess loved, so that 'for fifty-four years the kingship' was his, that is to say after he had usurped the throne. Under him the city states of Mesopotamia became an empire 'from the Lower Sea [the Red Sea] to the Upper [the Mediterranean]'. Sargon may well have conquered Cyprus, in the armed aristocrats' ever-pressing need for copper, Crete thus being saved by her lack of the metal. Sargon's dynasty lasted no more than a hundred years, the twenty-fourth century B.C. approximately. A rapidly expanded empire is not a settled land. There appeared an invading people from the north, the Guti, whom the unhappy Sumerians called the Vipers of the Hills.

It was next the turn of Egypt to suffer disruption. She had built her pyramids, she had extended her trade and her prosperity; under her successful Sixth Dynasty she had created an army and sent out her punitive expeditions in order to increase her trade—'the army returned in safety; it had hacked up the land of the sand-dwellers'. Her Pharaohs had delegated power to aristocratic rulers of provinces. Then Pepi II came to the throne as a child, extended his reign into doddering old age, and saw anarchy before he died. The governors of provinces revolted; the bedouins from without saw their opportunity and invaded. Egypt was suffering what historians have euphemistically called her First Intermediate Period.

It is worth while to reflect on what, in all this turmoil, the Minoans were so far, and for a long while yet, escaping. It was the common man who suffered most, the peaceful man. Poignant echoes come down to us from contemporary writings, just as they do from our own Dark Ages in the Saxon Chronicles describing the terrible depredations of the Norsemen. 'Who,' asked a Sumerian scribe in desperation and bewilderment, 'who was king, who was not king?' In Egypt we have *The Admonitions of a Prophet*. 'Nay, but the plunderers are everywhere . . . nay but the face is pale . . . Squalor is throughout the land; there is none whose clothes are white in these times . . . Nay but the crocodiles are glutted with what they have carried off; men go to them of their own accord . . . Nay, but laughter hath perished and is no longer made . . . Little children say, "He ought never to have caused me to live".'

Yet laughter came back, as mercifully it does, and the will to live returned, if indeed it had ever much departed. The generations passed, the wounds healed and the peasants, grumpily heedless of who were their new masters, worked undisturbed again. The end of the Third Millennium, as we know it, was approaching, as was also in due course a second and greater and more significant upheaval.

In Sumeria thrived the third and last dynasty of Ur, that city which long ago had given such a generously splendid funeral to Queen Shub-ad and from whose dying greatness Abraham in a couple of centuries' time was to flee. Egypt climbed back to even greater prosperity and greater artistic ability in her Middle Kingdom and in particular during her Twelfth Dynasty (c. 1990–1790 B.C.). She traded over the seas with Phoenician Byblos and she traded over the same seas with Crete. At last Crete comes into the light of history.

*

Already Crete had progressed considerably. She had settled down. In neolithic days there may well have been more than one wave of immigration into the island; but throughout the Bronze Age, at least until the first arrival of the Greeks in the island, which was not earlier than the fifteenth century B.C., the Minoans seem to have remained undisturbed and homogeneous as a race.* It is significant however that most of the early Bronze Age sites in Crete appear around its eastern coasts: whether or not the Minoans did in fact come from Asia Minor, their ties still seemed to come from there. The inhabitants of these new little towns, on or near the east Cretan coast, were likely to have been mainly seafaring people, merely using the hinterland as far as they needed to supply their agricultural wants and such excess of produce as they could afford to export. On the seal-stones, and, a little later, on the (pre-linear) hieroglyphics, appear images of ships.

These sailors, however, or perhaps rather the merchants who employed them, seem already to have learnt to appreciate their com-

---

* However, Leonard Palmer in his book *Mycenaeans and Minoans* poses linguistic evidence for a fresh infiltration of Anatolians, whom he calls Luvians, at the end of the Third Millennium.

forts. At the Early Minoan site of Vasilike (just south of the greater township of Gournia, of which more later) were unearthed some really fine houses. The one known as the House on the Hilltop is shown by Pendlebury* to have possessed at least a dozen rooms, probably already to have used the palatial 'light-well 'principle, and to have been built solidly, with a foundation of stone, below sun-dried brick bound by wooden beams.

In other ways the Minoans of the years before the entrance of the Second Millennium (and the Old Palace Period) show a steady growth of peaceful prosperity. The pottery, besides a guide to dates, can also be something of a guide to prosperity, or at any rate to the confident spirit that prosperity may be imagined to engender. The Early Minoan pottery, as well as growing in artistic merit, grows more fanciful in shape and much less dull and inhibited in pattern. There is an E.M. II squat jug with an enormous spout giving the impression (to a modern viewer) of a toucan's beak, and another of the same period with a lid the handle of which is a realistically relaxed dog, lying with its forepaws outstretched. Other pottery styles show a connection, and therefore the probability of trade, with both Egypt and the Cycladic Isles. Yet others show a willingness to experiment artistically: there begins to appear, for instance, the 'barbotine' style, which can only be described as knobbly and seems to have started with the sticking of shells on to the wet clay. Sophisti-cated taste would probably call it barbarous rather than barbotine: perhaps the late Minoan ladies did.

Another characteristic which the E.M. pottery shows is the people's piety, or rather perhaps the growth of a prosperity that enabled them to display an ever-present piety. The Minoans, like another pious people, lifted their eyes unto the hills and chose to believe their protective Divinity to reside in the caves of the moun-tains. Thither they carried and left votive offerings in great abun-dance, the indestructible part of which was in the shape of pottery, somtimes simple and crude, sometimes delicate and artistic. The cave of Kamares, lying between those twin peaks of the Ida range which so impressively overlook the Palace of Phaistos, is one such cave and the richness of discovery that it afforded the archaeologists has caused them to give the name to a whole type of pottery. Piety too is shown to ancestors, in the shape of the earliest Tholos or beehive tombs, filled, however, not with the bones of a single monarch

* The Archaeology of Crete, p. 62.

or a dynasty but rather with those of a whole clan. There is no sign of a unified control in Crete, nor even of a shared rule by a few noble families.

*

The second and greater upheaval already mentioned was now approaching. The cause, on this occasion, lay to the north.

There exists in Europe, and has existed since the ice retreated, a band of steppe country, running with few interruptions west to east and into Asia, north of the Black Sea, around the Caspian and beyond. And here have existed nomad peoples who throughout history have loomed like a dark, menacing, over-spilling cloud. They would one day help to destroy the Roman Empire; their eastern half, in the shape of the Mongols, would later terrify medieval Europe. Now the western half, the Aryan-speaking peoples, would begin an infiltration to the south.

The date: near enough to 2000 B.C. The effect: delayed and slow, but widespread and eventually overwhelming. The cause: perhaps no more explicable than the sudden flight of lemmings, though a good deal more forceful and directed in its execution—an overspill of population, a temporary worsening of climate perhaps, at any rate an urge.

Whatever the reasons, there must have lived in the wide steppe countries a very forceful, virile people. They permeate. They keep on turning up, if not as a people, then as an aristocracy that has conquered or has somehow achieved control of another, less forceful and virile people. We are careful nowadays not to speak of an Aryan race—Hitler has warned us off that mistake—and so we fall back on the indisputable evidence of language. But there must have been a race and people originally, and sufficiently forceful to make their presence felt in varied forms of dilution, with their cousinship always recognizable by a similarity of language.

Steppe-land is grazing land; and the supreme and also one of the most mobile of grazers is the horse. It is always dangerous to spotlight as a cause any single factor in history, lest one make it show up too brightly. But, whether physically or metaphorically, one can usefully make much of the horse. Horsey people are indisputably a different and recognizable kind of people, now and always and throughout the ages. They are self-confident, they do not seek to be over-intelligent but they do seek to be active and forceful and heroic

—it is not necessary to go further than that. They are also—to get on to less debatable ground—in possession of an advantage as conquerors. Cortes, in his advance upon Mexico City and faced with a surviving Bronze Age civilization, won a battle with the decisive help of his squad of cavalry that numbered exactly ten. He possessed therein that great military advantage of surprise, the unhappy Mexicans believing that they faced some strange new god-like monster which had two arms but four feet, what the Greeks had earlier called a centaur. In fact these early Aryan-speakers, when they began to penetrate south, may not yet have ridden the horse, but only harnessed him to the chariot. But even that was enough: the chariot slowly but inevitably became the coveted war-weapon of all the Eastern Mediterranean powers, Knossos included, and the potentates took to greeting each other with polite enquiries about each other's horses as well as each other's wives.*

This time had not yet come, however. The pressure from this first bursting at the seams of the great cosmic bag of horse-owning peoples would be slow in its effect if irresistible. At first the effect might appear as it were at second-hand, one set of people being overwhelmed by another who were themselves being pushed by the prime movers in the rear. In this way were the Romans to be threatened by the Alans and Vandals, themselves threatened by the Huns. So, now, one of the pair of founder-civilizations in the Fertile Crescent, Sumeria, found itself facing its end, though from yet another Semitic conqueror and not from any horsemen from the steppes. There enters upon the Middle Eastern scene Hammurabi, famous as a forerunner of King Minos in that he bequeathed to his people (once he had conquered them) the benefit of law and order.

Hammurabi was of the type of conqueror which the Aryan-speakers—including even the Mycenaeans, in spite of their Homeric reputation as 'sackers of cities'—seem sometimes to have had the sense to copy. He was a benevolent tyrant who, after his necessary conquests, took care to respect the culture of the conquered. His famous code of laws, besides proving a guide for future law-givers, took as a model what he found good in the established customs of his people's past. A significant aspect of these laws was that they recognized varying strata in society but expected, on the theory of *noblesse oblige*, a better code of conduct from the higher ranks, with

* The Amarna Letters, of which more later.

harsher punishments for the same offences, to match and offset their greater privileges.*

A good man, Hammurabi, and one would like to be able to record that his régime lasted for centuries. It did not. It suffered from the great unrest that had begun. Hammurabi's long reign ended about 1750 B.C., and before his son had been for many years on the throne his kingdom fell to the Kassites. The Kassites were an Aryan-speaking people.

There now appeared in Asia Minor the Hurrians, the Mitanni, the Hittites, all Aryan-speaking or Aryan-led. The Hittites made their home in the harsh uplands of central Anatolia; they proved themselves great conquerors, and they were also great charioteers: a manual on horse training has been discovered in their archives, written by a Mitanni. They will appear again in this history.

Invasion and upheaval came also to the other of the two founder civilizations. Upon Egypt descended the Hyksos, with the result that there ensued that country's second and longer 'Intermediate Period'. These 'people from a foreign hill country', somewhat wrongly translated as Shepherd Kings, were also Semites; possibly they included the seed of Abraham, still wandering for the last half dozen generations since their departure from the third and last city of Ur. They therefore come under the category of the pushers pushed by the Aryan-speakers: that they had had contact with these nordic marauders is shown by the fact that they brought the horse with them, the horse and the chariot. They have been described as a fertilizing influence upon Egypt, surely a painful one in operation.

Two other painfully fertilizing streams there are to be traced, and these come definitely from Aryan-speaking stock. One set of people sacks Troy, the fifth city on that site, inhabited by a prosperous Mediterranean people; it builds a sixth Troy which, through earthquake, will give way to a seventh that is Helen's. The other set of people reaches the Peloponnese. The first come down to history as the Trojans, the second as the Mycenaeans. They are in all probability closely related, speaking a closely related language—and that language, for the Mycenaeans at any rate, is Greek.

*

* The Code of Hammurabi rests in the Paris Louvre, on a black obelisk once captured by the Elamites and found in 1901 at Susa.

So there arrive, as yet unsuspected by the short and swarthy Minoans in their island safety, their new and racially different neighbours.

Can these Mycenaeans be spoken of as big and blond, Nordic in that sense of the word? They had a tendency that way, no doubt, but to go further could be unjustified. Homer speaks of some of his Greek heroes as fair or red-haired, Ulysses and Achilles for instance. Such colourings would admittedly be virtually impossible amongst the Minoans, but even amongst the Mycenaeans it may be mentioned only because it is a comparative rarity—and Helen had raven tresses. As a bigger-boned type the Mycenaeans may at least be visualized. What is important to realize is that, notwithstanding all their inter-connection, the frequent similarity of their art, Minoans and Mycenaeans are of two different races, temperamentally as well as physically different.

The Mycenaeans, these first Greeks in the Mediterranean, did not stop in their southerly trek until they eventually reached almost as far as they could. They settled round the Corinthian Gulf and in the Peloponnese as far south as Sparta. Besides Sparta, Mycenaean settlements which remained important in classical times are Thebes and Athens. But their major strongholds, besides Sparta, were Pylos on the western coast, Tiryns overlooking the Argolic Gulf (the space between finger and thumb if we imagine the Peloponnese as a three-fingered hand) and, most important of all and giving them (for us) their name, Mycenae. Mycenae commands the mountain pass that leads to the Corinthian Isthmus, which is itself a connecting link between the Peloponnese and the rest of Greece.

It is perfectly justifiable to give the name 'Mycenaeans' to these first Greeks in Greece, whom earlier historians had vaguely called Aegeans and Homer had dubbed Achaeans: it is a more justifiable name in fact than 'Minoan'. It is not necessarily so justifiable, how-ever, to assume that these real Mycenaeans, whose real relics have been dug up, are one and the same people as the people of a story, Homer's *Iliad*. That is a question that must be cleared up before proceeding any further.

The answer to it is, however, quite simply that we are completely justified. This is not the same thing as to say that Homer's picture of his Achaeans is in all ways historically accurate, far from it. That is what Schliemann hoped and seemed to expect, and in that he was wrong. But for the rest Schliemann was right, and there is no point in

trying to dispute it. Later excavation and philological research has
shown Homer to be wonderfully accurate in his reference to names
of places, his list of contributors of ships to the expedition and so
forth. Then, there are pieces of description in Homer which correspond strikingly with archaeological finds. There is the drinking
cup with doves on its handles, so like a real cup dug up at Mycenae.
There is the description of Hector's shield, hung over his back, which
tapped his heels as he walked, a description which only became
intelligible when the sword was discovered in the Mycenae shaft
graves depicting on its blade enormous body-high shields. There is,
strikingly, the boar's tusk helmet, an unexpected piece of armour
not much in keeping with the rest of a bronze-clad hero's outfit,
which has however been discovered both in clay-model form and,
though disintegrated, in actuality. Now the 'much enduring'
Odysseus, in the tenth book of the *Iliad*, goes on a raid into the
Trojan line. And here we see him, a grimmer figure than when
guest of the Phaeacians, donning practical protective armour. It is
exactly like a raid in the early part of World War I, when the 'tin hat'
or shrapnel helmet, not yet obligatory, is exchanged for the hard
khaki hat of ordinary parade. Odysseus's companion, Diomedes,
dons ' an oxhide casque without peak or plume'. And Odysseus himself is given by Idomeneus's companion Meriones a helmet also made
of leather. 'Inside it there was a strong lining of interwoven straps
under which a felt cap had been sewn in. The outer rim was
cunningly adorned on either side by a row of white and flashing
boar's tusks.'

Homer goes on to describe the helmet's history, a form of circumstantial evidence of which he was fond—as given by so-and-so in
return for hospitality, in this case stolen on one occasion by that
arch-thief, Odysseus's grandfather Autolycus, and so on. The
accuracy of that sort of evidence we cannot now prove, but it sounds
authentic enough. Homer was admittedly writing four or five hundred years after the event. He was nevertheless perpetuating epic
verse handed down by word of mouth by peripatetic court minstrels
who for many reasons saw to it that they kept their tales inviolate and
intact. They were titillating their hearers' ears with heroic tales of
their ancestors; and the more circumstantial they were with names
the better, though no doubt with a little juggling for the particular
occasion. They were achieving their rhythmic recitation and with an
effect of spontaneity by a liberal use of stock phrases which embalmed

ancient realities as clearly and timelessly as amber encasing a fly. All this would admittedly come to be mixed with description of what Homer's readers would expect and understand, thus creating some contradictions and obvious anachronisms which have afforded the experts material for unending dispute. But that fact does not alter the basic truth. The evidence is overwhelming that Troy was attacked and destroyed by the Mycenaeans, and that Homer's heroes—duly coloured by intervening memory—were those Mycenaeans.

We have, then, these new people whom modern historians have agreed to call the Mycenaeans. They are the Greek-speaking element of the wide sweep of Aryan-speakers spreading out from the steppe-countries. Their cousins will sweep through Asia Minor, will penetrate finally, duly mixed with the races through which they have passed, into Persia and India. They themselves will penetrate, as has been said, even to the fingers of the Peloponnese and in that peninsula and around the shores of the Corinthian Gulf they will settle down.

It was during the opening of the Second Millennium that they arrived. Yet it is not until the seventeenth century B.C. and probably not until near the end of it, that they seem to blossom forth into prosperity. The famous Mycenaean fortresses cannot possibly date before that time; most of them date considerably later. In fact, for the period under review here—or, rather, for the last part of it, when they may be said to have come into existence—the Mycenaeans can present us with an even lesser knowledge of their history than the Minoans.

Yet when they did begin to win some power and prosperity as a nation their progress must have been very rapid. Schliemann's finds in the shaft graves (which date at about 1650 B.C.) have only been exceeded in wealth of gold and artistic merit by Carter's finds in the tomb of the Pharaoh Tutankhamen. How had this sudden wealth been accumulated?

It may have been no more than the natural wealth of the land, which, before goats had helped to erode its protecting forests, must have been very considerable. There is reference in the Linear B tablets, both those found in Greece and in Crete, to 'unguent boilers'; and it seems that in both countries there grew up a consider-able and profitable trade in the manufacture and sale of perfumed ointment—or as the modern advertiser would call it, body lotion—founded on an olive oil base. So King Agamemnon and his fore-bears may have possessed, besides an heroic reputation, a profitable factory making this commodity that was to remain popular in the Middle East to the time of Mary Magdalen and beyond. It must be remembered, however, that the Mycenaeans came from a race more naturally warlike than industrial. If there were oil factories, then no doubt the aboriginal inhabitants were the factory hands. Piracy is a possible source of wealth, perhaps from some captured island base; robber barons ensconced in strategic positions were not a new phenomenon, and for that matter the word 'robber' might not have been acceptable. Troy was indeed in a strategic position to exact tribute from ships passing through the Hellespont, and what more natural or legitimate practice could be imagined? It is usually held that Homer's heroes had a more practical inducement for their expedition than merely the avenging of Helen, and their own experience of the lucrative practice on a lesser scale may well have whetted their appetite. A third suggestion is an ingenious but not an unreasonable one. It is made by Joseph Alsop in his book *The Silent Earth*.* Perhaps, he suggests, the Mycenaeans, possessed of no very great natural riches or great inclination to exploit such riches, sold themselves. Perhaps these warlike people, these sackers of cities as Homer called them, hired themselves out as mercenaries. The use of mercenaries is an ancient theme, and even at Knossos there was found, Mr. Alsop reminds us, a fresco which seems to show a file of negro, that is to say foreign, soldiers. At just about this time, too, the Pharaohs were wanting all the aid they could muster in order to drive out the Hyksos conquerors from their land. And finally it would be most likely from Egypt that Mycenae would get her gold. That last point is well made in any case. In whatever way exactly the Mycenaeans were earning their wealth they would have to be fetching it from abroad, they would have to be trading. By 1650 or so, they had reached the stage beyond mere consolidation in a new land.

The Mycenaeans must therefore have made contact with the Minoans, must long have heard of their reputation. As for the Minoans, no doubt they heard too of their new upstart neighbours in the north. But contact between the two, or mutual influence, was as yet insignificant. On a smaller scale the two were a little like China and Rome at the time of the latter's growth to empire: two strong peoples ignorant of and ignoring each other.

*

* Secker and Warburg, 1965.

The Minoans, with their much longer start in the as yet unacknow-
ledged race towards power and civilization, were by no means
standing still. Indeed, as the new millennium begins and as the
Aryan-speakers, future Mycenaeans included, spread southwards, the
Minoans may be said to have been entering truly upon their great
period of civilization. The 'E.M.' period of Arthur Evans has ended
and so has the Pre-Palace Period: in other words, as a sign of established prosperity on the part of both rulers and ruled, the first series
of great palaces were about to be built.

Though the wilder western half of the island was still not
populated, inland townships began at this time to increase. Three
kingdoms appeared, perhaps the mythological kingdoms of Minos,
Rhadamanthus and Sarpedon. The rise of the three great palaces of
Knossos, Phaistos and Mallia presupposes not only prosperity but
kingship, or at least some sorts of central authority that could
command a *corvée*, as well as an increased population to make such a
division of labour economically possible.

The wheeled cart arrives. From the model that has come down to
us it appears a somewhat clumsy affair, a farmer's tool rather than a
traveller's convenience. Nevertheless, roads do also begin to be
made, narrow tracks perhaps but suitable for the messenger, the
palanquin-borne noble and the porter with his pole-carried burden
or his string of asses. Pendlebury—who by the mode of walking over
most of the island mapped these roads—dates to this comparatively
early period the main highway of Minoan civilization, the road from
Knossos to Phaistos which was also extended north and south to the
palace ports of Amnisos and Komo respectively.

The first palaces were less grand editions of their later rebuilt
selves. When one set of buildings has been piled upon another and
both have been crumbled to ruins, it is not easy for the archaeologist to distinguish the new from the old. Nevertheless it has been
made clear that the first palaces of Knossos, Phaistos and Mallia
were by no means crude or embryonic affairs but had all the
essential characteristics of their successors, including differentiated
eastern and western wings and the central feature of a great open
courtyard.

Men do not live by palaces alone, and even more indicative of
growing prosperity is the picture that can be formed of the citizens'
private houses. The main source of information here is the famous
Town Mosaic. This, dating to the end of the Old Palace period at

about 1700, is in the form of faience plaques that may have served as inlays to decorate a wooden chest. The whole scene portrays the houses of a seaside town or port, and scraps showing animals, armed men and ships suggest the possibility of a siege being depicted, a significant hint that Minoan control of the sea was not always easy. Less subject to guesswork is the portrayal of the houses themselves. These are surprising: solid-looking affairs of two and even three storeys. The fact that some of the windows are painted red has suggested to perhaps optimistic interpreters that oiled parchment served as a substitute for glass and to help protect the householders from that strong south wind that blows in the spring and which was to be blowing on their day of catastrophe.

The designs on the seal-stones, now becoming so neat and clever, also give intimations of prosperity. They show for instance the pithos or giant storage jar, and the ship. Each of these could serve as a trade-mark for Crete—perhaps they did. There was carried abroad, by fine ships, in giant pithoi, a renowned product of the land. This was either neat olive oil or else that perfumed ointment to which reference has already been made as manufactured also by the Mycenaeans. Trade, which was as much the life-blood of an ancient nation as of a modern, was undoubtedly increasing in many ways. For it must be remembered that Crete was ideally placed for eastern Mediterranean commerce. She was more or less equidistant from three continents, the focus of sea routes from Cyprus and the eastern coast, from the Delta of the Nile, and from the head of the Adriatic where it is believed the ships met an overland route carrying tin and amber from northern Europe.

Much else the pithoi and the other vases may have contained; and they were so beautiful and distinctive that they were likely to have been exported for their own sake alone. They begin to turn up in Egypt and also at Ugarit, the town on the Syrian coast to which the finger of Cyprus points.*

Of the best pottery, however, no evidence of export abroad has been found. And if the Minoans valued their pottery as surely they must have done, then we may expect not to find such evidence but rather that they had the sense to keep it for themselves. (There may also have been the practical deterrent that much of it was very fragile.) Now there arrives, in these Middle Minoan or Old Palace

* In the reign of Senusert II (c. 1897–1877 B.C.) Minoan pottery was used by the men erecting the pharaoh's pyramid.

periods, perhaps the finest pottery the Minoans ever made, the Kamares ware, named after the cave already mentioned. The Minoans had learnt to use the geared or fast-moving potter's wheel, and they had learnt too to make and fire, when they wanted to, vases of almost eggshell thinness. The crudity of barbotine knobbliness or of toucan-like spouts had gone and the Minoans were displaying an exuberance that was sophisticated, self-confident and controlled. Here is the description of an expert*: 'It had a wonderful harmony of shape and ornamental design. Each vase has a personality of its own. Although the basic decorative motifs were often repeated, they were combined in an unbelievable variety of ways, creating an almost kaleidoscopic impression. The subjects were often drawn from nature but never lose their full decorative effect.'

An archaeological find of another type serves to show to what artistic heights the Minoans were beginning to reach in another medium, metal work. This is the gold brooch, found at Mallia, showing two hornets encircled round what is presumably a surface of honey which they are robbing. We are entitled to imagine that it held no deep or portentous symbolism, as any brooch in any other country would almost inevitably have held, but was just a very pretty thing to wear. One other find of this period shows a man with a dagger at his waist, or it may be a sheath knife: there is therefore no need to impute effeminateness to the Minoan of these times.

One other find is not artistic or masculine in its import but rather political. Near the Knossos throne room Arthur Evans found the bottom half of a diorite statue of a seated man, obviously Egyptian in style and with Egyptian hieroglyphics round its base. It dated without much doubt to the Twelfth Dynasty (c. 1990–1785 B.C.)† and it gave the name of the statue as that of an individual called User, born apparently in the Delta region. From the added epithet 'true of voice', it may be that he died in Knossos. Or it may be that he bequeathed the statue on returning to Egypt. But he must in any case have been an important person, the equivalent of a modern consul

* Nicolas Platon, at the time of writing curator of the Athens Acropolis Museum. This quotation is taken from page 145 of the English translation of his *Crete*, in the *Archaeologia Mundi* series.

† Egyptian dating is closely accurate, and so of great use in the comparative dating of other cultures, owing to two fortunate facts: careful chronology on the part of the Egyptians themselves—in particular by their genealogist Manetho (*floruit* 300 B.C.)—and secondly a reference in comparable Assyrian records to a particular eclipse of the sun which can be exactly dated (June 15, 763 B.C.).

or ambassador, or both. Thus it would seem that at the very beginning of the Old Palace period the Minoans had in the opinion of their established neighbours 'arrived'.

For another two centuries after the departure of User the Minoans, in and around the first edition of their grand palaces, prospered and thrived. Then came the first of the natural catastrophes from which they were to suffer: all three of the palaces were ruined, and no doubt much else besides. Says Nicolas Platon: 'Comparisons with data from Egypt and Mesopotamia show that it took place *circa* 1700 B.C. Such total destruction could only have been caused by a geological upheaval, as there was no foreign invasion to account for it, and it has in fact been proved that a violent earthquake did occur at the time.'

It was just the time when, on the other hand, the Mycenaean civilization was beginning to make its rapid progress.

Chapter VIII

Minoan Life at its Height

IT is all too easy to enthuse over the uniqueness, the beauty, delicacy, sophistication and happiness that must have accompanied Minoan civilization at its height. But it is also too easy to discount such enthusiasm, telling oneself that the discovery of so much that was both beautiful and unexpected would naturally lead to an exaggerated response, and that in any case to enthuse over such things is natural to anyone who wishes—and do not we all?—to be considered an artistic, sensitive and perceptive person.

It is necessary, therefore, to try to strike the golden mean—which is after all a Greek habit, though not perhaps in this case one inherited from the Minoans. The evidence left behind by the Minoans is extensive. It needs to be assessed with a careful mind, though certainly not an inhibited one.

First of all there is a significance in what the Minoans did *not* leave behind.

They did not leave any vast temples, wherein, impressive and heavy with symbolism, priests would have officiated. (And an idea of how heavy and oppressive that symbolism could be in primitive religions, with what deadly seriousness it must have been regarded, is borne in upon one from the early books of the Bible. The 28th chapter of Exodus, for instance, even on the minor matters of dress: 'And they shall make the ephod of gold, of blue, and of purple, of scarlet, and fine twined linen, with cunning work. It shall have two shoulder pieces thereof joined at the two edges thereof. And for Aaron's sons thou shalt make coats, and thou shalt make for them girdles, and bonnets shalt thou make for them, for glory and for beauty.')

Then, the Minoans did not wear beards. The Sumerians show dignitaries in heavy woollen skirts and equally heavy beards. The Mycenaean chieftains—at least judging by the gold mask that

79

Schliemann thought was Agamemnon's—wore beards and mous-
taches, which made them look fierce rather than portentous. The
Egyptians, unable apparently to grow good beards, tied a wooden
substitute on to the chin of their Pharaoh to add to his dignity. The
Minoans did without.

They did not go in for brooding, overhanging vastness of any
sort. Particularly, there were no vast statues. Nor did they seek any
imposing surface—whether it be on giant statues as in Egypt, or on
great upright slabs as in the land of the Hittites, or on inaccessible
rock faces as in Persia—on which to proclaim royal boasts of pomp
and power and victory in war.

They did not indulge in the tortuous voluptuousness and exaggeration of Indian art; they most certainly did not indulge in tortured,
brutal, bloodthirsty art such as that of the Aztecs and Mayas,
civilizations that though later in date were in much the same state of
material development.

None of the above is to say, however, that the Minoans were not
religious, did not have priests, were not affected by symbolism and
what we now regard as superstition. All peoples of Bronze Age
civilizations did all those things. In fact it will be as well, before
considering what was distinctive about Minoan civilization, to
remember what they did have in common with their contemporaries:
what may be called the basic Bronze Age mentality.

Every Bronze Age person, wherever he lived, was a neolithic person,
only slightly grown up. He was of the earth, earthy, which meant a
good deal more than that he was a little muddy of hand or dusty of
clothes. He had become a working partner with Mother Earth, and
this senior partner of his was a potent, not to say mysterious, person,
who needed to be propitiated and considered and worshipped.

Economic Man did not exist, any more than did Scientific Man.
Only Religious Man existed, if the term is taken widely enough.
Such a human being is certainly as anxious as any modern man to
live fully and to live well, as passionate and wilful in his desires. But
he will think in totally different terms when it comes to implement-
ing those desires. His prosperity he will consider as bound up with
the prosperity of his tribe or nation or people, governed by the king
who is also priest to the goddess. Be he merchant or sailor, aristocratic landowner, or craftsman, or peasant—and there is not much
else that he could be—he will think in that way. At the highest his
desires will be for prestige and power, and honour and the pride of

beautiful possessions; at the lowest it will be for a full belly and salvation from war and plague and such unhappy demonstrations of the powers of Nature as flood and tempest and earthquake, all of which will without doubt be the retribution for some communal sin. Fundamentally, human nature was much the same, the best part of four millennia away, as it is now. But the difference in thought would be very soon apparent. No doubt the pregnant girl of Knossos did take practical steps to protect her unborn child. But she did not go to a clinic but to the cave of Eileithyia, where among the imposing stalagmites she presented votive offerings to that particular personification of the Great Mother Goddess who took care of the likes of her. The Minoan merchant-skipper did not fail to insure against loss at sea; but he went, most likely, to an expert on omens—omens of the flight of birds perhaps, since Minoans thought much in terms of symbolism of birds—and this expert would tell him when and when not to sail. . . .

*

A Bronze Age people then, thinking and living in Bronze Age terms: that is a useful generalization. But the Minoans were, if nothing else, a distinctive people. They were distinguished by their home.

They were an island people; their home was an island home. And a home makes its people, a people makes its home and is thereafter influenced by it once again. Was Minoan Crete a rugged home like, let us say, Scotland, or an easy paradise comparable to a Polynesian island such as Tahiti, whose first discoverer, incidentally, named it romantically after an island of the Aegean, New Cytherea?

The answer is: something of each. Fly over modern Crete, and one's major impression will be of a land of harsh and arid mountains. But descend to its valleys, and walk those valleys in the spring, when the rains have ceased, and most but not all of the snow on the mountains has melted, and the strong south wind is dying down and there are beginning the long months of clear and uninterrupted sunshine—walk those valleys with a regard that can be closer and more intimate and more accurate, and one will be filled with the impression of a lovely and fertile and generous land.

Modern Crete is likely to differ from Minoan Crete only in two major ways and neither in the manner of an improvement. Nowadays, amidst the pale and barren limestone outcrops only a few gnarled and not too happy olive trees straggle up the mountain sides, petering out like the advance guard of some army already acknowledging defeat. But in Minoan times forest covered the mountain slopes—so the geological and biological experts tell us— almost to the snowline. This forest, when it strayed too far down-wards, cannot have been a direct blessing, but the reverse, necessita-ting hard work with the double axe, not the symbolic representation but the real thing. But in binding the soil, increasing the moisture, and so helping towards fertility, the mountain-side forests must have been a very great blessing to the Minoans.

The second difference is a particular aspect of that general contamination which modern worldwide industrialization produces, the contamination of the sea shores and the life of the seas that infringe on these shores. Modern Crete is by no means a greatly industrialized country. But the ecological balance is a delicate one. Any reader of Edmund Gosse's *Father and Son*, and of his descrip-tion of the unspoilt wonders of inter-tidal life along the south Devon shores which the two entranced botanists discovered, must be impressed by the obvious difference between those shores now and a century or so ago and the natural poverty that has been caused in the interval.

The sea shores of Crete three thousand years ago must have been spectacular with life. This may indeed seem a minor aspect of the influence of their home upon the Minoan people. But in practice it cannot have been. The Minoan artist did indeed love to depict human beings in familiar likeness, he did indeed love to depict the flowers and plants and patterns of leaves that he knew. But it was, for some reason, the life of the sea and the seashore that he loved above all to paint. As the Minoan made his merchant journeys over the Mediterranean the agile and sportive porpoise followed him, and the flying fish flew up out of the way of the jaws of the porpoises. The queen—if Arthur Evans is right in his allocations of the rooms of Knossos—had that very scene painted upon the walls of her megaron or boudoir. As the Minoan made his inshore fishing trip, he saw the pearly nautilus floating by, using his shell as a sail; he looked down through the wonderfully clear water, and saw the intricate rock formation and its animal-vegetable growth of waving fronds and tentacles; he watched the movement through the water of the octopus, and, apart from appreciating it as good food, had the time and sensibility to appreciate it as a creature of graceful movement and pattern.

In truth the Minoan was essentially an islander, and this is only one particular aspect of the truth. One can live in the middle of England and be very little conscious of the sea. One can, for that matter, live in the middle of such a vast city built on a tiny island as New York, and because of the city again be unconscious of the sea. But Crete, besides having no big cities, is long and thin: nowhere can one be much cut off from the sea.

As well as by the sea, the Minoan must have been affected by the mountains. Always he will have seen them, wherever he was, rising up from the plains, close-seeming because of the clear atmosphere, forming impressive silhouettes at the time of sunset. From the neighbourhood of Knossos he could lift up his eyes and see in the outline of Mount Jukte the profile of a recumbent god. At Mallia, though he was on a seaside plain, he had the mountains rising up behind him. At Phaistos, already at a height, he could look north over the fertile valley to Mount Ida, snow-topped and highest of them all, with next to it the twin peaks of the Diginis Saddle, below which an all-seeing eye seemed to gaze down on him from the distance, that eye being the holy cave of Kamares.

More practically, the mountains would have given the Minoans what they still give the modern Cretans, a variety of climate. Whereas on the plains an almost tropical vegetation can be grown—nowadays even bananas—some little way up the mountain slopes the fruit and vegetables of the temperate climes will flourish. When the summer heat has burnt up the grass, the flocks can be moved to higher pastures, still reasonably green.

Not that one must paint too sentimentally rosy a picture. The fact remains that the backbone of Crete is, and always has been while man has been upon this earth, mountain, and that there is a greater area where cultivation is impossible than possible. A Cretan would have to be a hardy and hard-working person if he were going to thrive on his beautiful island. He would also find it convenient and natural to be a sailor, or to put this point on the right and domestic scale, a boatman. There is a point here that modern man with his means of land transport cannot easily realize: on a mountainous, sea-girt small island such as Crete, with its much indented coast, transport over the water is, in contrast to that over land, both the easier and by far the more obvious method. The Cretan, then, would have had skill with boats.

But more than anything else the Cretan would need to have been a farmer and a hard-working farmer at that. And that is something to remember before one considers again the ladies in the frescoes and all in the way of sophistication that these suggest. After all, the prosperity of any society not industrialized, as we understand the term, cannot rest on a very wide or varied basis. Foreign commerce has greatly enriched a nation in any age, for not only does such exchange of goods bring in a profit but the introduction of new and exotic things creates a demand that did not exist before. The Minoans certainly engaged in foreign trade and sold and carried abroad their oil and scented unguents and their metalwork and beautiful pottery. A nation may also sell its services abroad, by way of mercenary soldiers for instance, or it may gain wealth by pure piracy; but though, as has been said, the Mycenaeans may well have done both these things there is no evidence that the Minoans did, and it does not seem in keeping with their character that they should have done so. Finally, a nation may extract and sell its mineral wealth; but again there is no evidence that the Minoans did this.

There remains only the wealth of the land itself which comes from its fertility. That is in any instance fundamental. The earth will grow its fruits—either to be eaten direct by men or eaten by the animals that men will later eat. And in either instance much activity, pastoral or by way of cultivation and husbandry, is needed. The Minoans, for all their sophisticated and cleverness and artistic ability, were not exempted from that life of primitive toil.

The mass of Minoans were, then, peasant farmers. But they too, since undoubtedly Crete in the sixteenth and seventeenth centuries B.C. was highly prosperous, must have shown cleverness and a considerable expertise.

They grew barley for bread and perhaps for sprinkling over their meat as they cooked it, as is described in Homer. They grew the olive and the vine. Those three are the typical products of the Mediterranean and they grew them well. They herded the sheep and the goat, the Linear writing showing that the numbers of the former were surprisingly large. They hunted the ibex, whose kingdom was the mountain crag and whom, with his magnificent curving horns, it is something of an insult to call a kind of goat.

There is no better way, if it can be achieved, of summoning up in one's imagination the aspect of a countryside than by visualizing what an exile of the time would have conjured up in his own imagination. The Minoan merchant-adventurer, the Minoan ambassador of his country's greatness, pining in the polyglot port of Byblos or in the dull flatness of Egypt, the Minoan sailor: of what would all those have dreamt?

They would have dreamt surely of their sunny landscape, their mountains that so lent enchantment to the view, their plains and valleys, soft to the tread, basking in the heat, smelling of thyme, and whispering with the stridulation of the cicada, that large and clumsy sort of grasshopper which flits from tree to tree like a miniature and inebriated bat. They would have thought of the serried rows of vines, cut back short and ruthlessly·in the winter—if they were cultivated then as they are now, which is a not unreasonable supposition—and raising up their green-decked arms like miniature suppliants to heaven. They would have thought, without a doubt, of the olive trees, spaced out on the hillside, old and gnarled, yet full of an unspectacular fertility, their branches sweeping over to the red-brown earth yet stopping short at sufficient height to give comfortable shade to man and beast—and always, always their grey-green leaves, more grey than green, shimmering faintly and rustling in the breeze. He would think of the profusion of wayside flowers, the pink and the rockrose and the little blue pimpernel, the very deep red poppy and the asphodel-like candelabra. If he had ever been a hunter he would think certainly of his distinctive beast, the crag-leaping ibex. There is an unexpected passage in a modern book, the second volume of Leonard Woolf's autobiography, where he describes how in the mountains of Ceylon he suddenly saw a deer launch himself magnificently out into space: the description makes it clear how such a sight can become indelibly printed on the memory. Something of the same impression then must have been registered on many a Minoan memory, and it was fitting, and is significant, that it should be so. He did not fail to show the leaping, the nobly horned, ibex in his art.

Yet it is also significant that the Minoan artist was sometimes pleased to show a less spectacular and heroic stance in portraying this most admired and loved of his wild beasts. There are two small faience plaques found at Knossos that show respectively a cow and a female ibex. Both are suckling their young, and both are showing an overflow of motherly love in doing so. These are lovely works of art, gentle things; it would not be altogether unfair to call them sentimental. They are as far removed from contemporary oriental art, or from American Indian art, or, with the possible exception of

Akhneten's, from Egyptian art, as shall we say, a Rubens cherub from a sphinx. . . .

*

Finally, in seeking to learn what life was like for the Minoan in the time of his heyday, which is the time of the flourishing of the second series of palaces, we should not forget those palaces, that is to say those other than Knossos, which has already been described. The Minoan himself, though he would most certainly have known of Knossos, might very well have never made the journey there, indeed would be more than likely not to have done so. He would, however, be likely to know the particular palace which afforded him protection and to which he owed allegiance, and to have nostalgic and sentimental memories of it, were he to be exiled.

No palace has yet been discovered for certain in the west of the island; and it is surprising how little, except perhaps at the end, the Minoans penetrated into what was presumably still the mountainous wilderness of that part. The discovered palaces, besides Knossos, are Mallia, Phaistos and Zakro.

Mallia, twenty miles east of Knossos as the crow flies, lies near to a beautiful sandy beach. Behind it rise suddenly and dramatically the mountains, but itself sits forthright on the plain.

The site, however, was not chosen for beauty alone, but rather for practical advantage. It lay on a wide strip of fertile land along which ran the road connecting eastern with central Crete; it was its own port and, as it faced the Aegean Sea, no doubt a busy one. One should not, however, imagine much in the way of jetties or hards, the more normal practice being to run at least the smaller ships up on to a shelving beach.

Mallia is remarkably like Knossos in plan, though not so elaborate nor so well built. There is no theatre or dance floor on which to welcome the returning king. But, beside the stairs on the west side of the central court, so like Knossos, was a slightly raised open logia; and, as remains of rich regalia were found in the room behind, it is thought that here the king might have ceremoniously appeared. By a process of elimination this king or dynasty should be Sarpedon, with Minos at Knossos and Rhadamanthus at Phaistos; Mallia is however a modern name only, Professor Marinatos opining that its Minoan name was Tamara.

There is here the same evidence as at Knossos of great storage capacity, lined pits that may have been grain silos being added to the usual giant pithoi. There is also more intimate evidence of religious observance. The great central court shows what no other of these shows, the remains of an altar, while at the court's south-west corner is a *keros*, a circular stone having all round its circumference a series of shallow cup-like indentations for small offerings, perhaps of first fruits or seeds—a gift to the goddess which is at the same time a hopeful bargain for reciprocal treatment, the reward of fertility.

Mallia, excavated by the French, has now none of the elaborate reconstruction of Knossos; and this is a lack that, if it precludes an easy understanding of the layout, does afford the imagination longer rein. Stand by one of the giant pithoi in the quiet yellow evening sunlight, with the mountains on the one side and the blue rim of the sea on the other; and it is at least a little easier to transport oneself back the necessary three-and-a-half millennia and to imagine the courts and corridors peopled with supple and bronzed Minoan men and delicate, white-skinned ladies in their rustling skirts.

If such can be said of Mallia it can even more truthfully be said of Phaistos. Phaistos is a lovely site. The modern visitor is fortunate in having more of the original building to view, its colour often the pale golden glow of Cotswold stone. To a visitor of any age the situation of the palace is magnificently regal.

Again there were practical reasons for the site: in the midst of the most fertile plain of Crete; near to beaches from which ships could sail to Egypt and Africa. Again, as at Knossos, there is evidence in the building of the palace of good engineering and good drainage; again there are storage corridors though not so extensive. It is for its theatral area that Phaistos is outstanding, it surely being here rather than at Knossos that Homer ought to have spoken of Ariadne's dancing floor. There might have been room even on this paved floor for the bull-game: it has been suggested that it was in the south of Crete that the county's wild bull mostly roamed. It was in the south too, it seems, that the best ceramic artist thrived, since the famous Kamares cave is near by.

One last thing needs to be said about Phaistos (which, though the most beautiful and evocative of the palace sites, yet did not produce a great deal in the way of significant artefacts). It is the fact that in the summer's torrid heat, when the little town in the valley would have sweltered, the palace lay in the path of a cool breeze blowing

from Mount Ida. 'So,' writes justifiably one enthusiast,* 'in the
olden days life was pleasant on the cool terraces, under the shady
colonnades and in rooms with large folding doors which could be
flung open to admit the fresh air from outside.' Pleasant that is to say
for the aristocracy, though no doubt the others found their
compensations in this peaceful land.

North-west across the Gulf of Mesara, from which the Phaistos
spur of hills rises, is a little town whose modern name is 'Holy Peace,
Hagia Gallene'. And between the two lies the villa or minor palace,
called after a Christian chapel dating from Venetian times, Hagia
Triada. A paved Minoan road connected it with Phaistos, and this
has led to the idea that Hagia Triada may have also been a royal
palace—a summer residence it is usually called, though if the
Rhadamanthines appreciated the cooling breeze, winter residence is
the more likely term.

It is sufficient to say of Hagia Triada—though again it is a beautiful spot—that here were found the three works of art of outstanding
merit, the 'chieftain cup', a rhyton showing boxing, wrestling and
the bull-game, and the 'harvester vase'. Those together are enough to
make any place famous. Indeed they make the place—and the time—
unique. What other art, of fifteen or so centuries before Christ, can
show such brilliant naturalness uninhibited by the heavy stultifying
hand of tradition, superstition, kingly commands or religious taboos
—such faithful but unexaggerated realism, such cheerful, intimate
humanity?

Zakro is the last of the palaces discovered, the land-owner, it is
said leading the archaeologists to the spot by seeking to pay his
Haraklion doctor's bill by means of a discovered gold ring. It lies on
the short Cretan coast that faces due east; and the presence in the
neighbourhood of villas and sanctuaries had already led to the belief
that the supporting focal point of a palace ought to exist. Nicolas
Platon and the Greek archaeologists of Athens started, with American
help, to excavate in 1961. They were rewarded as quickly and
spectacularly as had been Arthur Evans. Platon believes that Zakro
—again it is a modern name, called after the bay on which it stands—
was not only another commerical and shipping centre but also the
Minoans' main 'naval' base in exercising her command of the sea.

Again Zakro conforms remarkably to the traditional palace plan,
though it has its distinctive features: one is that there were not only

* Hanni Guanella, in *Ancient Crete*—see Bibliography.

Fresco from the palace of Knossos
nicknamed "La Parisienne"

Photo Mansell Collection

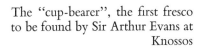

The "cup-bearer", the first fresco
to be found by Sir Arthur Evans at
Knossos

Photo Mansell Collection

The "young Prince", fresco from Knossos

The "gossiping ladies" of the restored miniature fresco from Knossos

The Vaphio cups. First scene: on the right the bull is being amorous towards the decoy cow, whilst on the left the capture of the bull is beginning. Second scene: in the process of capture one man is being tossed whilst another is in danger of being trampled to death

Photos Hirmer, Munich

The Chieftain Cup from Hagia Triada, thought by some to portray
children playing at soldiers

Photo Hirmer, Munich

Two beautiful *pithoi* or storage jars from Knossos. The one on the left was probably used for almond oil—hence its patterning

Photos Mansell Collection

Photo Mansell Collection

The "common touch": votive figures or idols from Knossos and Mycenae respectively

Photo Lord William Taylour

Photo Ashmolean Museum

Mycenæan culture, early and late: (above) replicas from finds from the shaft graves, including the gold mask thought by Schliemann to be that of Agamemnon, and, on the left, the dove-handled cup so like that described in Homer's *Iliad*; and (below) copy of a Tiryns fresco, showing the very marked Minoan influence

royal bath-tubs but also apparently, a small royal swimming pool. The palace is also distinctive in that there was no 'first' palace, the original building taking place at the same time as the construction of the 'new' palaces on the other site.

Another distinctive feature is the fact that the site does not ever seem to have suffered from robbers or plunderers. There is consequently a great deal of untouched pottery. Here we are back in a religious atmosphere, or at any rate ritualistic, with a bull's-head rhyton rivalling that found at Knossos and another rhyton depicting a mountain sanctuary, the chief artistic feature of which is the life-like depicting of the magnificent mountain goat. Evidences of trade and the importing of raw material for the Minoan artist are axe-shaped copper ingots (almost certainly from the island of copper, Cyprus), and a whole elephant's tusk, probably from Syria where it is believed elephants were still extant. Then there is great evidence of practical skills. First, enormously long bronze saws, no doubt more efficient than we should feel inclined to credit, since square-cut or ashlar stones could not otherwise have been created, either in Crete or in Egypt. Secondly, a wealth of kitchen utensils. These, together with, for instance, those found earlier at Gournia, give when collected together a considerable impression of culinary skill, something that we should perhaps have expected. Another significant find was what seemed undoubtedly a dye-house, with rows of tubs, whilst near by were found traces of violet dye: perhaps the Minoans and not the Phoenicians first discovered the famous royal purple.

Finally, a discovery at Zakro of more sinister significance. Excavation revealed, as Platon puts it 'huge lumps of volcanic debris which had been flung across during the eruption, a distance of eighty miles!' The eruption referred to is that of Santorin: the digging at Zakro has greatly strengthened the Santorin theory of the prime cause of the Minoans' fall.

Chapter IX

Government, Goddesses and Bulls

APEOPLE NEED not necessarily be shaped into beauty by possessing a beautiful home. In performing their part of an inevitable mutual process, that is to say in moulding the country that has moulded them, they may make an ill return and harm themselves in the process. Happily there is little sign of this in ancient Crete.

What the laws and constitution of the Minoans were before their decline it is not possible to say, though some reasonably informed guesses can be made. What the religion and the rituals were that bound them together it is easier to formulate.

We know nothing of Minoan laws as such. But we do know that Kings Minos and Sarpedon went down in legend as great and successful law-givers. Minos possessed in Greek legend something of the reputation of a tyrant. But that aspect is coupled with that of a conqueror and may do no more than reflect a foreign and weaker people's fear—and the Greeks were in an case congenitally suspicious of tyrants, benevolent or otherwise.

It seems likely that the Minoans were not worried on that account. Certainly the constitution under which they lived must have been a highly paternal one.

This fact is shown in so many ways by what has been found at Knossos and at the other palaces. There are the serried ranks of storage corridors in the palaces, either with their cubicles and lockers or containing those truly vast pithoi or urns of glazed pottery, a feat of the potter's art in themselves, that kept the central store of oil and wine.* There are the remains of many artisans' workshops within

---

* The question that will naturally occur to a modern potter is how could such huge jars possibly be made. It is believed that they were built up on a slow wheel, somebody else probably doing the turning. Only a few inches in height would have been possible at a time, a drying-off process being necessary between each operation. For the higher and more vertical parts, the pithoi may have been built up by bending round and adding pre-formed ropes of clay. It is believed

the palace precincts. There is the evidence for strict accounting of all dues in kind that came to the palace; there is even evidence of some centralized standard of value and exchange (though not of any sort of coinage) in those large ingots of bronze that were found at Zakro, cast in the shape of the royal and sacred double axe, a sort of mark of assay.

In fact the Minoan system of governemnt may be called a feudal system, though probably a loose one. We do not know whether by the time of the new palaces Knossos had gained hegemony over the other palaces and over the island as a whole, though much in the legends makes this seem likely. By this time a large number of smaller 'palaces' were being built, though it would really be better to call these mansions or simply houses—houses of the rich. Some may have been merchants'; one, from its contents, a plethora of ritual paraphernalia, is thought to have been an important priest's house. Perhaps such owners did not come within a strict feudal system. The fact remains, however, that often the big house takes the commanding position and the little houses cluster round it. This is the case at Gournia, the town in East Crete overlooking the Bay of Mirabello that was excavated soon after Evans began at Knossos by the American couple, Charles and Harriet Boyd Hawes. Certainly these two found a great difference between the size of the house of the lord of the manor and of the common person—as of course might have been expected. There is indeed a disconcerting discrepancy between the comparative grandeur of all the houses shown in the 'town mosaic' already referred to and the mean dimensions of the ground-floor plan of the common run of houses unearthed at Gournia. An effort has been made to resolve the difficulty by suggesting that the rooms of the Gournia houses were less meanly proportioned on the first floor; and another and more drastic way out would be to suggest that the town mosaic does not depict a Minoan town at all but a town that the Minoans were besieging. Perhaps, however, there is no difficulty to resolve: the Minoans were obviously capable of building magnificent houses; but a realistic assessment of any Bronze Age civilization will face up to the likelihood that the great majority of its people lived, not in the least squalidly, but nevertheless humbly, poorly and unspaciously.

---

that the firing of these huge pots was achieved by half-burying them in the ground and then burning brushwood over them.

One thing, however, may be taken as certain: if we say that the Minoans lived under a feudal system we must not envisage a strictly military feudal system. Perhaps what would now be called naval service, some patrolling of the coasts, was a feudal obligation. But there was no military obligation; that is a point which may well be stressed again: the palaces were not fortified, the armed and marching soldier hardly ever appears on fresco or pot or monument. In fact even when he is occasionally glimpsed he seems to give thereby added evidence of his scarcity and unusualness. One such appearance is on a fragment of fresco called 'The Captain of the Blacks', where the rank of soldiers appear to be negroes. Was King Minos not selling mercenaries but *buying* them? Another scene, on the Chieftain Cup from Hagia Triada, is undoubtedly martial—'Slope swords!' But the two figures look like children. Indeed they look completely like children—and such a scene is wholly in keeping with happy, cheerful, sentimental Minoan art. And if any objector wishes to make the point that if there were children playing soldiers then there must have been real soldiers, he is at liberty to make it. By 1500 B.C. soldiers had existed for a couple of thousand years, no doubt; and any society can have its soldiers and its sentries, its bodyguards, without being militaristic.

A further indication, dug up by the archaeologists, of an accepted and well-run feudalism is another of the Hagia Triada finds, the famous Harvester Vase. This is a beautiful and most sophisticated piece of work in black steatite, showing skilfully in semi-relief around the cup or vase a procession of men carrying their sickles and singing lustily and joyfully. A priest seems to be leading them, another man keeps time with a sistrum, and another man seems to be cheerfully, and perhaps drunkenly, trying to march the wrong way. Perhaps the artist idealized the scene. But at any rate, here is a harvest home-coming, and the point is that it is at once happy and roisterous and at the same time organized, with a backing of religious sanction and with apparently a total and willing acceptance of such. If there was an objector to the Establishment amongst that jolly crowd, a young 'leftist' seething inwardly with bitter indignation, he does not appear—unless of course he is the man going the wrong way, though one feels that, on the vase, he is doing so not to be difficult but to be funny. . . .

It may well be ridiculous, however, to talk of leftists and kickers against the pricks of Establishment in Minoan times. It has already been suggested that man of the Bronze Age was religious man. All societies were, no doubt to greater or lesser degrees, what Karl Popper has called 'closed' societies, where men did not begin to think of rebellion or of opting out, where the whole atmosphere was one of conformity and of a knowledge that only by conformity could prosperity be achieved. Quite possibly the Minoan was more individualistic, more intelligent, less conformity-minded than the flat-landed Egyptian or Sumerian peasant. But we have no right to take that difference very far.

*

What then was the Minoan like in his religion?

That is a very wide-ranging question, almost like saying: what was the Minoan like in his thoughts? His religion, like that of any Bronze Age person, was part of himself, informing unconsciously all his outlook; it was certainly not a Sunday, a one-day-a-week affair: such a concept would have been incomprehensible to him.

Yet it need not have been intense. One cannot imagine either the ladies of the miniature frescoes on the one hand or the harvesters on the jug on the other hand, being passionately religious.

Rather, his religion was all in a day's work. Indeed in some ways it was a work, the work of propitiating, persuading, influencing the God to order affairs as one wished or, if that were impossible, of making informed guesses as to the direction in which the said God in his omniscience was going to jump.

'The God'—is that correct? Or is it the gods, or the Fates, or the gods and goddesses, or, simply 'The Goddess'?

The answer is almost certainly 'The Goddess'. Minoan religion by all the signs was a relatively simple and primitive one: worship of the power and spirit that emanates from that Earth from which all fertility issues, worship of the Earth Mother, the Mother Goddess.

She had, the Minoan Earth Mother, many emanations and many aspects, each with their particular symbol and familiar. One of these was the bull, symbol of potency and strength. One was the dove, symbol of power—benign power?—from heaven. One was the snake, symbol of domestic protection. One was the pillar, symbol of —it is hard to know what, unless one accepts the obvious phallic explanation, which seems a little too crude and obvious.

In considering the worship of the Mother Goddess one comes much nearer, as near as one can ever come, to the common men and women of Minoan Crete. For those men and women went to the shrines of the goddess, which were usually within caves high up in the mountains, and having made their pilgrimage they presented their votive offerings. These might often have been something that in time would decay. But often it was a little figurine, a model in clay that is imperishable. The little model, just a few inches long, might be of an animal, a bull perhaps; it might be of a human limb, in which case one may be sure that the pilgrim came to seek miraculous health in that particular limb of his or her own body. Or it might be, and most often was, a model of the worshipper raising his arms in the accepted attitude of adoration. And all these models are crude. Obviously they are intentionally and acceptedly crude, with the face for instance no more than a pinch of the clay between thumb and forefinger. They contented the common people, who either made them or bought them; they contented, in those people's estimation, the goddess in her many forms to whom they were offered. But let there be no mistake about it. They are to the delicate bowls of the Kamares ware, or the fine filigree and granulated work of the gold ornament, as is the humble cromlech to the Taj Mahal. The crudity one may take as a sure sign of simple earnestness. But one cannot imagine a court lady offering up one of these figurines. There is therefore a suggestion of a class-structured society and some considerable difference of outlook between the classes. That, however, is to be expected in any case.

The differences, nevertheless, would be within the framework of a common religion, that of the worship of the Earth Mother in her many roles: even the court lady, if she found herself pregnant, would not scorn to visit the cave of Eileithyia, a place incidentally of enough potency to give its name to the classical Greek goddess of childbirth. The religion of court circles one would expect to be more sophisticated, more concerned with ritual and less with the simple giving and supplicating and bargaining with the god in which the peasant naturally indulged.* This idea is borne out by the discovery in the palace of Knossos of the effigies of the 'snake goddess'.

Here are accomplished works of art. Snake priestesses would be a more accurate description. They are not likely to please in conception a modern court lady, nor for that matter often a modern peasant either. The priestesses—there are two statuettes together with another of more doubtful provenance—are elaborately dressed. The

---

* With theology even—see Michael Ayrton's *The Maze Maker*.

snakes coil themselves over wrists and waist and head: the ladies are obviously expert snake charmers and manipulators. But, although there is obviously a potency in these snakes, there is no suggestion of an evil or frightening potency, as there is in the Greek Medusa head with writhing snakes for hair. Rather, it is much more like the snake-fringed shawl that the Greek goddess Athene wears, something that, spread out, affords protection, though it can be cast with magical and unpleasant effect upon an enemy. In fact the snake, besides being a fairly obvious symbol of Earth, over which it goes so closely upon its belly, is a symbol of protection. It has been pointed out that in all climes and times where snakes abound, the harmless and non-poisonous snake has been not only a symbol of protection but a protection in fact, becoming a useful scavenger and pet on a par with the farmyard cat, earning its saucer of milk and, in some instances, a man-made tube into which to slither as its home. Such tube-homes have been dug up out of ancient Crete.

Nevertheless, to have oneself crawling with snakes is not a natural idea in any age, however less squeamish than our own. One cannot help feeling that here there exists a sort of wilful, fascinated exaggeration, a pushing of things beyond the natural on the part of an upper stratum of society seeking sensation. That may be an unwarranted deduction; but there is another Minoan ritual, to be discussed shortly, where the imputation is scarcely escapable.

There is always an element of fear in religion. Whether or not the fear of the Lord is the beginning of wisdom, certainly the fear of the powers of the Lord is an example of very ordinary common sense. For if by the Lord one means Nature, which in any primitive religion one fundamentally does, then he is truly powerful, unpredictable, very doubtfully controllable by even the strongest magic or the extremest propitiation, and often in his actions catastrophic to puny man.

Now, though one always comes back to interpreting the Minoan's civilization as essentially and naturally happy, yet he must have had his fears, and it is obvious that he had one major one.

The minor fears can easily be guessed at, and should not be forgotten, lest one pictures too easily, and wrongly, a paradisical existence in Minoan Crete. No religion that is based on superstition and irrational beliefs can avoid producing such fears, however beneficial it may be in other ways and as a binding force to its participants. One can see how virulently it persists even in the modern world by reading for example the novels of Africa by Joyce Cary or of the Hindus by V. S. Naipaul. Minoans are not likely to have escaped the fear of some form of evil eye, for instance, or of bad omens, of the sinister influence of the unusual in any form, from the bird that flies strangely or alights significantly, to the child born unhappily with a sixth finger or a hare lip (caused, of course, by the pregnant mother seeing a hare).

But those sorts of minor fears are common to every people, and it is remarkable how easily men and women can live with them, seem indeed almost lost without them. The Minoans must have had one fear in a different category, a common and omnipresent fear. That was the fear of earthquake. Always, the archaeologists are finding evidence of earthquake; at least twice, it is firmly believed, the palaces and houses of Minoan Crete suffered major damage from this cause.

Here is the work of the Earth Mother at her most terrifying. And the Earth Mother, who in one of her emanations is Lord of the Animals, has many such servants and familiars.* In her most benign aspect she has the dove, the loving creature which alights delicately from the heavens. But in her most terrible aspect she has as her servant and familiar the roaring bull.

To experience an earthquake, even in a minor form, is a most impressive and frightening business: that is a universal opinion. To a people primitive in their religion but naturally sensitive, the experience must have shaken them to the core of their souls and imagination. Here beyond doubt was the Earth Mother's bull roaring and stirring below the ground. Arthur Evans, who was never unduly fanciful, gives evidence for this idea. Not only did he excavate two houses side by side just outside the perimeter of Knossos Palace, and find in one incontrovertible evidence of violent damage by earth-quake and in the other evidence of the sacrifice of bulls. But also he himself suffered a considerable earthquake shock while in his house, the Villa Ariadne, which he had built near the Knossos site. He describes how the actual movement was preceded by a rumbling,

---

*The 'lord of the animals' is also a Sumerian idea, and there are many representations of the hero-god Gilgamesh showing his prowess in this direction by such feats as holding up a couple of lions by the feet. Examples have been found of the same sort of masterful behaviour on the part of the Minoan Earth Mother; more usually, however, she is merely supported on each side by two animal familiars, the animals being the right way up.

which came from below the earth and which sounded to him just like the muffled bellowing of a bull.

This fear on the part of the Minoans, and also the terrible practical realizations of their fears, may not in fact have affected them adversely, though to say so may appear insensitive. It must have to an extent—perhaps a great extent—acted as a socially binding force, giving the people of all classes a common sentiment, a common experience, above all a common enemy. There is nothing more binding than a common enemy, especially when that enemy is overcome, as it was at least once in ancient Cretan history, by a heroic rebuilding of all that he had destroyed.

*

In any case, the fear gave the Minoans their major obsession. We arrive now at the second of the 'fascinated exaggerations'. It is the Minoan obsession with the bull.

Now, it is not necessary to ascribe the concern of the Minoans for the bull to their belief that by means of a magic animal of that breed their goddess caused the earthquake. We cannot know for certain that that interpretation is the correct one. It is obviously a very reasonable proposition; and the present writer found some corroboration in an unexpected place. Robert FitzRoy, writing in 1839 his *Narrative of the Voyages of H.M.S. Adventure and Beagle*, gives much attention to the Aurignacian Indians, the natives of northern Chile whose courageous fight against the Spaniards had attracted him; among much other information he gives the fact that they believed the earthquake to come from the roaring of a great bull underground. If all this supposition is wrong, however, the fact will remain that the Minoans *were* obsessed by the bull; and this is a surprising and significant fact, whether the cause of the obsession is known or not.

Why should the Minoans have invented and played their bull-games? And what can be learnt of their character from the fact that they did? In trying to answer those questions one may even gain some glimpses, by way of side-lights, into Minoan history.

First, the bull himself. He certainly impressed his image upon folk-lore and legend. The seventh labour of Hercules was to capture the beautiful bull of Minos, which Poseidon had driven mad in revenge for the king's refusal to sacrifice it to him. Hercules, of course, did capture the bull, but inconsiderately let it loose again in Greece so that Theseus had to do the capturing all over again. Then, apart from the Minotaur legend, the legend of the bull-headed man, there is the earliest story of the beast's finest hour when, filled with the spirit of the god Zeus, he carried the willing maiden Europa across the sea to Crete from Asia Minor. He was, in scientific and not legendary terms, *Bos primigenius*, and no doubt he did not swim to Crete but was left there when Crete first became an island. He had many millennia in which to breed undisturbed; and, since there is no trace of there having ever been lions on the island (unless perhaps later imported by sport-loving kings), he was, one may imagine, undisputed monarch of the island until man arrived to dispute and end his sway—a task that would most naturally impress itself upon the human memory.

Secondly, one has, simply, *bull*, the essence of bull. It is enough to impress any people, and it had impressed many races before the Minoans. It is one of the three forms of animal life, bull, lion and eagle, which, either separately or in fanciful combination, act through the ages as symbols for puny man pretending to the brawn and muscle and ferocity that he does not naturally possess. It is a self-advertisement for potency.

The Minoans did not worship the bull; they used him as a symbol in their worship of the Mother Goddess. They did not seek to tame or domesticate him; they let him run wild in their island and they captured him on occasion and proceeded to disport themselves with him.

To capture a wild animal intact is a more difficult and dangerous undertaking than to hunt and kill it. It seems likely therefore that the capture of the bull was at least as dangerous as playing with him in the bull ring, if not more so; obviously the difficulties encountered and the skills needed to be employed in the capture must have engendered the idea of the bull-games themselves.

There are many representations in Minoan art of men struggling with the bull; and, while some obviously represent the bull-game, more of them, it seems likely, represent the capture. There is a terracotta rhyton (of the First Palace period and from Koumasa in southern Crete) that shows a bull's head with enormous horns and pigmy men swarming all over them. This is a form of exaggeration of the task of capture, which did seem invariably to necessitate at least one person risking his life by entwining himself round the horns.

The most famous representation of the bull capture is given in relief round the two gold cups found at Vaphio near Sparta. That they were unearthed on the Greek mainland and not in Crete can help us to believe that either the games themselves or the artists who liked to depict them spread to the Mycenaeans; but it need not prevent us from interpreting what they show as a true picture of how the Minoans themselves set about the job of capturing their bull.

These two cups are a masterpiece of uninhibited, straightforward, story-telling art. They reside in the National Musuem of Athens and with the famous gold mask which Schliemann thought was Agamemnon's are perhaps the greatest of the Mycenaean exhibits. Gold is miraculously unharmed by centuries upon centuries of burial within the earth; and these cups shine now as they shone in the beginning as a reproach to modern men for what insultingly inadequate use they make of the most beautiful of metals. The scenes here depicted do not need to be described in detail. Suffice it to say that the pair of cups shows a series of events in sequence of time. First a tame cow is tethered as a decoy. Then comes the bull to make love to her—and with what a besotted expression he begins to do so! Then comes the netting of the bull, and the terrific fight to gain control over his daemonic strength, a struggle which, it seems obvious, will not end without casualties to the brave men who have set about the task.

How was the wild bull tamed? We do not know, but some sort of method similar to that used with the Indian elephant may be supposed, the influence of an already tamed bull being brought to bear. No doubt it was a long and slow process—and no doubt it was an incomplete one.

Then the game, the bull-leaping itself. There can be no doubt of the authenticity of this. Sometimes modern visitors to the Heraklion museum (which houses most of the Knossian finds) are disappointed and a little suspicious when they see how little of a fresco has been found and how much is a reconstruction by the modern artist— though they will discover, if they continue to look carefully, that Gilliéron always had justification for his reconstructions, if not in the fresco being restored then in some other similar fresco. The famous fresco of the bull leap is, however and in any case, more intact than most.

Again a time sequence is depicted. The acrobat will seize the bull's horns; he will turn a somersault on them; he will land on the bull's back; he will jump down into the arms of his waiting companion—

the two to make, no doubt, their bow and pirouette of happy achievement and relief to the ecstatic applause of the audience. In the
frescoes it is the convention always to depict men as brown-skinned
and women as white-skinned: the bull-leap fresco is therefore
without doubt showing that men and girls, dressed exactly alike,
both took part in this dangerous sport.

It is an extraordinary scene to have discovered, and it must
illustrate a remarkable skill, a skill which sometimes perhaps was not
enough, so that the crowd witnessed not a happy pirouette for an
end to the show but, with a fierce, half-horrified, half-pleased intake
of breath, the goring and the crumpled figure on the ground. Did
conceivably the acrobat obtain a lift from an obliging jerk upwards of
the bull's head? But then a bull's natural toss is a sideways one,
which would be worse than useless. No modern toreador has cared
to put such theories to the test.

It seems likely too that there were many variations of the leap.
There are figurines and seal-stones showing a sideways vault; there
is the beautiful slender acrobat in ivory, who, divorced from his
bull, seems almost as if he were diving down on to it from a height. It
is surely not too fanciful—when we remember that clay rhyton of
tiny men swarming on a pair of huge horns—to imagine sometimes a
clown-like figure amusing the populace, that sort of clown who is
really the bravest and most expert acrobat of them all.

But what was the purpose of the bull-games? Perhaps there was no
purpose, that is to say no purpose explicable in logical terms. The
circus analogy must obviously not be stretched too far. Yet all
peoples have been fond of spectacle; and the Minoans, by their
appearance and by the evidence of other relics, were obviously a fit
and athletic people: there is the rhyton from Hagia Triada showing
besides the bull sport a wrestling bout and a boxing match (the
boxers incidentally wearing helmets, a fact which seems to point to
the Minoans being sensitive and sensible enough to guard against
brain damage). We have, too, the evidence from the miniature
frescoes of crowds obviously watching a spectacle. But no Bronze
Age crowd, no crowd of people who were in some ways ancestors of
the classical Greeks, would find themselves going to watch merely a
circus show. Obviously there was a dramatic, and a religious
significance. What it was is hard to see; and one may be at least
allowed the guess that it had to a very great extent become lost in the
evolution and elaboration of the spectacle. Many of the legends

insist upon the Minoans being great dancers. Possibly, then, this spectacle was preceded, or accompanied, by dance and music. Perhaps the bull was finally sacrificed. Undoubtedly the bull is among animals, the great sacrifice. One practical reason for this would be that he was good eating—and no people in the ancient world would see anything wrong in taking their cut after the god or goddess had had his or hers. Also, the bull must surely satisfy as a sacrificial beast by the spectacular quantity of his blood. There is no suggestion that the Minoans indulged in the messy and disgusting ritual of the Roman neophyte entering into the mysteries of Mithras, who sat below a grille over which the bull's throat was cut. But there is the much more spiritual practice of pouring a libation of bull's blood to Mother Earth, to see it actually absorbed by Earth as one pours it; and that practice is depicted by the Minoans. There is also the Minoan habit of making rhytons or jugs in the shape of bulls' heads, and very beautiful and striking replicas they are.* It is tempting to imagine these, at a feast, pouring out wine the colour of blood —and the wine being drunk communally with very great and significant solemnity, as indeed it was in Plato's legend of Atlantis.

But, to return to the games; perhaps the bull was not finally sacrificed. Perhaps he was too precious; having been trained at great expense of time and risk, he would be jealously guarded from a fate which in the old days might well have been his, and by a coterie of interested persons who as time went on were growing increasingly powerful. Mary Renault, in her novel of the Theseus legend, *The King Must Die*, has most persuasively suggested that the bull-leapers were a set apart, self-conscious and famous 'toreadors' with great popularity and so with some power. That is a wholly reasonable proposition.

*

There arrives at this juncture in fact, unavoidably, the scent of over-sophistication, indeed the smell of decadence.

This idea must be examined carefully. Is it justified?

We come back to the Theseus legend and to that band of youths and maidens which he led and which he saved from sacrificial death. It has been assumed by Mary Renault—legitimately, since she is writing a novel—that in fact those youths and maidens were being shipped to Crete to be trained for the bull-leap, this being an exercise

* There is one from Knossos, one from Zakron, and one from Mycenae.

which the Minoans themselves were becoming disinclined to practise. And this has seemed such a reasonable supposition that it is creeping into works of non-fiction and being cited by guides on the Knossos site as a fact. It must be made quite clear that there is no justification for this idea whatever, save as a reasonable guess. But guesses are not facts. It is best to forget this possibility that the Minoans had reached such a stage of moral cowardice. However, a not entirely healthy scent remains.

The Aztec civilization before its end had games which it is thought may have involved human sacrifice. The Roman Empire had games, which in its decadence became increasingly degraded and utterly brutal, with matinées of pure butchery. There is a slight similarity to Minoan Crete there, perhaps, but not much of one.

It is not in that sort of similarity where significance lies. It is rather, as has been suggested, an unnaturalness, an air of over-sophistication, of exaggeration. Those ladies, are they the Bright Young Things of 1450 B.C., blasé and discontented, and hedonistic, and willing and anxious to try everything new and anything once? And did their counterparts exist among the young men? There is a fresco where a Minoan young man seems to possess a red glove. There is nothing very much wrong with a red glove, but one could hardly imagine a chariot-driving Mycenaean with a red glove—let alone Achilles. There was only one Homeric hero who could have worn such a thing, and that was Trojan Paris. And he came to a violent end.

*

Societies have their imprint, their aura, their definable and all-permeating outlook and tradition. One such may be romantic; another has reached a stage of classical conservatism but is still strong and thriving. One is religious. One is hedonistic. All of them in the end will decline and expire.

The Minoan civilization at its height and before its ending was, surely, hedonistic, and with an active undercurrent of religiosity. Yet the religiosity, though it may be superstitious, though among the simpler and poorer strata of society it may be very earnest and even intense, is never masochistic, nor portentous, nor darkly cruel, as Mother Earth religions most certainly could be. The Minoans in fact, if perhaps they did not spare enough time from aesthetic appreciation and enjoyment to attend to such serious matters as self-protection or, in the modern idiom, 'national defence', yet did at least have the sense to know how to enjoy themselves and how to express that joy.

*

And to the hedonistic there always seems in the end to come nemesis or the wrath of offended Zeus, though it would be false to a modern interpretation of history to discern a matter of cause and effect as Plato did with his Atlantians.

Civilization had reached a time about fifteen hundred years before the birth of Christ (these dates are uncertain and the vexed question of chronology will be discussed in a later chapter). The Minoan prosperity and the Minoan influence were at their height. For two centuries the dreaded Bull beneath the Earth had been quiet. Then came rumblings and rumours from across eighty miles of sea to the north, news that the volcano of Thera was erupting, darkened skies perhaps; torrential, muddy rains; floating pumice on the sea; refugees and terrible stories from sailors.

But, the Minoans must have thought, this could not affect them very intimately; this time they would be lucky. For a long while this situation must have continued, with fluctuations and for as much as twenty-five years. The volcano of Thera was spewing its heart out and leaving an emptiness in its place.

Then one awful day the emptiness caved in. The cold sea rushed in to fill its place and to meet the red-hot heart not yet dead. The result: one fantastic, incredible explosion, causing an island of nine miles across to become no more than a broken ring round a deep lagoon.

The Minoans were saved from utter catastrophe by their distance, just as the Mycenaeans were saved even more completely, though there are legends of floods and of torrential rains. Lumps of pumice seemed to have arrived all the way by air—they have been found at Zakro. There would have been darkened skies, lurid sunsets and— more terrifying—a heavy descent of fine ash. There may have been secondary results in the way of earthquake, then or later. Most likely of all, a great tidal wave must have arrived from the north, destroying especially Minoan shipping on which depended so largely her prosperity.

This was not the end by any means. But it was certainly a sliding down from the peak, the beginning of a long and eventful decline.

The Minoans were weakened. And there were those who would take advantage of that weakening.

Chapter X

The Rise of the Mycenaeans: Prowess and Wealth

THERE ARE, it has been said, two kinds of invaders, those who ruthlessly and even vindictively destroy the civilization which is greater than their own, and those who have the sense and magnanimity to learn from those they conquer. The Mycenaeans were of the latter kind. More than that, they learnt from the Minoans and copied them long before they ever dreamt that they would one day rule at Knossos.

It has also been said, and rightly, that no ancient people can have taken half as much notice of their art as do the archaeologists who dig up what they leave behind. That the archaeologists should take such great interest is natural: it is more or less all they have to go on for their theories and reconstructions. But that the people themselves are not likely to have been so obsessed is something that needs to be remembered.

This fact would apply particularly to the Mycenaeans. They were, it is repeated, a horsey and warlike people. In any age the hunting squire or the army general is not likely to have been a connoisseur of the arts. This is not to say, however, that the squire's or the general's lady wife would not be interested in fashion, or that he himself would on the one hand not fail to use 'those artist chaps' if it served his purpose and on the other follow unconsciously, in his conservatism, some fashion even in the matter of military apparel which had once been borrowed from abroad.

The Mycenaeans aped the Minoans in many ways, and yet often with a significant slant or difference. The art they left behind must be carefully considered even if they did not necessarily set much store by it themselves. In particular what is left of their palaces will be of interest: here the differences from the Minoan are great, though by no means entire.

The Mycenaeans we left having suddenly achieved a great show of wealth, their fiercely moustached king and his family lying buried in a panoply of gold. This new-won prosperity was to last, no doubt with fluctuations, for the best part of five hundred years, the second half of the period being the time of greatness when the palaces were either built, or, as in the case of Tiryns and Mycenae, refortified and enlarged. Whatever copying of the Minoan there may have been earlier there was likely to be an increase after the Thera disaster, when many Minoans, artists and craftsmen included, must have migrated abroad, fleeing from the devastation caused by the wrath of the Mother Goddess in her most terrible mood.* This increase in in the amount of copying does in fact exist.

The bulk of the unearthed Mycenaean artefacts are to be seen in the National Archaeological Museum of Athens, but there are also lesser collections in the local museums, at Nauplion for instance, near to the sites of Tiryns and Lerna and Asine and not far from Mycenae itself, and at Chora, near to Nestor's palace of Pylos. In all, the same story is told: significant similarity to the Minoans, significant difference.

There are bead-seals, those equivalents in both countries of the owner's personal signature and identity disc. There are frescoes from the palace walls. There is everything from the most sensitively worked ivory to the crudest of votive offerings.

Men are shown naked except for the tight-waisted belt and the loincloth. The women are bare-breasted but wear the exaggerated flounced skirt. There are portrayals of the bull-leap; and there is a bull's-head rhyton. The sign of the double axe or labrys is shown, and the distinctive figure-eight shield. The sacred shrine is portrayed, and the goddess with doves, and also the cord tied in the shape of the sacred knot (giving an impression sometimes remarkably like the the life-giving, good-luck *ankh* sign of Egypt). In decoration, the motives of the octopus, the dolphin and the lily occur.

But there are differences. There is a pretty sauce-boat in the shape of a goose, there is a little gold toad. No significance there, perhaps, except that there was no slavish copying. On a pot appears what seems to be cock-fighting. There are in the frescoes many dogs, large greyhound-like beasts but sometimes with fluffy tails. There are

* In subscribing to the Thera theory as cause of the beginning of the end of the Minoan civilization, one must beware of the enthusiasm of those who like to stress the quite terrible and far-flung effect of the eruption. The Mycenaean palaces are only half as far again away from Thera as the Minoan. At this time the former seem to have survived intact.

horses and chariots and their drivers. There is a boar-hunting scene. There is a rhyton in the shape of a lion's head, and a small relief of a lion attacking a horse. There is a two-headed eagle, and a brooch in the shape, not of two bees round the honey but of a warrior's helmet. There are one or two examples of men not naked except for the loincloth but wearing tunics and also greaves on their legs. There is an actual suit of bronze armour.

Surely something of a pattern emerges. Here, in short, is the Minoan theme unmistakably; but it is masculinized and militarized. The dog, the horse, the hunt, the chariot, the warrior, all those are new.

Then there are the palaces, of which Mycenae, Tiryns and Pylos are the outstanding examples.

Mycenae first. Mycenae does indeed have its throne room, its shrine, its megaron and bathroom, its drains, its grand staircase, but on a very reduced scale compared with the Minoan. Mycenae's palace is a small affair in the middle of a vast surrounding fortification. It is the site as a whole that counts, the total entity, and not the palace perched in the middle of it. And that total entity is, without doubt and quite simply, a fortress. It stands commanding a pass through the mountains between Corinth and Argos; its situation is magnificent. It is rugged and the way to it is steep. There is in fact not enough flat space on which to build a larger megaron or a larger palace; there is no room at all for serried ranks of storerooms. But the great fortified wall, skilfully following the contours, with its sally-port, of over-all length three-quarters of a mile, is overwhelmingly impressive and a major feat of military engineers, who must incidentally have been in command of a large and willing labour force.

The noble lord for whom all this was built must have been a proud man. 'King of men', king of kings, *primus inter pares*, lord of all he surveys, he can look down from the court of his palace (ignoring or ignorant of the fact that it is a good deal smaller than that of Knossos), and see the houses of the village that nestles below for protection; the distant view of a rugged but also fertile land, and, enclosed within the rampart wall for piety's sake, the shaft graves of the mighty ones who had founded Mycenae's greatness. He may be the very man himself, Agamemnon, planning the Trojan expedition and unaware of the end that awaits him on his return. He may be Agamemnon's father, Atreus, who with bloodshed founded

Mycenae's second dynasty and whose remains would rest without the walls and within the great beehive tomb or tholos, whose imposing entrance is in the same style and tradition as the fortress's own recently built Lion Gate.

So, standing where the king stood, does one's imagination run at Mycenae, whereas at Knossos or Phaistos or Mallia the visitor is more likely to try to conjure up lithe, small, brown-skinned, decorated men and rustling, sophisticated women. One stands beside the ancient shaft graves and the curious walled-in path that encircles them—a processional way, another later act of piety?—or looks up to the sloping way, protected by its great bastion of cyclopean stones, that leads to the Lion Gate; and one imagines a horse-drawn chariot emerging from the gate and clattering down the slope. One may imagine too, perhaps, curbing romanticism, that the scene is not quite so noble as intended. The chariot is light and the way stony: the noble lord being driven finds it hard, as he is shaken up and down, to retain a noble attitude. But one thing is certain: the lord is trying to retain a noble stance, and he has already ensured a noble and romantic send-off, with the horses made to prance and froth at their bits, the dogs being loudly and masterfully controlled, and the ladies there to wave their fluttering farewells and to show off their unnecessarily flounced dresses.

*

Tiryns lies less than twenty miles from Mycenae and at the head of the Gulf of Nauplion, the waters of which may in the times of its greatness have reached to the walls. These walls are even more impressive than Mycenae's, so that the later Greeks who came to destroy them could only wonder and think that giants, the cyclops, could have built them—an impression that might be entertained by anybody who had not had his senses dulled by too much familiarity with machinery. There is a sally-port here too, or exit or entrance through the quite tremendous thickness of the wall. Its sides are smoothed at a height not of humans but of sheep—men must live and even in the most heroic age the occupations of peace are more frequent than those of war. Tiryns, nevertheless, was connected in legend with Hercules, that most hard-working of warrior-heroes; and remains of frescoes of war chariots and hunting scenes were found fallen from its walls.

The palace of Pylos impresses in a different way. If we are

entitled to imagine Agamemnon at Mycenae, then we may equally picture Nestor at Pylos, for though there was long dispute as to the site of Nestor's palace the perseverance of the Greek archaeologist, Nicolas Platon, and in particular the American veteran, Professor Karl Blegen, has proved beyond a reasonable doubt that the correct site had at last been found: there can hardly have been in the neighbourhood two palaces of the order of the one they found and excavated. The Palace of Pylos lies in the south-west corner of the Peloponnese, overlooking the Ionian Sea, not far from where the nineteenth-century naval battle of Navarino was fought. It is a most beautiful and fertile part of Greece, where, besides the vine and olive, wild flowers grow in variety and profusion, from a poppy of the deepest red and the larger-flowered pink-and-white cistus to a pimpernel that is not red but blue: they grow now and there is no reason to believe that they did not grow then, to gladden the heart of old Nestor when in more peaceful mood. Nestor, it will be remembered, is the veteran of the Greek heroes of Troy, a sort of mixture of Polonius and W. E. Gladstone. Besides advice he was full of reminiscences, particularly of the daring cattle raids in which he used to indulge in his youth under King Neleus, the father and founder of his line. In whatever way this Neleus acquired his wealth, if he owned the valley of Messenia as well as the coastal strip, as he is reputed to have done, he must then have been a rich man indeed.*

Pylos, though on an impregnable enough site, gives, much more than either Tiryns or Mycenae, the impression of a Minoan palace wearing the prosperous smile of peace rather than the formidable frown of war. Fortifications seem absent, at least from the final set-up. Remains of frescoes have shown the Minoan themes of porpoise and octopus. An archive room full of Linear B tablets was found, and also more than one room containing in all such a store of *kilikes*, drinking cups much in the shape of our champagne glass, many still lying there in broken confusion, as to make one feel that Nestor's famous post-Troy hospitality as described in the *Odyssey* must have been, far from exaggerated, a mere shadow of the splendid reality. There is a difference nevertheless between Nestor's throne room and that of King Minos at Knossos. There is nothing sacerdotal about this room, no lustral area for anointing. Beside the throne is a curious little drain, where, it is imagined, the king, with royal

---

* As also Nestor after him, since, by the legend, he was the surviving son, the other eleven being slaughtered by Hercules.

extravagance, could pour out his libation to the gods or the goddess of Mother Earth. In front of the throne, at a convenient distance, is the raised circular platform for the central hearth and fire. Here in fact is the megaron, not of the Minoans but of the Mycenaeans and as described by Homer, draughty but magnificent, more accustomed to roistering and feasting than anything else, presaging in a curiously exact way the open feasting halls of that much later warrior people, the Anglo-Saxons.

*

Yet there at Pylos, just next to the entrance, were the archive rooms, the offices, where the hoard of over a thousand Linear B tablets was found. So one comes to the apparent paradox, which must be carefully considered, that the Mycenaeans seem to have been at one and the same time a band of carefree militant swash-bucklers and the careful employers of a meticulous bureaucracy. There is something of the same paradox in the case of the Minoans, at any rate after they came under Mycenaean influence and used the Linear B script.

The owner of the archive room and the Homeric hero do not at the first glance seem possibly the same person. But the very impressive-ness and surprise of the Linear B discoveries may have led one to exaggerate the extent of bureaucracy that they presuppose. And on closer examination the heroes of the *Iliad* and *Odyssey* are by no means the simple, innocent, vacant-minded fighting machines that they might seem. If one examines Homer, and then the Linear B tablets, the paradox will be dissolved and at the same time a clearer idea obtained of what the Mycenaeans in their times of greatness were really like. There is no need to make any excuse for taking Homer so seriously. It does not matter even if no such people as Achilles and Agamemnon, Odysseus and Nestor, ever exactly existed. The poet has had enough material handed down to him without break for him to be able to delineate the character of the Mycenaean Greeks with accuracy, and certainly enough inherent wisdom and wit to do so with insight.

And it is the character of the Mycenaean, his outlook and his code, that is significant. The *Iliad* will be examined first, and may in fact seem to show a very different person from the owner of archive rooms. But the *Odyssey*, while not contradicting the *Iliad*, will show how the reconciliation can be made.

The *Iliad* is the story of an unnecessary quarrel between proud men and of the evil that it caused. The *Odyssey* is the story of the lawlessness of men whom Odysseus left behind when he went to Troy and of the nemesis that overtook these men at his hands when the gods at last let him end his adventures and return to his pestered wife and his home.

The famous quarrel of the *Iliad* took place before the walls of Troy and in the tenth and last year of the siege—ten is a good round number, the same number of years as it took Odysseus to get home after the fall of Troy, and it would be foolish to set too much store by its arithmetic accuracy. It was between on the one hand Agamemnon of Mycenae, King of Men, brother-in-law of the errant Helen and leader of the expedition to avenge her, and on the other Achilles, King of the Myrmidons of Thessaly and greatest of all the Greek warriors. The subject of the quarrel was a matter of prestige, of honour. The Greeks, filling in time presumably, have sacked another city and taken away, amongst other girls, one Chryseis, who is the daughter of a priest to Apollo. The priest, affronted, has appealed to Apollo, who, equally affronted, brings down plague on the Greeks. It is to Agamemnon himself that the girl Chryseis has been allotted; and at a conference of the Greeks the obvious suggestion is made that Agamemnon should forthwith restore his prize to her grieving father and angry god. Agamemnon, however, will have none of this simple solution. He is, he explains naïvely, very fond of the girl; he prefers her in fact to his wife Clytemnestra—which, as things turned out, was not saying much. Is he in any case to be left without a prize, he, Agamemnon? Nevertheless he will after all consent to the plan if Achilles will give up *his* girl in Chryseis's stead.

Now, of course, Achilles is affronted—he is more than affronted, he is furious. When finally it is agreed by the assembly that he must give up his girl to Agamemnon, he vows that he will under no circumstances continue to fight for the Greeks, and he retires to his tent to nurse his wrath.

Now this may seem absurd; and there are times when Homer, who is not above laughing gently at his heroes on occasion, lends himself to that interpretation. But not often. The real point that he makes is that the two warriors cannot really behave in any other way. They are *proud*. Their reputation amongst their companions as warriors is what matters, and the outward signs of that reputation, such as prize slave-girls, therefore matter too.

What has even more significance to the Mycenaean warriors—or

Achaean warriors as Homer calls them—is not so much their reputation amongst their contemporaries as their reputation in the eyes of posterity. In their religion there is no heaven, no immortality, no after-life that really matters, but only a dim, wraith-like existence, where, as Achilles himself says, to be king is worse than being the lowest of property-less peasants on earth. So there is only one kind of immortality possible to achieve and that is the immortality of fame, to live on in the song of the bards as they tell of the deeds of past heroes.

So Achilles—who though brutal is a tragic figure—has to work out his destiny. His inclination is to pack up and go home with his Myrmidons. In that way he would in fact save his skin. Whereas if he stays—and so the nymph Thetis, his mother, tells him—he is destined inevitably to final death before the walls of Troy. The choice is in fact between safety and old age and mediocrity on the one hand, and on the other an early death but imperishable fame.

There can be no question as to which will be Achilles's choice. It is not taken until the Greeks have suffered the deaths of many of their brave soldiers and are on the brink of defeat; it is not taken until his squire and the companion of his youth, Patroclus, has been killed. It is only then that Achilles's proud and deep and noble wrath is appeased. But appeased it is, and Achilles once more enters the fight to slaughter the slaughterer of his friend, the greatest of the Trojans, the Prince Hector. There—with the giving back of the body of Hector to his father by a relenting Achilles and the magnificent ritual of the burning of the body of Achilles's friend—the *Iliad* ends. The sack of Troy by means of the ruse of a wooden horse, the death of Achilles, all that is left to other tellers and other tales of the heroes; Homer has finished his task of showing what he had set out to show, the epic tragedy of ungainsayable pride in action.

Nor are things very different within the walls of Troy. King Priam does not blame his daughter-in-law, Helen, for all the trouble she has caused: it is the nature of proud men to contend for beauty when they find it. Even Hector, a much gentler character than his enemy Achilles, displays perfectly the code of the bronze-clad warrior. It comes at the end of that most human of scenes, when Hector says goodbye to his wife and child before returning to the battle. Andromache begs her husband not to go. But there is no question of that, though Hector admits that deep in his heart he has an unshakeable foreboding that Troy will be taken, and he will be dead and

Andromache carried off shrieking into slavery. 'As he finished,' the story continues:

> glorious Hector held out his arms to take his boy. But the child shrank back with a cry to the bosom of his girdled nurse, alarmed by his father's appearance. He was frightened by the bronze of the helmet and the horsehair plume that he saw nodding grimly down at him. His father and his lady mother had to laugh. But noble Hector quickly took his helmet off and put the dazzling thing on the ground. Then he kissed his son, dandled him in his arms, and prayed to Zeus and the other gods: 'Zeus, and you other gods, grant that this boy of mine may be, like me, pre-eminent in Troy; as strong and brave as I; a mighty king of Ilium. May people say, when he comes back from battle, "Here is a better man than his father!" Let him bring home the bloodstained armour of the enemy he has killed, and make his mother happy.'

'May the people say!...' And all this grandiloquence on Hector's part just after he has been making his hearers' blood run cold with a description of the probable fate that awaits them all! There is no inconsistency, however. Such is the code, and the way of life, of the hero, be he Trojan or Greek, and there is no way, indeed no thought, of escape.

That is the essence of the Mycenaeans, or Achaeans, as Homer sees them in the *Iliad*. One minor practical detail may worry one. Were the heroes fighting in the unflamboyant boar's-tusk helmet whilst stripped to the slim waist and the Minoan loincloth, or were they really bronze-clad warriors? Perhaps sometimes one, sometimes the other. But there is that suit of bronze armour found near Nauplion and now in its museum. That is real enough, and heavy and imposing enough—it looks, in fact, with its overlapping cape and skirt, rather like the corroded cape of a nineteenth-century cab-driver. It must have been a very different thing, however, when shining and new, a trophy and prize worth while for anyone who could slay its wearer and strip it off his back, as was the habit of the Trojans and Achaeans.

This conception of Trophy is reflected, too, in the holding of games at the great funeral ceremony. These funeral games are serious things and the winning of a prize important, and for the ever-same reason: it bestowed prestige, it advertised prowess. In the modern use of the word, one was careful in all ways of one's *image*.

*

Whereas the *Iliad* is an epic the *Odyssey* might be called a novel of adventure. Nevertheless it has its serious theme, which is nothing less than that lawlessness will in the latter end reap its due punishment from the gods. The importance of this will emerge later; what concerns us now is the character and code of the Mycenaeans, and how these can be reconciled with the ledger-keeping propensities that the Linear B tablets seem to show.

The story of the *Odyssey* is that of the return of its hero from the Trojan war to his wife and palatial home on the island of Ithaca and of what happens when he arrives. His adventures—as told in person by this 'talkative, bald-headed seaman'*—are, to say the least of it, somewhat improbable. The point and purpose of the long wanderings is, however, that Odysseus is being held back by the gods, while the sins of the lawless suitors (who are extravagantly despoiling his estate and importuning his wife Penelope to believe him dead and marry one of their number) may pile up and merit the fate that at last the hero will mete out to them. For the present purpose the story may be joined where Odysseus's son Telemachus sets out on his own particular journeyings. Telemachus, a babe in arms when his father leaves for the Trojan war but now reached to man's estate, has thought it wise to sally forth to see if he can discover any news of his father, whom Penelope faithfully believes to be still alive. He determines to visit not Agamemnon, who has already met his fate, but those two other heroes, Nestor and Menelaus, who have both settled down in peace again, the latter with his restored wife, Helen.

The boy makes his first journey by sea. On arrival, he and his companion disembark, to find King Nestor and his people holding a ceremonial feast on the sea shore. They are welcomed without question and invited to join in, which they do. Telemachus then reveals his identity and his mission, and has to listen to a long statement by old Nestor, which is rather more about the old man himself than Odysseus and tells him nothing that he wants to know. However, the storytelling over, Telemachus is invited with ceremony to spend the night at the palace. Another meal, with vintage wine that has 'stood ten years'; and then Telemachus is bedding down in the traditional place for the guest, in the portico to the great hall, and

* Odysseus is taunted with baldness in the *Odyssey* but only when impersonating a beggar and after his patron goddess Athene has most effectively helped in the disguise; for Flecker to call him bald is therefore perhaps a little unjustified.

having, for courtesy's sake, Nestor's only unmarried son, Peisistratus, as companion.

In the morning comes the further ritual of hospitality. The palace bathroom comes into use—it is bigger than the queen's at Knossos. There is a step for easy access into the bath (as may still be seen) and various containers wherewith to pour water over the bather (as were duly unearthed). Telemachus had the fullest honours given him, as was no doubt due to a royal guest, for 'the beautiful Polycaste, King Nestor's youngest daughter' gave him his bath. 'When she had bathed him and rubbed him with olive oil, she gave him a tunic and arranged a fine cloak round his shoulders, so that he stepped out of the bath looking like an immortal god'—a habit incidentally of most Homeric heroes.

Meanwhile King Nestor was proceeding with his ritual as royal host. The heifer to be finally eaten at the feast must first be sacrificed to the gods and, as this is a special occasion, must have its horns gilded. The goldsmith was accordingly summoned, the requisite amount of gold being carefully doled out by the king himself. Then Peisistratus, the king's son, expertly dealt the fatal blow, the women 'raised their cry', the dark blood gushed on to the ground, and the carcase was swiftly dismembered for gods and humans alike to have their share. With men of gentle birth to serve him, Telemachus was fed. He was then presented munificently with a chariot and horses, for his journey on to King Menelaus, and lent the king's own son to accompany and drive him. The two young men in due course made their ceremonious adieux. All has been according to protocol and as it should have been—except that Telemachus is no wiser about the fate of his father.

The young man's treatment at his second stop is even more over-whelming, Homer going out of his way to describe it so. Nestor may have possessed great wealth and great holdings in land, owning not only the coastal strip but also the 'Further Pylos' or the famous Messenian vale.* But Menelaus, brother of Agamemnon and so of the great Atreid dynasty, King of Sparta or Lacedaemon and lord of

---

* In the Annual of the British School of Archaeology at Athens, 1966, R. H. Simpson seeks to define the dominion of Pylos and shows that it must have been extensive. There is a difficulty, however, in that some of the towns which seem identifiable seem also to tally with some of the 'seven cities' with which Agamemnon at Troy tried to bribe Achilles out of his wrath. Was the great and somewhat devious king offering something he did not possess?

the land of Argos, brought to him by his marriage with Helen, is richer still. Just before the pair of visitors arrive there has been a farewell feast to Menelaus's daughter, for whom a dynastic marriage with the son of Achilles had been arranged.*

After a two-day journey—and it would be over a high mounatin pass—the two young men duly arrive.

Their horses are outspanned and their chariot leant against the wall by the gate. They are then led through the lofty palace, wondering at what they see. They are bathed, they are placed on high chairs next to the king. Before they eat, a maid pours water over their hands from a golden ewer into a silver bowl. The housekeeper offers them bread and dainties; the professional carver carves; and they drink from golden cups. And all this before anyone knows who they are. Indeed Menelaus's equerry has already been reprimanded for his lack of taste and gumption in presuming to ask his master whether the strangers shall be admitted, for—as the king is at pains to tell them—'your pedigree has left a stamp upon your looks that makes me take you for the sons of kings, those sceptred favourites of Zeus, for no mean folk could breed such men as you are'. The meal over, Telemachus, as impressed as it was intended he should be, leans over to his companion: 'Look round the echoing hall, my dear Peisistratus,' he whispers. 'The whole place gleams with copper and gold, amber and silver and ivory. What an amazing collection of treasures!'

And then comes the rather revealing and unexpected answer of Menelaus, who has overheard the aside. He admits complacently that indeed few mortals can rival him in wealth 'considering all the hardships I endured and the journeys I made in the seven years it took me to amass this fortune and get it home in my ships'. The voyage, he explains, was made whilst his poor brother Agamemnon was being murdered, and so must have been recent and presumably on the way back from the Trojan war. He had visited Cyprus, Phoenicia, Egypt, Ethiopia and Libya.

Such a fortune however, Menelaus continues, is worthless when you have lost your companions in adventure: even Odysseus must, he feels, be presumed to have gone. Whereat Telemachus dissolves

---

* It was to this man, Neoptolemus, that Hector's unhappy widow Andromache was rewarded as spoils. He met an unhappy end, the legends tell, being killed by Orestes to whom the beautiful Hermione (nearly as beautiful as her mother Helen) had been promised.

into tears, and his identity is revealed, and all dissolve into tears in sympathy. . . .

The arrival of Helen from her upper room causes a welcome diversion. She does the proper thing as royal mistress and house-wife—and the passage that follows is revealing for what it tells:

> Adreste drew up for her a comfortable chair; Alcippe brought a rug of the softest wool; while Phylo carried her silver work-basket, a gift from Alcandre, wife of Polybus, who lived in Egyptian Thebes where the houses are furnished in the most sumptuous fashion. This man had given Menelaus two silver baths, a pair of three-legged cauldrons, and ten talents in gold; while in addition his wife gave Helen beautiful gifts for herself, including a golden spindle and a basket that ran on castors and was made of silver finished with a rim of gold. This was the basket that her lady Phylo brought and set beside her. It was full of fine-spun yarn . . .

Helen in fact proceeded to cheer the company up considerably, though not before having a good cry with the rest of them over the probable fate of Odysseus. She had something put in the wine, and she told them amusing tales of Troy. Menelaus capped them with a tale from his adventures in Egypt—which in fact did have a bearing on the probable fate of Odysseus. At last they all went to bed, and in the morning, the two young men, politely resisting the pressing invitation to stay longer, duly made their ceremonial departure. . . .

Not, however, before they had received their gifts. Telemachus is offered horses. But, he says, there is not much grazing for horses in Ithaca. Very well then, says King Menelaus, 'I'll give you a mixing bowl of wrought metal. It is solid silver with a rim of gold round the top . . . I had it from my royal friend, the King of Sidon, when I put up under his roof on my journey home.' When Telemachus finally takes his leave he is also given a two-handled cup from the king's 'scented store-room', whilst Queen Helen removes from her chests a long decorated robe that glitters like a star and which she presents to her departing guest as a gift for his bride-to-be. Then, before leaving, Menelaus, loth to part with Odysseus' son, makes the naïve suggestion:

> Perhaps you would like to make a tour through Hellas and the Argive country. letting me take your companion's place; in which case I should provide the car and horses and serve as your guide to the

various cities? Nobody will send us away empty-handed: we can count on each of our hosts for at least one gift, a copper tripod or a cauldron, a pair of mules or a golden cup.

*

So, in these and other passages of the *Odyssey*, the reader gathers the indelible impression, as he is meant to do, of an Achaean aristocracy that is not only proud but wealthy, and subscribing religiously to a tradition of lavish hospitality, which is coupled always with a gift-giving.

It is this fantastic gift-giving, or rather gift-exchanging, that is so striking, although one should not perhaps be surprised at it. The system has existed, and still exists, in primitive society; an ambassador to Persia in the nineteenth century (in fact the archaeologist and decipherer of the cuneiform, Sir Henry Rawlinson) resigned his post because he felt he was going to be restricted by the Foreign Office in participating in what he realized was a normal and necessary practice in the Middle East. It will also be met with again, when reference is made to the Amarna letters during the time of general Minoan unrest. Nevertheless, its full import, and also how exactly it worked, are hard to grasp. Did the Menelauses of the time really go touring round the eastern Meditarranean collecting a rich store of presents, only to have to give most of them away in due course? We may believe that they did, or at least some of them. We may believe that it was in fact a thinly disguised form of merchanting, though they themselves would have been shocked at the word. It may have been partly diplomatic; a way of sealing alliances. It may have been that the best man, that is to say the most powerful and already most successful man, usually came off best over the apparently so friendly and generous transactions, thus illustrating the truth that to him that hath shall be given.

What is significant is that the Mycenaeans, as shown in Homer, besides being warriors with the very particular code of conduct of warriors, are also men of property and very conscious and proud of such status. They have two great prides in fact, one in prowess and one in possessions, both redounding to their prestige. Homer will always go out of his way to tell of a man's genealogy. But he will equally go out of his way to tell the genealogy of a man's possessions, his articles of 'treasure'—the cup with doves on the handles for instance, so signally duplicated in archaeological discovery, the possessions of Helen, and so forth.* Such treasure will be acquired not blatantly by trade—those gain-conscious Phoenicians may follow that practice—but, in a gentlemanly manner, by exchanging gifts, and the gift system will be tied up with the strict and exacting etiquette of hospitality, which is also a gentlemanly occupation.

*

So one can begin to see that a Mycenaean may employ his scribes and his store-accountants and still be a Homeric hero.

* The Homeric word for treasure is '*Reimelion*', literally something that can be stored up or laid away.

Chapter XI

Uncertainties, Probabilities, and Recapitulation

ONE MIGHT speak of the long agony of the decline and fall of Knossos, a tragic epic such as Gibbon told of Rome. But agony is probably the wrong word. There was a decline and fall undoubtedly, and it was not quick. But neither was it steady, no deadly down-sloping straight line on the graph of history but a wavering one. There were, at least, interludes of continuing prosperity.

The Minoans had responded brilliantly to their first great disaster of around 1700, building even more splendid palaces and houses than those that earthquake had ruined. What the effects of the Thera explosion upon Crete were we do not know, whether falling ash and débris, tidal waves or delayed secondary earthquake shocks or a combination of all three. What does seem reasonably clear is that the recovery after this second catastrophe, though considerable, was not as complete as on the previous occasion, and that the up-and-coming Mycenaeans took their chance to gain ascendancy over their one-time tutors and their present rivals in power and wealth and trade. There follows, therefore, the first half-century of Mycenaean rule, or influence, in Crete, dating approximately 1450 to 1400; and though some of the glory must have departed and the Minoans must have suffered much, yet the archaeological signs, including the Linear B script, show on the whole a continuing prosperity and even in some ways an increased one.

The Linear B script is a great source of information. Admittedly it might have told us much more if it had not so disappointingly been used only for utilitarian purposes; but archaeologists and philologists have contained their disappointment and made the most of what they have been given. Some critics have felt that they have made more than is warranted. Nevertheless it is surprising what may be legitimately deduced from entries of rationing, store accounting and the movements of goods and workmen; and it can even be argued that some of the more literary uses that contemporaries of the Minoans were making of their script—the inaccurate boastings of the pharaohs, for instance—have provided less worthwhile information rather than more.

However, the decipherment of Linear B did cause considerable consternation amongst the experts by showing that the language in which it was written was an archaic form of Greek. This conclusion led to increased difficulty in the interpretation of the probable course of events, and difficulties had not entirely been absent already. The time has come to consider these problems, before reviewing the early years of the Mycenaean influence at Knossos as illustrated particularly by the tablets written in the Linear B script. It will necessitate a little recapitulation; it must also entail a realization— something that perhaps needs to be stressed—that in writing the Minoan story one is not so much recounting events as trying to piece them together and to make sense of the tenuous, patchy, slowly increasing and sometimes contradictory evidence. Neverthe- less—and this also must be stressed—there is one other realization which is necessary, and this is a more comforting one. Whatever are the present differences of opinion as to the true course of events, they do not alter this basic historical fact: there were two main cultures in the Bronze Age Aegean, Minoan and Mycenaean, the latter first learning from the former but finally assuming the ascen- dancy; and the two between them form a synthesis which consti- tutes their legacy to the classical age of Greece and all that came after. Exactly how soon or how late in time the Mycenaeans super- seded the Minoans, and how exactly they did so, are fascinating problems and important. But they are not half so important as the problem of trying to elucidate just what was the combined contribu- tion of the two to the cultures of the future or their combined influence upon later history; and that contribution will not be greatly affected by a shift in likely dating or a changed accent here or there on the relative influence of the two contributors.

*

Arthur Evans found evidence that the second and last palace at Knossos had not merely crumbled slowly to ruin but had met a day of disaster, with signs of fire on smoke-blackened stones, the famous day of spring, in Pendelbury's phrase, when the wind blew from the south. This discovery presented at the beginning no particular problems. That was that, that was the end; and by stratigraphical evidence and the presence of a few ceramic imports from Egypt which could be dated with reasonable accuracy, the destruction of Knossos was placed at about 1400.

But how had it happened? There was always the tempting interpretation of a Greek invasion and conquest as shadowed forth in the legend of the triumph of Theseus. There was no evidence of slaughter, however; and surely there would have been some such. Had it then perhaps been revolution, an uprising of the people against their rulers? But that, from all the signs of a happy and prosperous civilization, did not seem very likely, though there was the apparent confusion that the throne room showed and that had so impressed Pendlebury. Had it then been another outburst of Crete's ever-threatening danger, earthquake? But, as at least negative evidence against this theory, it was pointed out that fire was by no means a necessary concomitant of earthquake in ancient times, when no such things as gas mains or electric cables were there to be broken. Nobody at that time seems to have put forward the Thera proposition, partly perhaps because the date of this volcanic explosion was very hard to estimate (as to a lesser extent it still is).

The question of the true fate of Knossos was left open, and Evans got on with his job, in particular with his efforts to decipher the two more sophisticated scripts which he had called Linear A and B. Though his efforts must not be belittled, he did not get very far. Then came the discovery, in mainland Greece, of Linear B tablets almost exactly similar to those found at Knossos. That also gave Evans no cause to worry: to him it was merely another example of the comparatively uncivilized and unimportant Mycenaeans learning from the Minoans.

Then, in the years after the Second World War, there came upon the scene the young architect, Michael Ventris, who as a boy had had his enthusiasm fired by hearing a lecture by Sir Arthur Evans and who had vowed that he would decipher the Minoan script. In 1952 came his announcement—hotly disputed at the time, as was natural, but now almost universally accepted—that Linear B was written in an archaic form of Greek.

That really put the cat amongst the pigeons; it was rather as if Doomsday Book had been discovered to have been written in Anglo-Saxon. But the new fact had to be faced. Here were Minoan palace records written in Greek; here were Mycenaean palace records written in exactly the same Greek. Another surprising fact emerged. Evans had dated his Linear B finds at Knossos at about 1450. Blegen dated his Linear B finds at Pylos at about 1200. Could both those dates be right? Was it reasonable to suppose that a method of writing should remain to all intents and purposes entirely unchanged for something like a quarter of a millennium?

Leonard Palmer, professor of philology, thought not. The Pylos dating seemed indisputable; Evans must therefore be wrong. The accusations were unfortunately taken to the Press: Evans was accused of old man's forgetfulness or carelessness at the best or of deliberate falsification in order to back up his preconceived theories at the worst. The date of the Knossos tablets, said Palmer, should obviously be put much nearer those of the Pylos tablets; this would mean another two hundred years or so of Minoan hegemony before the appearance in Crete of the Mycenaeans.

The dispute has died down, but has not been resolved. Palmer has elaborated his theories in a carefully, courteously and forcefully written book.* Nevertheless, he has not carried many of his expert colleagues with him, the majority feeling being that, surprising though it may seem, Linear B did stay put for something like 250 years, and that indeed it was not so surprising, since the use of the script was so circumscribed and so thoroughly unliterary. An added support for the anti-Palmer theory was the discovery of further tablets at Greek Thebes which were dated at just about halfway between the two extremes of 1450 and 1200.†

Even so, the date of the appearance of the Mycenaeans at Knossos does remain uncertain. To complicate matters, there are those who suggest that this date should not be later than Evans's 1450 but even earlier still. Nor does the method of the Mycenaean coming, whether all-out military invasion or comparatively peaceful penetration and a mere change of dynastic rule, cease to be a matter of dispute. If the physical catastrophe dated at 1400 was the real date of a Greek conquest or raid, in fact the Theseus episode, then Greek would have been fighting Greek. Even that, however, is not an impossibility: the Trojans are shown by Homer as very like the Greeks, as they may well have been, and such exultant sackers of cities as the Homeric heroes would have been perfectly capable of attempting to sack a Hellenized Knossos.

---

* *Mycenaeans and Minoans* by L. R. Palmer, revised 1965 edition.
† As reported in the *Illustrated London News* of December 5, 1964.

But then—or rather now, at the time of writing—there has grown up the Thera theory: Knossos and the rest of Crete suffered, somewhere not very much later than 1500, in a sufficiently serious manner to send thousands of victims overseas even if the palaces were not irretrievably ruined.

What sense or certainty can one extract from this long series of complications?

There is no certainty. Not one of the solutions offered lacks some sense and probability behind it; the only answer, in the light of evidence to date, is to choose the most probable.

It will already have become apparent which choice the present writer has been making. After the finds of pumice at Zakro there are obvious grounds for thinking that the Thera explosion did seriously affect Crete, and the likelihood that Plato's story of a catastrophic end to 'Atlantis' bore some Cretan truth behind it is increased. That it was the end of Knossos is, however, far from probable. Archaeological finds increasingly show that after 1450 Cretan prosperity was not at an end, not by a long way and not for a long time.* The peak was passed, certainly; the sceptre had moved into the hands of the Mycenaeans. But no more.

So therefore, to recapitulate, and now to take the story further, the chain of events that seems the most likely from present evidence is taken to be as follows:

- *c.* 1700 First destruction of palaces, followed, after a possible, interval of recession and recuperation, by—
- *c.* 1600 The great age of ancient Crete and also the slow rise to prosperity of the Mycenaeans.
- *c.* 1450 The great Thera explosion, causing, either immediately or after a time-lag with secondary effects, widespread but not universal or irreparable damage to Crete. The Mycenaeans approach the height of their power, and, taking advantage of their neighbour's weakness, gain control at Knossos, though not by anything approaching a full-scale conquest, and not in the process destroying Minoan culture.
- *c.* 1400 Knossos and the other palaces seem likely to have suffered a further cataclysm, in the way of earthquake, invasion or

---

* See, for instance, *The Last Mycenaeans and Their Successors* by V. R. d'A. Desborough (O.U.P., 1964), particularly Chapters VII and X.

popular revolt; though it may finally become clear that this is a non-event and a confusion in date with the Thera catastrophe.* The Minoans, in a sort of provincial backwater and outside the main course of Middle East history, continue, with no glory but some prosperity, until—

c. 1200 The great age of unrest in the area begins. And, as one of the major results thereof, both the Mycenaeans and the Minoans suffer final eclipse: the Iron Age is at hand.

After this recapitulation, the narrative can now return to consider Knossos under its first experience of Mycenaean administration. With the Minoans possessing something like half a millennium of relatively high civilization behind them, with the Mycenaeans inhibited by something of awed respect from indulging in any of

* In September 1969 an International Scientific Congress on Thera Volcano was held, at which Professor A. G. Galanopoulos, the co-author of the book *Atlantis* already referred to in Chapter IV, gave the final address. The view prevailing at this congress, he says, is that the Thera eruption started rather at the end of period LMIb (about 1450 B.C.) than earlier and that the collapse of the roof of the volcano occurred probably later on in LMII, about 1400 B.C. Part of his final address runs as follows:

All of us are aware that the greatest puzzle we face is the mystery of the decline of the Cretan-Cycladic civilization in the middle of the Bronze Age.

Some of us believe in the Marinatos theory that this was an aftermath of the gigantic explosion of the Santorin volcano. Some others prefer to seek historical explanations according to human behaviour, wars, revolutions and the rest. The boldest of us are convinced that the Cretan-Cycladic civilization, known after Evans as Minoan civilization, is nothing else but the civilization of Atlantis, which disappeared in a similar way in the Bronze Age. According to archaeological findings a destruction of palaces is observed on Crete Island in LMIa. The destruction apparently was more severe on Santorin Island; the civilization on the island seems to have abruptly ended at that time. On the contrary, on Crete Island the civilization continued up to the end of LMIb. At this time a widespread devastation with burning occurred throughout most of central and eastern Crete; the devastation included sites of Rhodes, Kythera, Milos and Keos. After this occurrence a gradual decline of Minoan civilization is observed... The seismic destruction of the palaces of Crete Island combined with the failure of the vegetation of the island due to tephra-fall, and the annihilation of the Minoan fleet through the sea waves set up by the collapse of the central part of the Santorin Island at the great paroxysmal climax of the Thera eruption, or possibly later on in LMII, could explain quite satisfactorily the decline of the Minoan civilization which is observed after the end of LMIb.

their more ruthless habits, the change may not be expected to prove noticeably drastic.

This will prove to be the case. If, however, Minoans were stubbornly conservative, Mycenaeans were a forceful people, and changes there were. The Linear B tablets help to show them.

Chapter XII

Knossos under the Mycenaeans: Evidence of the Linear B Script

THE LINEAR B script is not a medium for writing poetry, or narratives, or love letters. Its vowels are strangely arbitrary; it deals in syllables and not a single letter for each sound as does our own alphabet; its groups of signs may often be transliterated in a disconcertingly different number of ways; even for its contemporary readers its meaning had usually to be made clearer by the use of supporting pictograms. As examples of the difficulty in reading the script—a difficulty not necessarily confined to the modern decipherer—here are just two of the rules which have had to be evolved so that it can be read. Firstly, the signs invariably represent a vowel followed by a consonant; when there is in fact no such sound in the word depicted, that is to say where two consonants come together, the next following vowel will be inserted—e.g. *krusos* will be written KU–RU–SO. The second and equally unhelpful rule is also illustrated by the word just quoted. At the end of a word, *and* at the end of a syllable, the following consonants are omitted: L, M, N, R and S.

When the Minoan-Mycenaean civilization died it is therefore not very surprising to find that this way of writing died too, the Greeks and Cretans presumably remaining entirely illiterate until the Phoenician signs were borrowed and improved to form the classical Greek alphabet. Similarly one may safely assume that the great majority of Minoans and Mycenaeans remained illiterate even at the height of the use of Linear B. Neither peasant nor aristocrat would have any use for it. Everyone would have left the job to the expert, the scribe and the tax-collector and the accountant, just as everyone would have left the bronze-smith to work bronze, or the unguent-maker to make unguents or the carver-of-the-meat to carve the joint. One can certainly not imagine Homer's Achilles deigning to learn to write, but neither can one imagine the real Mycenaean baron so lowering his proud and very peculiar code of conduct.

What may seem surprising is that such an intelligent and vital people as the Minoans never evolved a less stiff and anchylosed sort of writing medium. Perhaps it seemed too utilitarian for them to take much notice of it. What must be realized, however, is that for their writing to develop as it did is not in the least unusual. It was following the usual course of such things. Always, in the centralized economies that characterize the ancient world, there had existed a practical need for an accounting and control-keeping medium. The art of numbering therefore grew up; and there developed after it a crude art of lettering good enough to show the kind, the provenance, and so forth, of the things or people numbered.

That, it seems clear, is exactly the use for which Linear B and its preceding scripts in ancient Crete were developed. This statement may yet, of course, be refuted and a sherd turn up at some archaeological site with a poem upon it, to amaze and delight the digger. But that is not likely. Another use of most early writings may yet be exemplified. This is the use which takes advantage of the magic which, it seems to the primitively superstitious mind, it must possess, in that it constitutes utterances from the mind of one person that first die and then magically come to life again in the mind of another person, the reader. Hence the magic curse, or the incantation to the god or goddess, which must surely in the very nature of things be effective. However, none even of these has been found at a Minoan or Mycenaean site—though it would be leaning much too heavily on purely negative evidence to deduce from the absence that these peoples were too open-hearted or too unsuperstitious to use the power of writing in that way. One thing must be remembered in this connection. The Minoan scripts are not primarily designed, like cuneiform, for incising upon clay. More probably, the usual method was to write on papyrus or the equivalent, the clay tablet being only a secondary and (in the short, contemporary view) more ephemeral record. Even these clay tablets were not baked, and we only owe their continued existence in every case to the accident of fire. The tablets therefore that have come down to us by chance must only be a tithe of what once existed.

Nonetheless, the fact remains that what we have may all be broadly called administrative and accounting documents. Whether or not any other use is later proved to have been made of the Minoan scripts, we must accept the fact that the material and non-literary use was always their main and intended one.

*

That Linear B was a Minoan and not a Mycenaean invention is a reasonable assumption, since it is only the Minoans who have ever shown us any earlier scripts or evidence of evolving a method of writing.

In short, the evolution of Minoan writings is as follows. First came a pictographic script, owing much to Egypt. It was this, it may be remembered, that first caught Arthur Evans's interest, written on the ancient seals that were still surviving amongst the Cretan peasants as 'milk-stones'. Evans distinguished a first, and then a second and more developed of these primitive writings, Hieroglyphic A and B. There followed, at about the time of the building of the old palaces, the considerable development represented by Linear A, still largely undeciphered and written, it is assumed, not in Greek but in the Minoan language. Then there appeared in the decipherment story—coming merely to confuse the issue—the discovery at the palace of that name the famous 'Phaistos disc'. This was a roughly circular disc of clay covered on both sides with a spiral succession of hieroglyphics quite unlike in design any found in Crete previously or since. All attempts to fit it into the evolution of Minoan writing have failed, and it is now regarded as a fortuitous import, probably from Anatolia or at best the effort of some ingenious Minoan scribe with a passion for experiment and an esoteric knowledge. Whether it was an experimenting scribe or some innocent but enquiringly minded sailor importing a souvenir, this particular individual certainly caused more mental exertion three and a half millennia later than he can ever have envisaged. At least it may be said that on either hypothesis an intelligent interest in writing was shown.

At length, there comes Linear B. It has appeared so far only at Knossos in Crete and at several Mycenaean sites, notably at Pylos. It has many signs the same as Linear A, but also many new ones. It is, as has been said, now almost universally accepted as having been written in an archaic form of Greek.

The deductions from these facts are inescapable. Linear B is an adaptation of the Minoan Linear A for use in a new language, just as the Sumerian and Babylonian cuneiform would later be adapted to the language of Darius's Persia. It was the invention of Minoan scribes faced with the need to work in Greek, either the scribes at Knossos or Minoan scribes employed by the Mycenaeans on the mainland; and the fact that the discoveries so far show an earlier date for the Knossos tablets makes the first of these alternatives seem at present the more likely.

It is the Linear B tablets in Crete and not in Greece with which this chapter is concerned. The first fact to be recalled is that so far they have only been found at Knossos. This again is only negative evidence and one must not assume from it that the Mycenaeans remained at Knossos during this period and penetrated no further, an idea which in fact other evidence does not bear out. It is a reasonable deduction, however, that only at Knossos was an active Mycenaean administration established.

First to be considered will be the general impression that the tablets give—an impression of an elaborate bureaucracy which so surprised many experts—and then the signs that can be gathered of changes in the Minoan way of life which the arrival of their powerful neighbours, so different from themselves, affected.

The usual form of tablet known as the 'palm-leaf' type, is—to quote Ventris and Chadwick in their great book on the subject*—'of the approximate proportions of a modern cheque-book, with rounded, pointed or square-cut ends, at Knossos often reinforced by a string down the middle.' These were for single or comparatively short entries, which were summarized on to larger page-type tablets. The entries on the 'palm-leaves' are usually in the form of first the object or animal or person concerned, then what there is to say about it or him or them, and then an explanatory ideogram. From the analogy, Ventris and Chadwick continue, of contemporary tablets from other countries, Hittite for instance, 'we may expect that the scribe was called upon both to catalogue commodities and personnel arriving at the palace, and to record those sent out or assigned to particular purposes; and in addition, perhaps, to inventory the state of a particular store-room or labour group at a given time. In some cases we are helped by an explicit description, as in an introductory sentence like [here they are quoting from Pylos as well as Knossos] "Olive oil, which Kokalos delivered to Eumedes", "Contributions by the wood-cutters to the workshops", "Contributions of bronze for arrows and spears" . . . In other cases, when the

* *Documents in Mycenaean Greek* by Michael Ventris and John Chadwick (C.U.P., 1956).

tablets merely contain lists of proper names and ideograms, it may be a matter of guesswork for us to determine whether the tablet records receipt or dispatch. Where place-names occur with large amounts of agricultural staples, we may suspect that these represent actual or expected tribute *to* the palace; but when men's names are listed in the dative with small amounts of the same commodities, they are probably the recipients of rations *from* the palace.'

That quotation gives a good idea of the kind of transaction recorded by the tablets as well as of some of the difficulties of the modern decipherers. The general impression is of a busy and prosperous economy run centrally and in much detail by the palace.

One of the first more particular points to notice is that the 'large amounts of industrial staples' referred to above were in fact often surprisingly large. One series of tablets concerning rams reaches the very considerable figure of 25,051. It is in fact sheep that form the major figure for livestock; but there are others, and the following entry is interesting for its comparative numbers:

> Rams 202, ewes 750, he-goats 125, she-goats 240, boars 21, sows 60, bulls 2, cows 10, **At Kudonia**: 50 working oxen.

Kudonia was in the western and less populated part of the island, but it nevertheless comes under Knossos control. It is on the face of it surprising that the number of bulls and cows is so small. But Crete can never have been a land to support many cattle (in England's West country one cow is usually allocated as much grazing land as seven or eight sheep); and presumably the bulls for the ring were allowed to run wild until captured and then kept in a special training establishment, which would have had no connection with an entry such as the above, presumably a landowner's contribution in kind to the palace. The pictographic signs for livestock are interesting because they do seem to show, as one would expect, a degree of stylization proportional to the commonness of the entry (see illustration on next page).

Again there is a minor surprise in that there seem to be no separate signs to differentiate an ox from a bull. The Minoans of all people must have known the difference; perhaps the context always made matters clear. It does not seem at all likely that the Mycenaeans on their arrival would have stopped the bull-games; they were, one would imagine, far from being spoil-sports or squeamish in their

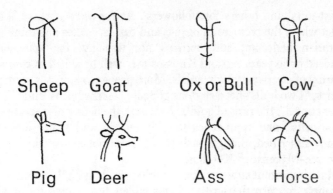

Sheep Goat Ox or Bull Cow

Pig Deer Ass Horse

outlook, and in any case many representations have been found on the mainland of the bull-leap or the bull-capture—witness the famous Vaphio cups, for instance.

Entries of rations seem to show a fertile country and a fairly liberal dole. (The original entry is in cupfuls and it has been assumed that his cup would have been the same as the standard cupful of the contemporary Middle East.) Here is a typical entry:

At Pharai, wages for 18 men and 8 boys: grain per month, 1,170 litres of barley.

If one treats men and boys alike and gives thirty days to a month, the daily ration works out at one and a half litres or just over two and a half pints. As for meat, the wage earners had presumably to find their own, or more probably they seldom got it—one must remember that the ration for even Julius Caesar's soldiers was usually grain and grain only. The issue is sometimes in flour rather than grain, and as the trade of baker is mentioned one need not fear that the ration receiver was unable to produce a palatable meal for himself. Another rationing tablet runs, 'Total men of Amnisos, nine; the rations to be from there.' Amnisos was one of the two ports of Knossos, and the entry suggests possible imports of corn, most likely from Egypt.

Cloth and clothing, and household utensils, are all looked after by the Knossos palace records. Women are the weavers and spinners, as one would expect. Linen as well as woollen garments are listed and there is reference to dyes, including the ancient world's beloved purple. There are clean-edged and dirty-edged clothes, which may lead one to think of stream-side laundries, though not necessarily overlooked by a Princess Nausicaa. There are cloaks suitable for 'guest-gifts' and others for 'followers'. As for utensils there is one tablet where the pictogram, of jugs and basins, makes one think of a Victorian bedroom, and perhaps not wrongly, for Windsor a hundred or so years ago and Knossos may well have had in common an army of ewer-carrying menials. More proper to Knossos seem the entries, 'Two bulls'-head rhytons gilded[?] on the horns' and 'Three silver cups . . . the rims of gold'. Here, with the listing of treasure and 'guest-gifts', one approaches the Mycenaean and Homeric world already described, though such things were not necessarily absent from pre-Mycenaean Knossos.

More important subjects than clothing and household utensils did of course concern the scribes. Pylos tablets have much to do with land tenure, where it is shown that there can be common land, feudal fief land, royal land and even land belonging to the gods. Unfortunately such tablets at Knossos are scarce; there is, however, reference to communal and fief land.

The gods receive tribute as well as own land; and in this connection the Knossos tablets are more forthcoming. Evans, amongst his early finds, came across eleven tablets now known to show the monthly issue of olive oil to various destinations, the dedication being, with catholicity and caution, to 'all the gods', and we obviously have here a sort of ritual calendar. Knossos also shows under this heading something more specific. First there is an offering of honey to Eileithyia, who it will be remembered was the goddess of childbirth and who remained known to the Greeks even down to classical times. Then—and here one surely begins to see the Mycenaean influence—there are records of offerings to *Potnia*, the Lady (or Our Lady) and then to Athena Potnia, the lady Athene. Finally there is offering, as one would expect, to the Earth Shaker, but he is now definitely the Greek god, Poseidon.

We come now to the one unmistakable sign of Mycenaean influence upon the Minoan way of life that the Linear B tablets produce. It is the appearance of the horse and chariot.

Never before have either appeared on anything Minoan. Now, in this early Mycenaean period, there comes first, to support the evidence of the tablets, a seal-stone picture of a horse being carried on board ship, an import presumably, and, since it overshadows the whole ship, by far the most important import. Then the Knossos Linear B tablets show a new pictogram, and being new it is unstylized, the light-framed military chariot. Not only so, but there are two further signs, the complete chariot but without wheels, and the bare frame of the chariot alone. Here one is sent straight back to Homer, who in the *Iliad* explains how chariots are carefully dismantled and stacked and covered with a cloth when not in use, and that when required (even by the impatient goddess Hera herself) the wheels have first to be refitted. Here are a few of the Knossos entries (the italics and so forth of the decipherers denoting uncertainties of translation being omitted):

Two horse-chariots without wheels, inlaid with ivory, fully assembled, painted crimson, equipped with bridles with leather cheek-straps and horn bits. Forty pairs of wheels of willow-wood, with studs. Eighty horse-chariots not inlaid, not fully assembled. The feudal contribution of Alexinthos.

It seems evident that the chariots were not only important items, carefully described, but also splendid affairs: to supply forty of them Alexinthos (by the ending of the word presumably a town and not a person) surely entailed being heavily taxed. The number of chariots recorded on the discovered Linear B tablets of Knossos reaches the surprisingly large total of over four hundred.

So we have a major change at Knossos. Tiryns and Pylos had Minoan-like frescoes painted on their wall, which yet were different; and one of the great differences was that hunting dogs and men with spears, and horses and chariots were shown. Now we have Knossos, if not painting chariots, at any rate possessing them. The question of the chariot will be elaborated when describing the waves of war and unrest that were soon to strike the civilized world of the eastern Mediterranean. Here we see the first portent, in peaceful Knossos, and it is significant. The horse-chariot is essentially an instrument of war; it can also be used for hunting or at least for going to the hunt; it is undoubtedly a status symbol. If one can legitimately imagine Agamemnon or some other king of Mycenae making the most of his spectacular exit from the Lion Gate, then one can now imagine the same sort of splendid scene as a similarly magnificent equippage speeds over the viaduct of Knossos, the stone balustrade echoing back the clatter and the sound of the horses' hooves. The curled, over-dressed, under-dressed ladies of the palace, perhaps even a little more exaggerated in their attire as unsuspected decadence begins to descend upon them, would surely accord to the Mycenaean hero in his chariot a favour decidedly marked.

Chariots are not the only warlike item listed by the Linear B tablets of Knossos. Sometimes with the chariots are enumerated corselets, that is to say body armour. There is reference to fifty swords and forty-two spears with bronze points. And there is one tablet (to be seen at Heraklion museum, as may the famous Phaistos disc) which shows the pictogram of a helmet. All this does not amount to very much, and Knossos has never been envisaged as so unmilitary as not to possess at least a guard; but, with the chariots, it helps to show something new. . . .

Before leaving the tablets, one other probable result of their obviously increased use after the arrival of the Mycenaeans may be mentioned. It is the opposite side of the coin and the corollary of the general illiteracy. If the lords of the palaces wanted records but did not wish to do the job themselves, then they had to ensure that scribes were trained. There must have grown up in carefree Knossos what had developed a long time before in the cities of Egypt and Babylonia, the school. The unlucky boy who showed a precocious intelligence, leaving the mere learning of manual skills or tribal lays within the family, was indentured to become a scribe. He took the equivalent of his satchel; and while his fellows enjoyed the sunshine, he pored over the hieroglyphics at his desk. One must hope that he got at least some satisfaction from a consciousness of superior intelligence and knowledge precious and exclusive.

*

We turn now to what evidence exists to supplement that of the script in showing how the Minoans were changed by the arrival of the Mycenaean influence.

So far in ancient Crete's history remarkably little evidence has come to light of royal graves. Perhaps there was cremation, perhaps interment, but whatever happened it does not seem that much of a fuss was made: no rich grave goods, no places of continuous dynastic burials. But in Mycenae, it was entirely different. Already one elaborate method of burying the great dead has been invented, the shaft graves with their amazing richness of sacrificial wealth in the form of gold; now, at about this time, there is coming into use the second method, even more elaborate, the tholos or beehive tomb, with its corbelled roof, its imposing portal that is so striking a piece of architectural engineering, and its long *dromos* or approach cut into the side of the hill. Here we have on the one hand a copy in a general way of the Egyptian idea of the pyramid, a home for the great and still influential dead which shall be so spectacular as to satisfy the spirit of the corpse and impress all those left behind. Here we have on the other hand the idea that, in the mid-centuries of the Second Millennium, there was spreading out, from the Mediterranean to the shores of north-west Europe, the idea of the megalith builders, the builders in great stones, who produced, besides the ritual sites for the living in the shape of Carnac and Stonehenge, the great tumuli, the so-called passage graves, for the dead. It is not suggested that the Mycenaeans were the father of the megalithic builders, but rather that both were heirs to a similar idea. There is even this curious correspondence: that when the next king in the dynastic line came to be buried, despite the great work of uncovering the entrance to the tumulus or the dromos leading to the beehive tomb, despite the imposing ritual that must have accompanied so important an occasion, yet it was the practice to bundle aside most unceremoniously the bones of the previously buried king to make way for the new one, a practice that must have emanated from some belief that only for a little while did body and spirit have any connection.

So much for this habit of the dynasty-conscious and aristocratic Mycenaeans. True to expectation, the same type of burial of great men begins to appear in Crete after 1450.

First there are the so-called Warrior Graves at Hagios Ioannis near to Knossos. Here are buried fine weapons, swords and rapiers and spears, and one of the swords has been identified as very similar in workmanship to that found at Dendra on the mainland where the only suit of Mycenaean bronze armour yet to be discovered was also found. Then there is the burial at Isopata, also near Knossos. This is a true tholos burial, but there are differences, an uphill dromos for instance and a rectangular and not round chamber—the Minoans, it seems, are not going to allow anyone to impose his own ideas completely.* What was found in this Mycenaean-type tomb is very revealing. Fine alabaster vases from Egypt give evidence of foreign trade—or else the sort of royal souvenir hunt that King Menelaus boasted of to Telemachus. Another pointer to an increasing foreign trade by the Mycenaeans, and to a share in it by Knossos, is the trace

---

* Such tombs must not be confused with small and unimportant Cretan tombs in the Messara region, which may be called of the tholos type and which date from the end of the Early Minoan period. Nicolas Platon considers, however, that in these much earlier tombs lies the origin of the Mycenaean tholos.

of items of amber at this time; and amber is not known to have come from anywhere but the Baltic area, travelling across land to the head of the Adriatic. The second significant find at Isopata is a gold seal ring. It is both highly religious and highly conventional. Here are priestesses or sycophants dancing round in a flowery meadow, and they are so thoroughly Minoan in costume that their waists are ridiculous, their breasts the same at the other extreme, and their faces, which do not matter, conventionalized into something like beaks. And at the top of the picture, similarly dressed but floating in the heavens, is—presumably—the goddess.

So we see the Mycenaeans, on their arrival, making their presence felt not only in the military and heroic aspect but in the religious too; and the religiosity, though more conventional than deep, has individualistic, and again heroic, motives behind it: the highly prestigious burial of the chieftain. As has often been pointed out, Homer was anachronistic in having his dead heroes cremated rather than interred; but otherwise he may have been right, and there are likely to have been games at the royal funerals, so that the living princes could have a chance to enhance their honour and prestige as well as the dead. Perhaps, as in Homer, they quarrelled a little over the awarding of the prizes; and perhaps, as not in Homer, this being Crete, there was bull-leaping included in the games.

However, this introduction of heroics and dynastic burial cannot have affected the common run of Minoans very much. Once again there is need to look at the other side of the coin. The invaders show an increased religiosity that is hardly true religiosity at all, that is merely an emanation of the search for prestige. The invaded show an increased religiosity that is personal and genuine.

This is a likely development. If it truly happened it will for-shadow a later period in history, the time of Christ, when throughout the Roman Empire peoples were being taken over by a foreign power (which even if benign was still foreign) and had been suffering a period of great unhappiness from one cause or another; they therefore sought solace in the personal, so-called mystery religions. Because it may be expected to have happened also in Bronze Age Crete one must be careful not to bend the evidence in favour of the proposition. It does not seem, however, to need to be bent.

There is the famous sarcophagus of Hagia Triada. This dates within our period 1450 to 1400 (LMII or New Palace, Phase III, that is to say).

The custom grew up at this time, both in Crete and on the mainland, of burial of the common people—no doubt the more prosperous of the common people—in clay sarcophagi (known to the archaeologists as larnakes). Sometimes these were genuine chests with legs, sometimes they were much more like bath-tubs, indeed some of the Cretan examples are just like their baths and may even have been so. The outside of these larnakes are painted with patterns or scenes.

The Hagia Triada larnax is painted with highly revealing scenes. First, the more perfect of the two panels that go the length of the chest. This is divided into three scenes. On the left a bare-headed woman wearing what looks like a sheepskin skirt is pouring liquid from a large vase into what we may legitimately call a mixing bowl. This bowl is raised up and stands between two columns bearing at their head the duplicated emblem of the double axe, and on the axes are perched two birds. A second woman follows carrying two more vases or buckets, and she is followed by a man playing a large lyre. The woman wears a headdress reminiscent of that worn by the man in the Young Prince fresco. The background now becomes greeny-blue and the scene changes. Three young men, also clad in sheepskin skirts, come bearing gifts: two calves, life-size and presumably alive, and something that may be taken as the model of a boat. Finally, against a white background again, a man stands very straight and stiff and upright, clad fully in a sheepskin cloak that envelopes his arms. Behind him is what looks like his own sarcophagus, and before him are steps and a tree.

On the other side are four scenes, or at any rate four different backgrounds. On the left, where a large piece is missing, five pairs of feet suggest two pairs of women following a single one. This leader seems to be the same crowned figure as on the other side. She walks ceremoniously, holding her arms before her. Next comes an unmistakable sacrifice. A bound bull on an altar seems to watch sadly his own life-blood drain away into a vessel below. Beside this vessel patiently wait two goats. Behind, a man plays on the double pipes. Next, a skirted woman, with the same gesture of outstretched arms as the crowned one, rests her hands on an altar. Behind is the same double-axe stand and above the altar a jug and a bowl of fruit. Finally appears what looks like a large edition of the altar. Its top is edged with those formalized representations of bulls' horns known to the archaeologist as horns of consecration, and above it grows another tree.

The two end panels have a similarity and a difference. In both, two people, pale-faced, are driving a chariot. But in one they drive a pair of horses (though some say a goat); while in the other they are driving mythical creatures, splendidly winged griffins, and at the same time are facing a strange and menacing bird.

In interpreting these scenes one must guard against being too bold or fanciful and so piling up on the object more than it can stand. But the likely explanation of the meaning of the scenes is fairly simple and fairly obvious. Here is a man—the figure in the sleeveless cloak—watching his own funerary rites. There is first a libation to the Earth Goddess. It might be of wine, it might be of blood, it might be a mixture of the two; the mixing bowl may have a hole in it so that the liquid seeps down into the earth. There is a bearing of gifts, again either to the deity or deities, or to the dead man himself, for his succour in the world to come. There is a sacrifice, principally of a bull, and an offering of wine and the fruits of the earth at a sanctuary. As to the end panels, although it is the Minoan custom to show women as pale and men as brown, yet it is also a more universal custom to show also a dead man as pale. The griffin scene may therefore depict him flying off to heaven; and the bird may be an evil spirit trying to prevent him. The other panel might have that optimistic aspect common in Egyptian tombs, where the dead man is shown indulging in the heavenly equivalent of the activities he most delighted in on earth, fishing in the river or driving his chariot: the Minoan, having arrived, reverts to his more homely mode of transport, his buggy and mare.

The usual Minoan religious symbols are there, the double axe, the pillar, the birds, probably doves. But for the rest, nothing like this of any earlier date has been found in Crete. Evidence of sacrifice, yes; but only of communal sacrifice, to ward off the earth-shaker, for instance. Evidence of personal votive offerings, yes, in plenty, but not evidence, as here, of supplication for a happy, personal, after-life. Such, in all conscience, is a common practice of mankind. But it has not manifested itself before in what seems from all other evidence to be light-hearted, vividly-living, Minoan Crete. From the evidence of this painted sarcophagus of Hagia Triada (one-time home of the jolly harvester cup), it does not seem far-fetched to compare the Minoans under their first experience of Mycenaean tutelage with the seekers after mystery religions of the Roman Empire.

A foreign occupation does not have to be harsh, however, for the people who experience it to feel unhappy or unfulfilled or to seek solace in religious rites. There are no signs that the Mycenaean occupation was harsh.

Nor are there any real signs, despite the Linear B, that the Mycenaean rule was highly bureaucratic, more bureaucratic than had been its predecessor. What seems more likely—if we have judged the Minoan character correctly—is that it became more *efficiently* bureaucratic. It has been pointed out, and very rightly, that no amount of accounting documents need make one assume that the system which produced them was necessarily an efficient one. It may have been quite otherwise—and, judging by modern experience, one might say that the greater the number of documents the less efficient is the system likely to be. The heroic type, while scorning to perform the menial task himself, is quite capable, with his stern sense of honour and duty, of seeing that his menials perform their tasks reasonably well. When the Mycenaean lords came to easy-going Knossos, then, they may at least have tightened the slack reins just a little.

Here, and in other ways too, a comparison with the British empire-builder of the nineteenth century may be appropriate. One of the causes of the First Afghan War was not over-taxation by the British occupation but more efficient taxation: the Afghans were affronted that taxes should really be enforced. There may also be a parallel, and with the Romans too, in that the Mycenaean occupation at Knossos seems to have been uninterfering and unexacting. A particular style of pottery for this period is traced by the experts, the so-called Palace Style. 'It stiffens,' writes one commentator, 'the marine designs and the older plant and architectural ornaments into a more majestic symmetry.'* Perhaps, what is more significant, it introduces the drinking cup, in design like a modern champagne glass and which the site of old Nestor's palace of Pylos was to produce in such profligate profusion. Of these Mycenaean rulers who took their opportunity and came to Knossos when Thera had weakened her one may say this. They brought their heroic and aristocratic customs and ways of thought with them; the Minoan people, however, they left largely alone, though this leniency may have seemed less apparent to the Minoans than to the Mycenaeans themselves. One interesting fact is that most archaeological evidence

---

* Page 142 of *Greece in the Bronze Age* by Emily Vermeule (University of Chicago Press, 1964).

of this period of occupation at Knossos comes from buildings outside the palace. Apart from repairing and making more grand the throne-room, the hub of dynastic rule, the Mycenaeans seem to have left the rest of the great sprawling palace largely alone: perhaps it was already really badly ruined; perhaps: like most less cultured conquerors throughout history, they felt instinctively unwilling to have much to do with the place that was the heart of that culture. Let the scribes and the artisans and artists work where they had always worked, but the military gentlemen of Mycenae would create their own sterner, plainer, workaday administration outside.

Chapter XIII

The Spread of the Heroic Tradition and the First Growth of Turmoil

THE TRIBULATIONS of the ancient Cretans were only just beginning.

That as a generality is hardly deniable. As to detail, we are, with our present knowledge, in a quandary. The real and final collapse of Knossos, it is being insisted, comes, with the fall also of the Mycenaean kingdom, at the hands of a widespread and destructive movement of peoples in the whole area. But something highly unpleasant, something that in a wide view may be said to start the rot, must have happened to all the Minoan palaces, and so presumably to Crete as a whole, soon after the appearance of the alien Mycenaeans. To repeat the argument, one must envisage three possible reasons for this probable misfortune of about 1400: yet one more geological upheaval, and caused perhaps by the death-throes of Thera; civil war; or a military invasion by another force of Mycenaean 'sackers of cities,' even though a Mycenaean dynasty already ruled at Knossos. The fact that the Mycenaeans were already there in 1400 gives a little more credence than originally to the civil war theory. Yet, on the other hand, nothing so far disinterred gives credence to a rule harsh enough to have so soon given rise to a major revolt. It is useless, with our present knowledge, to continue to speculate or to come down in favour of one theory rather than another. We must accept the fact that *by* about 1400—and perhaps one may accentuate the 'by', rather than 'at', for somebody's dating may yet prove wrong—the palaces of Minoan Crete, those superb witnesses to her cheerful, sprawling vitality and greatness, had come to the end of their splendour. The power and importance shifts definitely to mainland Mycenae—and that power and importance is not yet over, though the portents of final destruction may already be visible to the historian.

We have the best part of two centuries to cover, and during them Crete will be out of the limelight. Mycenae will continue to develop what may legitimately be called an empire, will over-reach herself as another before her, and will suffer at the hands of those who will take advantage of her weakness, as she in the past had taken advantage. Yet even Mycenae will not be the focus of attention. There is no focus, or at least the beam is much wider and more diffused. The theatre is the eastern Mediterranean and its surrounding lands; and of the actors some have new names though some have very old ones.

The particular act of Mycenae's over-reaching may be safely taken as their war with Troy, the great punitive expedition around which the story of Homer's *Iliad* is woven. Professor Blegen's date for this, of about 1250, will be taken, though there are others who put it later and nearer to the date worked out by the Greeks themselves, 1194–84. Though, however, one accepts the central fact of the legend —and, as has already been done, the basic truth of the portrayed character of the Greek warriors—yet one must, of course, shy away from the sort of romanticism that led to Marlowe's 'topless towers of Ilium'. It will create the setting and tone of this chapter much more correctly to quote from a book already referred to, Emily Vermeule's *Greece in the Bronze Age*: 'Troy is one of the two great stone-walled cities of Asia Minor which seem directly comparable to the palace-citadels of the mainland—the other is the huge Hittite capital of Bogazköy or Hattusas. . . . The Hittites, Trojans and Greeks shared a common Indo-European heritage to some extent.' No ancient people, in fact, lived in isolation, though it is all too easy to accept unconsciously that they did do so and to experience surprise when one people, for long considered separately, are shown to have been in contact with, or even merely contemporary with, another people so considered. It may come as a shock to realize, for instance, that Moses and Agamemnon must have been very near or actual contemporaries and that the Mycenaeans were struggling outside Troy at the same time as the Israelites were struggling across the Sinai desert. As the fourteenth century dawned the history of the Middle East—which was the history of the forerunners of the Western World —was increasing in pace. And into that history the Mycenaeans were pushing themselves, to affect it and to be affected by it.

*

Egypt's third phase of greatness is essentially different from her previous two: called her New Kingdom, it would be better called her Phase of Empire.

It is almost as if the Egyptian rulers were now to be shamed into becoming imperially minded. The Hyksos occupation had been a shaming experience. When therefore the Pharaoh Khamose, first of the great Eighteenth Dynasty, liberates his country he also takes his vengeance upon the collaborators. 'I razed their towns and burned their places,' he boasts, 'they being made into red ruins for ever on account of the damage which they did within this Egypt, and they made themselves serve the Asiatics and had forsaken Egypt their mistress.'

That is a curtain-raiser, and the real expansion of an erstwhile peaceful and unexpansionist Egypt comes with the fifth pharaoh of the dynasty, Tuthmosis III. Here is an heroic figure, as legendarily athletic as Achilles, as strong in bending the bow as Odysseus. But he has a mother, and he cannot get rid of her when he ostensibly comes to the throne: Queen Hatshepsut, ancient Egypt's female Pharaoh, only releases the reins at death. Tuthmosis III immediately breaks out into activity: he is shamed, or frustrated, into a violent policy for the rest of his reign of 'extending the boundaries'. The date is about 1460, a decade before the Mycenaeans arrived in Knossos.

Most of the campaigns of Tuthmosis III were in Syria, around the headwaters of the Euphrates. There lived in those parts a people called the Mitanni; to the east of them were the Assyrians and the Babylonians, to the west the Hittites. A start in the Pharaoh's progress of victory and subjugation was made further south, against 'the vile enemy of Kadesh' and at the strategic town of Megiddo (where the Israelites were later to fight battles and which was to give its name, Har Megiddo, to the Armageddon of St. John's vision). Tuthmosis entered the battle 'on a chariot of gold equipped with his panoply of arms like Horus, Brandisher of Arm, Lord of Action'. He won it, and draped his slain enemies around the walls of Megiddo, though he took seven months to complete his investiture of the town. There followed—according to the Pharaoh's boast—no less than fourteen successful campaigns, culminating in a foray across the upper Euphrates and the consequent discomfiture of the Mitanni, great breeders of horses. On his way home, Tuthmosis had to meet his old vile enemy of Kadesh again, people who were apparently unbeaten, unrepentant and also knowing a thing or two about horses themselves. They let loose a mare at the beginning of the battle and as the Egyptian chariots were drawn by stallions there was grave danger of chaos and of a Pharaoh ignominiously being taken in the wrong direction. Fortunately, one of the Pharaoh's generals slew the mare and presented its tail to his majesty as a souvenir.

So we are very much in the heroic, horse-and-chariot atmosphere. The son of Tuthmosis III, Amenophis II, equally a great bowman and athlete, continued in his father's footsteps, parading his strength before the turbulent kinglets of Syria but apparently avoiding a head-on clash with either the Mitanni or the Hittites. He came home, he says, 'with 550 prisoners of the Maryannu [an Indo-European word for knights who fought in chariots], with 240 of their wives, 640 Canaanites, 232 children of princes and 323 female children of princes', unhappy hostages whose lives would depend on the good behaviour of the compatriots they had left behind. The next Pharaoh, Amenophis III, the magnificent, the *Roi Soleil* of ancient Egypt, left soldiering to his generals and endeavoured to retain his country's dominance by means of diplomacy and diplomatic marriages. The King of the Mitanni was sufficiently powerful to insist that his daughter should not be a mere member of the royal harem but the Pharaoh's principal wife. This she became and was handed on at the death of Amenophis to his son and successor, who was none other than the famous 'rebel' king Akhneten, an aberration in the line of heroic pharaohs and one who had no concern with foreign diplomacy or foreign conquest. The second quarter of the fourteenth century has been reached—and the Mitanni and the Hittites are about to come more strongly into the picture.

These two peoples possessed similarities to the Mycenaeans, and also to the Trojans, in that they were, all three, part of the first great wave of Aryan-speaking Indo-Europeans that had come south from the steppe-countries in the early centuries of the Second Millennium. By now they were either mixed with the indigenous population or remained an aristocracy ruling over them, the Hittites being in the former position and the Mitanni ruling over a Semitic people called the Hurrians. Much is known of the Hittites but little of the Mitanni, except that they were once powerful and were a great nuisance to the Hittites, with whom they were in much closer contact than the Egyptians. One small item of knowledge about them has its interest. Among the prolific Hittite archives a manual of horse training has been discovered; and it is written by a man of the Mitanni. Here is another connection with the Trojans, whom Homer likes to call 'trainers of horses', whilst at the same time it seems to show the Hittites as similar to the Mycenaeans at least in that they were not too proud to learn from their more skilful neighbours.

The Hittites are an important people, not only in their own right, but also archaeologically, their archives being the main source of our recently improved knowledge of the history of these times in the Middle East and of the evidence that the Mycenaeans were more intimately connected with it than had ever had been previously suspected.

The history of the Hittites themselves is a turbulent one, as might be expected of a people living in the harsh mountain plateau of the centre of Asia Minor, and as might also be expected from our general knowledge of these centuries in this part of the world. These people enter the scene with what seems a premature brilliance in the early sixteenth century; they peter out around the eleventh century as an unimportant minority of displaced persons in the neighbourhood of Carcemish, only fit to be duped, as was Uriah, husband of Bathsheba, by more forceful persons such as David, King of Israel.* Their appearance, in self-portraits and as portrayed by the Egyptians, is distinctive and neither Semitic nor obviously Aryan, with a large aquiline nose; the nearest similarity is with the Aztecs, though there is nothing whatever known to connect the two.

The Hittites traced their introduction to greatness to one Labarnas, as important a dynastic figure as was Atreus, grandfather of Agamemnon, to the Mycenaeans. He reigned from approximately 1680 to 1650, the time when the Minoans were about to enter upon their own period of greatness. Then came the Hittites' premature burst into fame at about 1600. They swallowed up the ancient town of Yamhad, where now stands Aleppo, and continued on down the left bank of the Euphrates, until they came to Babylon, peaceful under the Amorite descendants of the great law-giver Hammurabi. Babylon the Hittites captured. And then they marched home again, leaving the city to be taken over by the Kassites, another people of Indo-European elements, and to carry on in relative obscurity but not total unimportance, rather as Knossos was to continue for a while under the Mycenaeans.

* The story of David, Bathsheba and Uriah the Hittite is told in II Samuel, Ch. XI.

The reason for the Hittites' precipitate return was unrest at home. The trouble was dynastic, the kingship being a matter of intrigue and dispute. This is perhaps a recurring problem with such forceful and individualistic peoples as these Indo-Europeans seem to have been, a problem that the Persians were to experience and the Mycenaeans under Atreus—judging by the legends and the change of grave-sites —were shortly also to experience. In the land of the Hittites the outcome was serious, a usurper climbing to the throne and then losing all the territories won by the arms of three preceding kings. For a whole century or more the Hittites seem to have lived under a cloud, unable to do much more than maintain their survival under the pressure of enemies of which the greatest were the Mitanni.

With the rise of a new dynasty in the middle of the fifteenth century, the fortunes of the Hittites began slowly to mend. It was at this time that Tuthmosis III made his spectacular foray against the dreaded Mitanni, and the Hittites may have improved their position by a temporary alliance with the Egyptians. It was obvious, however, that, for all the long trail of captives that the Pharaoh took back with him, there were plenty of horses and chariots and Maryannu to man them left behind, together with an undiminished martial spirit. For a while yet, so the Hittite annals tell, the 'Hatti-lands' as they called their country, and the capital itself, Hattusas, were to suffer from invasion and despoliation from all sides, from the Mitanni in particular.

But then at last there came to the Hatti-lands their great saviour and leader and fighting-monarch, the king with the great con-temporary reputation and the very musical-sounding name, Suppiluliumas.

The date is about 1380. Now began a century and a quarter or so of turmoil at the further end of which stood the milestone of the Trojan War. It was a time unlike any that had been seen before. It must have been a period of mental upheaval as well as physical; it was an age of warring empires, all fighting with the weapons of diplomacy as well as with horse and chariot. It foreshadows a time of even greater turmoil, coming from without; and whether those who caused this first upheaval were the cause also of the second or only the victims of it, it is hard to say; though it is true that violence and a tradition of violence usually lead to more of the same thing. Rather as the Anglo-Saxons, those heroic-minded warriors of a later day who are so reminiscent of the Mycenaeans, were to suffer from a heightened form of their own aggressiveness at the hands of the Danes, so these earlier kingdoms on the other side of the dividing line of the birth of Christ were to suffer from their own treatment magnified and worsened. The Bronze Age was approaching its break-up, though no one knew it.

King Suppiluliumas was not going to obtain much help from Egypt: *le Roi Soleil* was approaching the end of his reign and resting more than ever on the laurels that others had gathered for him: in five years' time he would be succeeded by a young man who would change his name and his religion and be no more interested in international prestige than would be England's Richard II or Edward the Confessor. The Hittite king would therefore occasionally turn his attention both to such old-stagers as the Babylonians and such newcomers to the imperial scene as the Ahhiyawa.

Now, there is no mystery about this. The Ahhiyawa are believed, and with good reason, to be synonymous with Homer's Achaeans, that is to say the Mycenaeans. Their country is shown to have had connections with the Asia Minor coast and to have been approached by sea; when it is realized that the Achaeans were spelt in Homeric Greek with the *digamma*, which makes them the Achaiwoi, the similarity between the two words is close. There is no other people to fit the double evidence. It has been suggested that some particular part of the Mycenaean empire may have been meant; Rhodes for instance or even Crete. But there seem no good grounds for creating this refinement. The narrative can therefore proceed, embodying the assumption that the Ahhiyawa and the Mycenaeans are one and the same people.

During the reign of Suppiluliumas the two kingdoms were on friendly terms. The Hittite king was troubled by a certain person who was being a nuisance; he therefore prevailed upon the Ahhiyawa to take him or her—there is a suggestion that the recalcitrant person may even have been the king's wife—into their custody as a political exile. That is all; the Mycenaeans were not very important within the international scene as yet, and Suppiluliumas was merely making minor use of them. The main task of the Hittite king was to destroy once and for all his country's inveterate enemy, the Mitanni.

The first attempt at this was a failure: the Mitanni king, named Tushratta, was victorious and sent some of his booty as a present to the Egyptian Pharaoh, now his ally. Suppiluliumas next made a more careful attempt, attacking the Mitanni from the rear and subduing the wild tribes in his path by force of arms together with the diplomatic gift of one of his daughters in marriage, a signal honour, no doubt. This time the Mitanni king submitted, apparently without much of a fight, as did his satellite kingdoms to the south: Suppiluliumas extended his sway as far as the Lebanon, encroaching upon the sphere of influence of an Egypt that was at the moment only interested in its own internal affairs. Within the kingdom of the Mitanni this Egyptian weakness now caused a palace revolution. The pro-Egyptian Tushratta was assassinated and a new king was installed who saw more hope in allying himself with a fresh and growing power and not an old. This new power was Assyria, whose king was showered with gifts. The Mitanni could not have made a more significant, or dangerous, move.

At just this time in the slowly degenerating situation in the Middle East the conduct and diplomacy of the monarchs concerned is brilliantly lit for us by the chance find, in 1887, of the famous Tell el-Amarna tablets. These, stored in the new capital city that the rebel king Akhneten had built for himself, are part of the royal archives and record some of the correspondence between the Egyptian pharaohs (in this case Akhneten himself and his proud predecessor Amenophis III) and their 'brother' monarchs of the surrounding realms. These documents are as naïvely human as anything in the *Iliad* describing the vituperative quarrellings of King Agamemnon and Achilles. That they show a gaggle of minor emperors fiddling while the Middle East burns would perhaps be an exaggeration; but they do give the impression of people playing at power politics and who are a little inexperienced and crude at the game.

There is only one letter from Suppiluliumas and it is to Ahkneten on his accession to the throne. It begins in this wise:

> Thus hath Suppiluliumas, the great king,
> king of Hatti-land, to Huria
> king of Egypt, my brother spoken:
> I am well. With thee may it be well
> With thy wives, thy sons, thy house, thy warriors, thy chariots,
> and in thy land, may it be very well.*

* From *The Tell El-Amarna Tablets*, edited by S. A. B. Mercer (Macmillan, 1939). The lines are not, as might first appear, some form of blank verse but correspond to the cuneiform originals.

The penultimate line is certainly revealing. It is the usual form of preliminary inter-monarchial greeting; and if it had not been unearthed it would be quite incredible: chariots lumped together with wives! Sometimes horses are included with the chariots.

The rest of the meassage concerns, as do so many of these letters between potentates, the matter of the exchange of presents: here is further evidence that Homer was historically correct in showing this business as so important. 'I used to exchange presents with your father', says Suppiluliumas in effect, 'as token of mutual friendship; I hope therefore that we two shall continue to do the same':

> Whatever was requested of thy father,
> thou, my brother, withhold it not!

The determination, and avidity, with which the kings collect presents for the enrichment of their treasury and their prestige is positively shaming. As has already been said in connection with Mycenae's great show of gold in the shaft graves, it was Egypt who was the great source of the prized commodity, and she was not allowed to forget the fact. Tushratta of the Mitanni put it as succinctly as anyone: gold in Egypt was as common as dust elsewhere, and of course the Pharaoh would not miss it if he gave away a little more. The King of Babylon had occasion to complain bitterly:

> In respect of thy messenger, whom thou didst send
> the twenty minas of gold, which he brought, were not complete;
> for when it was put in the furnace, it did not come forth five minas.

The bargaining over the giving of kings' daughters in marriage is as close and at times as sordid. The Mitanni king and the Egyptian pharaoh are fairly dignified in the matter; but there is trouble once more where Babylon is concerned. On the Babylonian king complaining that he has had nothing from his daughter and does not even know whether she is alive or dead, the magnificent Amenophis II replies that, incidentally, he did not complain that she was not beautiful, and that in any case the reason why there have been no gifts coming from the king's daughter to the king is that there have been no gifts lately from the king to the king's daughter. Another letter from Babylon makes the improper suggestion that if the Pharaoh has no more daughters he is willing to send out as diplomatic concubines then any beautiful girl will do—for, after all, no one need know the difference.

There is, finally, another side to these Amarna letters, and one that may be considered more historically important, though all the haggling under cover of brotherly well-wishing as to wives and horses is surely significant of a malaise of some sort existing amongst the kingdoms of the Middle East during the last centuries of the Bronze Age. Letters come not only from the Pharaoh's royal 'brothers' but also from his own colonial governors. They come from Syria and Palestine, and they tell a clear tale of unrest and a deteriorating situation.

The Egyptian throne was by now occupied by Akhneten, who became Pharaoh at about 1375, five years after Suppiluliumas's accession, and who was soon busy writing his hymns to the sun and having his new capital built for him. First, a certain Abi-Asratu asked for help, describing himself as the Pharaoh's dog and reminding the Pharaoh that he guards for him the whole of the land of the Amorites. But then it seems that Abi-Asratu turned traitor, and his sons with him, and there came impassioned appeals for help from the governor of Gubla, which is the same as later Byblos and a port with which both Minoans and Mycenaeans had long been trading. Only just a few archers and chariots and charioteers, the governor pleads, but a small show of strength, and the position will be transformed. Akhneten did on this occasion reply, but it seems to have been a very unhelpful answer. 'The king, my lord,' replied the governor in his turn, 'says, "Protect thyself, and protect the city of the kings that is in my care." I say: With whom should I protect myself and the city? Formerly a royal garrison was with me ... What are the dogs, the sons of Abi-Asratu, that they act according to their hearts' wish and cause the cities of the king to go up in smoke?'

By the time of the last years of the reign of Suppiluliumas, the short, strange, troubled reign of Akhneten was over in Egypt and the young but ineffectual Tutankhamen was on the throne of the pharaohs.* Suppiluliumas, taking advantage of Egypt's weakness, staged one last campaign, invested the great fortress of Carchemish after an eight-day siege, and became master of Syria from the

---

* Tutankhamen's virtually sole claim to fame lies in the lucky chance that his tomb had remained unrifled by robbers until discovered by the archaeologists in 1922. It showed what wealth could be buried even with a poor sickly pharaoh who had ruled for only a few years. One item among the piled-up grave goods is of significance here: a magnificent chariot. And, as did both the Minoans under Mycenaean tutelage and Homer's heroes, so did the Egyptians store their chariot chassis and its wheels separately.

Euphrates to the sea. The Hittites had most certainly arrived. There remains one other letter of these times, not from Tell el-Amarna but from the Hittite archives, which shows most dramatically and surprisingly the shifts and changes of power that were taking place in these regions.

The short five-year reign of Tutankhamen was by now also ended. The letter comes from his widow, Queen Ankhesnamun (daughter of Akhneten and Nefertiti), and it is addressed to King Suppiluliumas; it runs as follows:

> My husband has died and I have no son but of you it is said that you have many sons. If you would send me one of your sons, he could become my husband. I will on no account take one of my subjects and make him my husband. I am very much afraid.

The throne of Egypt, though filled by a male, went by the female line: the widow was therefore virtually offering nothing less than the age-old throne of the pharaohs to the prince of the Hittites. The fact reflects a most amazing rise of one power and decline of another. Suppiluliumas did send a son, though after an understandable hesitation; the boy was however assassinated on the way, and the young widow was probably forced to marry one of her own subjects, the odious Priest Ay, who sat on the Egyptian throne for four unruly years and who had probably engineered the murder. So was the chance of a very powerful alliance missed.

Before his death in 1340 King Suppiluliumas, at the height of his fame, did two things of considerable future consequence. One was to interfere in internal Mitanni affairs and to depose the pro-Assyrian usurper of Tushratta. This for a time put a buffer state between himself and the growing power of Assyria. The king's other act was to avenge himself upon Egypt for the murder of his son. This was to have a double consequence. The more immediate was an introduction of the plague into the Hittite lands by Egyptian prisoners-of-war; the less immediate but of greater consequence was an increase in the determination of those in power in Egypt to be avenged for the degradation they had suffered from without during their country's time of weakness under Akhneten.

The plague carried off Suppiluliumas himself and his eldest son. It continued during the reign of his second son and successor, Mursilis II. Like Greek Oedipus and Agamemnon, Mursilis sought to discover what had caused this sign of displeasure of the gods and to expiate the sin. He also—no doubt on the principle that every little helps—asked the Ahhiyawa to send an effigy of their god with instructions as to the proper ritual: once again the Ahhiyawa are shown as still a friendly power. Incidentally, this sending of images of gods for prophylactic purposes seems to have been fairly common: Mursilis also sent for the god of Lazpa (? Lesbos); and a little while earlier Tushratta of Mitanni had obliged in the same way to help the ailing Amenophis III. Mursilis seems to have repaid his debt to the Ahhiyawa by inviting some of their king's family to come to the Hatti-land for lessons in chariot-driving—lessons which if they had been better handed down might, one would imagine, have shortened the Trojan war.

The time of the Egyptian efforts at vengeance upon the Hittites was not to come until the accession of Mursilis's successor. Mursilis was not, however, without his external troubles; and they came from the north and from the west. To the north lay an agglomeration of small unruly tribes who could never be pinned down and against whom repeated campaigns had to be staged; they were so persistently a nuisance that there must be a suspicion that they were receiving help from even further afield. To the west were a string of states along the eastern coast of the Aegean Sea, one of which was called by the Hittites the Lukka Lands and may have been Lycia. The Hittites' story of their trouble with the Lukka Lands brings in the Mycenaeans once again.

A certain Hittite subject by the name of Piyama-radus had turned freebooter and was causing trouble in the Lukka Lands. Now, the Lukka Lands seem to have been a kind of No-Man's Land between the Hittites and the Ahhiyawa. Piyama-radus was operating from the southern part of the Lukka Lands at a place on the coast called Milawata; and Milawata (perhaps the later Milatus) was an Ahhiyawa town. Would, then, the Ahhiyawans, asked the Hittite king, please have the man extradited and handed over to justice.

The matter was not so simple, however. Ruling in the Lukka Lands was a relative of the Ahhiyawa king, and he was proving difficult. The Hittites had therefore to send a punitive expedition against him. Mursilis,* in a conciliatory letter to the Ahhiyawa king, explains that he is sorry about this but that it is necessary, adding

---

* Actually the report of this correspondence in the Hittite archives does not say which king is concerned; other evidence makes it clear, however, that it was Mursilis or possibly his immediate successor.

however a renewed demand that the freebooter be captured and handed over. There is also an additional personal touch which shows a close friendship, or at least connection, between Hittites and Mycenaeans: the messenger carrying the letter is explained to be a man of importance, who has in fact ridden in the chariots of both Mursilis and of the brother of the Ahhiyawa king. The outcome of the affair was that the rebel was in fact handed over as requested and friendly relations were maintained; it looks, however, as if they had become a little strained during the process of the negotiations.

The next landmark in the generally deteriorating situation was the set battle between the Hittites and the Egyptians at Kadesh on the river Orontes.

Egypt had been rapidly developing out of her short period of pacifism and spiritual introspection under Akhneten: it is rather as if again her rulers had felt shame, shame for an aberration that had been disastrous from a diplomatic and imperial point of view. The usurper, Ay, had been soon got rid of (and with him presumably the unhappy and importunate widow, Ankhesnamun). An army general, Horemhab, became Pharaoh. He chose as his successor a young officer already in an important post, Superintendent of the King's Horses. This man called himself Rameses: the last truly famous native Egyptian dynasty, the Nineteenth, was about to be born, and the land to experience her last period of imperial glory. As for the Egyptian people, however, this is what their modern historian, Sir Alan Gardiner, has to say about them: 'It is impossible not to notice the marked deterioration of the art, the literature, and indeed the general culture of the people. The language which they wrote approximates more closely to the vernacular and incorporates many foreign words; the copies of ancient texts are incredibly careless, as if the scribes utterly failed to understand their meaning. At Thebes the tombs no longer display the bright and happy scenes of everyday life which characterized Dynasty XVIII, but concentrate rather upon the perils to be faced in the hereafter.'

Rameses I had little chance to show his prowess, reigning for less than two years. His son, Sety I, did not waste much time. Following the example of his illustrious predecessor of a hundred years ago, Tuthmosis III of Megiddo, he mounted his golden chariot and advanced victoriously through Palestine to the banks of the Orontes, which was on the Syrian border. The Hittites considered Syria their domain. King Mursilis, forgetting such minor matter as Piyama-radus the freebooter but remembering that he already had another enemy facing him in the south-east, where Assyria had finally swallowed up the land of the Mitanni—Mursilis marched to meet the Egyptian army with a large army of his own. The two monarchs surveyed each other and their forces from each side of the river, and decided to leave it at that. Each side retired: the clash was not yet.

It came when Sety died and Rameses II came to the Egyptian throne. One of the many titles of this famous Pharaoh was Ozymandias; and Shelley was more perspicacious than he knew in selecting him to illustrate the irony of dilapidated greatness. Rameses II was probably the most untrammelled boaster of all time—when one considers the uses to which the ancients sometimes put the invention of writing one can almost commend the Minoans for restricting it to a practical and at any rate truth-telling use. Until the Hittite archives came to light it had been the habit of historians to accept Rameses's description of the battle of Kadesh as a resounding personal victory at something like its face value. Now it can be seen that—though the Pharaoh may have indeed been very brave in extricating himself from a highly dangerous position into which the folly of himself or his generals had placed him—the battle for the Egyptians was at the best a draw and in its results pretty disastrous.

There is no need to describe the battle, for what matters is firstly its result and secondly the peoples who were taking part in it. A little of the Egyptian scribe's boasting on behalf of his proud monarch is worth quoting, however; for it is like a bad edition of Homer and may serve to show how the heroic tradition had permeated, at this time, into the most ancient of civilizations as well as into the new:

> His majesty issued forth like his father Month [or Mont, a war god], after he had seized his panoply of war and had put on his corselet; he was like Baal in his hour. The great span [horse-chariot] which bore his majesty was called Victory-in-Thebes and was from the great stable of Rameses. His majesty rode at a gallop, and charged the hostile army of Hatti, being all alone and having none with him.

For this great battle both sides had mustered as large a force as possible. On the Egyptian side are mentioned the Shardana, possibly men from Sardinia. On the Hittite side were Philistines and Lycians and Dardanians, which is the name that Homer gives to the men of

Troy, as well as other names not easily recognizable. Here were tribes and peoples of all the coastal areas that lay across the sea, northward from the Nile Delta, men willing to take advantage of the unsettled times and to fight for those who wanted them to fight.

They were to become an increasing and significant phenomenon, and the Egyptians were to call them the Peoples of the Sea.

Chapter XIV

The Turmoil Continues: the Peoples of the Sea

ONE MAY detect a recurring theme of opportunism on the part of the Mycenaeans, though to be fair to them they were not necessarily being more opportunist than any other militant and ambitious people of these times. The Minoans suffer from the aftermath of the Thera eruption, and the Mycenaeans appear at Knossos; the Egyptians cease to try to spread their influence in the Middle East after the battle of Kadesh, and there are signs that Mycenaean expansion receives another fillip; finally the long-lived and splendid city of Troy, known as Troy VI, collapses, possibly from earthquake, at about the same time as the battle of Kadesh, and within fifty years or so the Mycenaeans are staging their great expedition against its not-so-splendid successor.

As for Knossos, she has been described in her initial decades of Mycenaean occupation as not so very greatly harmed or changed. Nevertheless it may not be wrong to think of her also as unhappily dragged at the wheels of the juggernaut car of Mycenaean militarism. Admittedly, when the time came, Homer's King Idomeneus does not seem to have been an unwilling participant in the war against Troy. But centuries of a peaceful way of life cannot be easily abandoned, and it seems very likely that the people of Crete were at the least not enthusiastic supporters of their Mycenaean king. The final fall of Knossos may have been inevitable, but it cannot be called deserved, as might be termed the fall of Mycenae. If the Mycenaeans by their conduct were asking for trouble, then the Minoans were to have trouble once more thrust upon them, and through no fault of their own except perhaps the over-eagerness to be helpful of the naturally easy-going.

*

The narrative of these centuries of turmoil is resumed with the battle of Kadesh. Its date is put, with accuracy to within a year or two, at 1285, and the ensuing treaty between Egypt and the Hittites at 1269. Egypt, with two-thirds of a century in front of her before she had to meet the fury that was to come, proceeded to retire from the international Middle-Eastern scene.

Not so the Hittites nor the Ahhiyawa. The Hittites, after yet another sacking of their capital city by the ever-unruly tribesmen of the north, and after another palace revolution, settle down to a decade or two of prosperity and relative peace. The Ahhiyawa figure as givers to the Hittites of worthwhile gifts and then in a more important role. In a treaty with the Amorites, the Hittite king cites his brother of Ahhiyawa as one of those 'who are of equal rank to me, the King of Egypt, the King of Babylon, the King of Assyria'. If King Suppiluliumas of the Hittites had 'arrived' when, a century earlier, the Pharaoh's widow had approached him, then the King of the Ahhiyawa had also arrived when the Hittite monarch cited him as an equal.

Was that king the Homeric Agamemnon? Posterity is not very likely to know. But the date is about right. This Amorite treaty was made in the reign of that Hittite king who acceded to the throne about 1250; and it is 1250 that Professor Blegen, who is the greatest excavator at Troy after Schliemann, gives as the most probable date for the beginning of the legendary siege. There is also one other reference in the archives to this same Hittite king that helps to make the identity probable. This states that the King of the Ahhiyawa 'withdrew' from the Land of the Seha River. Now the land of the Seha river is another of the Hittites' outer dependencies along Asia Minor's Aegean coast, and it looks as if this is an incident similar to that of the Lukka Lands, when the Ahhiyawa, after backing the troublesome freebooter, had caved in before Hittite pressure. The Ahhiyawa king is now in Asia Minor in person—but again he caves in.

Whatever the exact truth, the Ahhiyawa—that is the Achaeans, that is the Mycenaeans—did besiege and finally destroy the city of the Trojans. The first thing to say about this great final fling in the aggressiveness of the Mycenaeans is that it is not shown even by pro-Greek Homer as wholly a success. It took ten years to accomplish; it succeeded in the end only by means of treachery and a ruse—though it must be allowed that most ancient sieges only ended in that way. At least once the Greeks were nearly beaten; and their outstanding characteristic was the inability to agree amongst themselves.

It is the return of the legendary Greek heroes that has particular historical import. It is tragic and tells of failure and growing lawlessness. Only the aged Nestor and Menelaus with his restored wife Helen are fortunate, and not even they for long. As for the others— Diomedes of Argos, Odysseus of Ithaca, Idomeneus of Knossos, and Agamemnon himself—all returned to overwhelming trouble.

One legend, already referred to, ascribes to Idomeneus the usual fate of anyone who, to save himself from disaster—in this instance shipwreck—promises to the gods the sacrifice of the first creature to meet him on safe arrival home, such creature proving to be, of course, his own child. The heartless keeping of the vow is considered to be the cause of a visitation of plague upon the Knossians and they expel their foolish and Jonah-like, misfortune-bringing king. Another version gives Idomeneus a faithless wife living in sin with a usurper, a failure to regain his throne, and—as before—his departure from the land he once had ruled and so rashly left unguarded.

The stories of Agamemnon and Odysseus both have the same primary theme of lawlessness and usurpers, in the first instance successful and in the second by no means so.

All the legends about Agamemnon and his family point to a long-draw-out and complicated dynastic quarrel of ferocity and intensity: the Mycenaeans, it seems likely, had no more learnt to solve the problem of trouble-free kingly leadership than had their brother Indo-Europeans, the Hittites.

Agamemnon had early been deprived of his kingly expectations by the murder of his father (or possibly grandfather) Atreus, done to death by the king's own brother Thyestes and that brother's son, the wicked Aegisthus. Agamemnon, however, returning from exile in Sparta, where he had married Helen's sister Clytemnestra, duly regained the throne. He may have done this by peaceful means, but in any case the usurpers, Thyestes and Aegisthus, were not disposed of. There then came for Agamemnon prosperity and the building up by him of personal power and leadership of the Mycenaean world: he was a forceful if not exactly a likeable person. Then ensued the abduction of Helen by Paris of Troy. Helen was twice over Agamemnon's sister-in-law, both his wife's sister and his brother's wife: he had to do something about it.

What he did was to organize the greatest city-sacking expedition that the Greeks had ever staged, the expedition to which every Mycenaean princeling was either proud or persuaded to offer his quota of men and ships and his own bronze-clad arm. The great fleet collected at Aulis, near to Thebes and on the strait between Euboea and the mainland. There it stayed, for lack of a favourable wind. The Greek cure was drastic: the sacrifice of Iphigenia, daughter of Agamemnon and Clytemnestra. Whether or not Agamemnon had ever told his wife that he preferred slave girls to her, as Homer makes him confess to his fellow heroes, Clytemnestra had little cause to love her ambitious husband, nurturing a large grievance on which to feed her hatred.

And so, through the long years, Clytemnestra helped to keep the kingdom of Mycenae from falling to pieces, and did it as consort to her husband's cousin and previous accessory to a royal murder. To turn for a moment from legend to archaeological evidence, there are, according to Desborough, signs that at his time Mycenae suffered her first attack and received a further strengthening of her defences; though until we can be more certain of the date of the siege of Troy we cannot be sure that this occurred in Agamemnon's absence. Always, however, there was in the minds and upon the conscience of the guilty couple the day when the rightful king would return. Always on one of the two peaks that overshadow Mycenae was stationed a sentry looking out for the beacon fire which, relayed across the peninsulas and islands, would herald the victory of the Greeks. Then, one day, after three thousand fruitless vigils, a man may be seen leaping and stumbling down the stony slope, and in through the guarded sally-port and so through the 'echoing' portal of the megaron to confront his mistress and master. And Aegisthus and Clytemnestra—'perjured lioness, wolf-mated' Euripedes calls her— are left to make their preparations and steel their resolution.

Agamemnon, recompensed for his loss of the slave-girl Chryseis by the greatest prize and status symbol of all, the daughter of the King of Troy, duly arrives back at his great fortress capital. He is afforded the travel-stained hero's ritual welcome, being bathed in his silver bath. But he does not step from it refreshed and god-like. While Trojan Cassandra describes the doom that she cannot see but knows is about to be enacted, King Agamemnon is murdered in his bath.

There is something appalling in this story, even though it is hardly unique in the annals of dynastic crime. That it has truth behind it we need not doubt: it made such an impact on the Greeks themselves that it appeared at least twice in the plays of their great classical dramatist, by Aeschylus as well as Euripides. Nor was the dynastic tragedy finished.

The story of the return of Odysseus has a similar theme, but with a happier if no less bloody ending. After the Cloud Cuckoo Land adventures of the hero, the tale gets down to its real purpose, to tell of treachery and its just reward: Odysseus is approaching the goal of his homeland. It is this detailed picture of a Mycenaean home-coming in these very troubled times that can help us to visualize their reality.

It is not a clear picture but it is an intriguing and suggestive one. The story is well known. Odysseus, King of Ithaca, when finally persuaded to join the Trojan expedition, leaves behind him his wife Penelope, a Spartan princess, and also a baby son, Telemachus. When Odysseus seems unlikely to return, the local lordlings and landowners cluster round and pay court to the unprotected lady, whether grass or real widow nobody knows, wishing both for her person and her inheritance. Penelope, unlike Clytemnestra chaste and faithful, endeavours to procrastinate by announcing that she must fulfil the duty of weaving a shroud for her ageing father-in-law before making a decision and by employing the ruse of undoing at night what she has woven during the day. Though this ruse serves its purpose for a remarkably long time, it cannot be expected to work indefinitely and it does not. The suitors, now becoming permanent lodgers, continue to eat her out of house and home. It is a curious and not easily believable situation though it may approximate more nearly to the truth than we feel inclined to imagine: the suitors observing a romantic conception of courtship, willing to let the best man win and for the winner honestly to add his own inheritance to that of his lady, yet at the same time leading a life of gross, gentle-men-at-leisure laziness and gorging themselves with meat in a way that only a still prosperous and peaceful pastoral economy could afford.

Then, only a little while after the grown-up Telemachus has made those fruitless journeys of enquiry to Menelaus and Nestor, the much-travelled Odysseus returns. Having ended his incredible adventures at the court of the Phaeacians (in whose description, it has been suggested, lie memories of the greatness of the Minoans), he reappears at his palace in Ithaca, to be recognized at first only by his old and faithful dog. Trading on this lack of recognition, the wily Odysseus lays his plans with care. Finding out whom he can trust, he gradually makes himself known to these and then finally, in a memorable scene and using his great bow which no else can string or shoot, he lays about him and kills off his rivals one by one. He follows this by a further winnowing of the faithless from the faithful; and almost the final scene is of carnage within the megaron and a line of lolling-headed maidservants strung up without.

This horrible scene of the hanging of the treacherous women slaves, besides remaining in the memory, is probably of real historical significance. Odysseus is seldom shown as a cruel man. But he has nearly lost his throne and his heritage, and there is no question but that incipient rebellion must be ruthlessly crushed. Odysseus, like the rest, has come back to turbulent times, when hate and vengeance and ruthlessness are the natural order of the day.

*

This picture of the times is borne out by the last of the references to the Ahhiyawa, and also by the contemporary Egyptian archives.

Towards the end of the reign of the Hittite king who had listed his Ahhiyawa brother as his equal (King Tudhaliyas IV, c. 1250–1220) there appeared a cloud on the western horizon of the Hatti-land. A certain Madduwattas found himself driven out of his kingdom, probably on the Asia Minor coast, by one named Attarissiyas of the Ahhiyawa. Some have seen in this second name an elongation of the Mycenaean dynastic name of Atreus, but the spotting of similarities is a dangerous game, with the bending of philological rules in the spotter's favour all too tempting, and the credibility gap is in this case too great: let it suffice that this man was an Ahhiyawan and that he had the power and the effrontery to turn out of his kingdom a vassal knight of the Hittites. This kinglet ran to the Hittites for protection and redress, and was given another small kingdom as compensation, a compromise solution.

This was not the end of the affair, however. Tudhaliyas died, and we find his successor—the last but one of the recorded Hittite kings—writing a letter of indictment to his one-time protégé Madduwattas, accusing him of rebellion and not only of rebellion but of allying himself with this 'man of the Ahhiyawa' who had turned him out of his original kingdom. The two of them had apparently fought a pitched battle with the Hittites, in which the Ahhiyawa general with the name vaguely like Atreus had commanded no less than a hundred chariots. What had been the result of this battle is not made clear.

But there is reference to a further marauding adventure by these two anti-Hittite allies upon 'Alasiya', which could be either on the Syrian coast or the island of Cyprus. What a tale of confusion and lawless opportunism, and how different from the courtly friendliness and assurance of the times of Suppiluliumas a century and a half before! Do we have here the reflection of some city-sacking raid undertaken by the Mycenaeans while the Trojan war dragged itself out, or some adventure undertaken by one of the heroes of that war, unmentioned by Homer, after it was over?

One of the other heroes, it will be remembered, seemed strangely loth to hurry back, and that was Menelaus. In the *Odyssey* he boasts to Telemachus of the successful adventures he has had in Egypt on his return journey from Troy, besides suggesting another journey abroad in search of treasure, which may be euphemism for loot, so easy to pick up round the Delta of the Nile.

The Egyptians, from about 1230 onwards, ran into serious trouble. Their scribes saw as the source of it the fact that 'the Northerners were disturbed in their isles', and they named those who were causing the disturbance 'the Peoples of the Sea'.

The historians find it as hard to pin down the Peoples of the Sea as did Odysseus the sea-god Proteus. This is unfortunate; but the fact does help to show up the inherent turbulence of these times and lack of any authoritative power. They were, these Sea Peoples, as one historian has said, 'a phenomenon, not a race'. From the time of the battle of Kadesh they become increasingly prominent as a phenomenon, and as a threat too. In 1221, in the reign of the Pharaoh Merenptah, successor to the boastful Rameses II, Egypt had to repel a combined invasion of the rich Delta lands by the Sea Peoples and the Libyans. As with the battle of Kadesh, the Egyptian scribes gave names to some of these peoples. Again it is philological guess-work to tell who they are: Philistines apparently, and Sardinians, and also 'Akwasha'.

Are these the same as the Ahhiyawa? It is generally considered so. But if so, what are they doing amongst the Peoples of the Sea, who surely were as much their enemies as enemies of the Egyptians? The only possible answer to the question may give us the best clue of all to an understanding of the situation: everyone was attacking everyone; every other person was an adventurer or a mercenary or, finally and most significantly, a displaced person.

One other juggling with names may be mentioned, the Pulsati, which has been taken for the Egyptian equivalent of the Philistines. In the earliest translation of the Old Testament known as the Septuagint there is a reference to their origin which might be either Capadocia or Crete. This is the sole evidence for the oft-repeated suggestion that the Philistines originated from Crete. It is altogether too flimsy. Professor Marinatos, however, is of the opinion that it might well mean that people had in fact arrived in Palestine from Crete, these people however being some branch of the 'Peoples of the Sea', who had entered Crete and then moved on, rather than indigenous Minoans. Such a situation does in fact seem likely in many places from the archaeological evidence: the Peoples of the Sea were by no stretch of the word colonizers; they entered, caused havoc, and—with perhaps some of their victims accompanying them—moved on. Crete was no more escaping their visitations than the rest of the lands of the Middle East.

*

Soon after 1190 Egypt had to try to beat back a more determined invasion through Palestine, and eventually succumbed to it. At the same time the last of the recorded Hittite kings came to the throne. He was named Suppiluliumas the Second—perhaps hopefully. The hope was not fulfilled. The by now brittle Hittite Empire collapsed and its people retreated into Syria. Then, after a period of darkness, they formed, with a mixture of other peoples, a so-called Neo-Hittite kingdom round Carchemish, with which the Israelites were to have their dealings.

Now great empires, however effete or disturbed or brittle, do not fall to mere raids of adventurers, sackers of cities and displaced persons. Here was something more like mass invasion. By tradition the Hittites fell to the Phrygians; and by tradition the cities of Mycenaean Greece and Minoan Crete fell to the Dorian Greeks. The movement from the north *behind* the Peoples of the Sea had begun.

Thucydides, in the opening pages of his history of the Peloponnesean war, follows this tradition. And this is his summing up of the situation:

> After the Trojan War Greece was in a state of constant movement and was being settled in a way that left her no peace to grow strong again. For the return of the Greeks from Troy took many years and brought many innovations, and civil wars happened in most cities, from which people escaped to found new places.

Chapter XV

'Rowers for Pleuron': the Coming of the Dorians

KING NESTOR'S splendid palace at Pylos, with its timber framework to its walls and its rich store of oil-filled pithoi, must have burnt very well. There are signs that it did so. At Mycenae it was the granary that in particular showed signs of burning. The Dorians had arrived.

The date was around 1150; if Troy fell, after its desultory ten-year siege, at 1240, and if Herodotus is right in giving the Achaeans eighty years of grace before their downfall, then the date would be 1160, not very different.

Even Nestor, living by repute twice the normal span, must have been dead. The heroic victory over Troy was already no more than a memory, though a sedulously forested memory because for some time now victories had not occurred and the Mycenaean world was patently deteriorating. A certain King Echlaon (by the Linear B tablets Ekhelawon) was on the Pylian throne.

'Thus,' say his tablets, 'the watchers are guarding the coast.' Suddenly the new danger has become imminent. The king sends his rowers northwards to the neighbourhood of Pleuron, at the entrance to the Corinthian Gulf. There are, by the count of the tablets surviving, 443 of these rowers, enough by Homer's reckoning for nine ships. Perhaps there were many more; but this, if it is all, is a poor showing, very poor indeed by comparison with King Nestor's contribution of ninety ships for the expedition to Troy.

The Linear B tablets at Pylos dealing with naval and military matters have been made much of as an interpretation of dramatic action on the part of the Mycenaeans in an endeavour to stave off the inevitable end. So much has been made of them in fact that there has come an understandable reaction against such an interpretation.

But there is no need for the reaction. An interpretation that fits better can hardly be thought of; strokes of luck do occur to archaeologists and philologists. The experts, Ventris and Chadwick, while giving a cautious evaluation of the relevant tablets in their book *Documents in Mycenaean Greek*, favour the romantic interpretation. The tablets as a whole do seem definitely to show a military set-up existing at the time. There is a king of Pylos, a *Wanax* as opposed to a mere feudal lord whose title is an archaic form of the later Greek *basileus*: this ties up with the obvious importance of Nestor in the Homeric epic and the equally obvious modern signs that Pylos was an important palace and seat of an important and wide-ruling king, second only to Mycenae and Agamemnon. There are also *equeta*, companions to or 'followers' of the king, staff officers perhaps acting as liaison between him and the local feudal lords who would be nominally in command of their own areas. There is also a *lawagatas*, a very important person and, it would appear, the Commander-in-Chief—he might well have been appointed specially when the threat of war arose. Incidentally the same title is mentioned once on the Knossos tablets, which cover, it will be remembered, the initial period of Mycenaean occupation of the Minoan capital, and this fact lends some support to the idea that the occupation was a military one and not a full-scale political affair.

There are three naval tablets found at Pylos. 'The first'—to quote the Ventris and Chadwick book* 'is a list of the number of rowers to be provided by various towns for an expedition to Pleuron. The second is probably somewhat similar, but the heading is almost all lost, and the numerals are much larger . . . The numbers make it certain that we are not here concerned with a peaceful mercantile venture, but a naval operation; and it would be unlikely that the business of trade would be thus organized by a central authority . . . The third tablet is more enigmatic . . . the heading speaks clearly of "rowers who are absent" (without leave?)'

The military as opposed to the naval tablets enumerate a total of 740 troops. One of these tablets, apparently introducing the whole series, starts with a heading that says specifically that the soldiers listed are for the duty of guarding the coastal regions. The numbers are preceded by the names of commanders and subordinate commanders and also by words—not always translatable—which denote either their town of origin or the particular 'trade' (in the modern army sense) to which they belong. Two of the towns of origin read as if they were Olympia and Erymanthos, both in Elis, north-west of Pylos's fertile Messenia: either the King of Pylos had increased his

* Page 183.

relative importance since the siege of Troy or he had been given by the Mycenaean king special and general responsibility for the defence of the western coast.

*

Did the Dorians in fact come by sea, and so to attack the western coasts of Greece? Tradition does say that they came from the north-west, and the evidence of dialect appears to bear this out. Desborough, however, favours the greater likelihood of a land invasion. However, people who come to Greece are likely to become sailors if they are not so already; and a combined influx by both land and sea seems highly probable: the later attempted invasion of Greece by the Persians, though not wholly comparable, was certainly a combined sea and land affair. Herodotus (Book I, 56), after listing several places in Thessaly where they sojourned, says simply that the Dorians finally migrated to the Peloponnese. However, with the passes south of the Corinthian isthmus so heavily guarded by Mycenaean strongholds, they would be likely to have taken at least their last step into the Peloponnese by sea as well as land.

What the Dorians did when they had arrived is difficult to say with any exactitude. It does seem clear that their arrival led in many instances to a flight of the Mycenaeans. There is archaeological evidence that the population at this time suddenly decreased. There are even suggestions that this was a time of drought, and that the Dorians, like perhaps the Mycenaeans in Crete, were not doing much more than seize an opportunity, thus benefiting from the plight of their enemies and holding on to once fertile land until the fertility returned. In his book *Discontinuity in Greek Civilization*, Rhys Carpenter develops this theme, basing his argument on the theory that the latitude reached by the trade winds varies with the intensity of the polar front, that this results in a cycle of wet and dry periods in the Mediterranean and that a dry period occurred at this time. One feels, however, that there is a certain amount of special pleading in this book; and there does not seem any good reason for presupposing any other reason for the Dorians' success than superior force of arms. All we know for certain is that the great cyclopean fortresses of the Mycenaeans came to an end, as did also their once mighty and rich and heroic princely occupants.

There is one curious myth covering these times in Greece, which are in truth the beginning of a Dark Age, dark for those who lived through them but also dark in the way of giving very little light to the historian. This is the myth of the 'return of the Heraclidae'. It says that the descendants of Hercules, having disappeared up into the north when the hero died, returned after a couple of generations and conquered the Peloponnese. In other words the Heraclidae were the Dorians. It is significant that the worship of Hercules in later times was always to be more prevalent amongst the so-called Dorian part of the Greek population. The legend must in fact be dismissed as little more than an attempt by the later Greeks to claim for themselves an ancestry that could be traced back to the Homeric heroes. It is at least possible, however, that certain displaced Peloponnesians of the earlier disturbed times had allied themselves with the Dorians when they arrived.

There are two other legends that may be nearer to the truth. One is that the grandson of Agamemnon, one Teisamenos by name, was defeated by the Dorians, who divided the lands of the Peloponnese between themselves, leaving, however, the district of Arcadia to its rustic simplicity and the district of Achaia to the mercy of Agamemnon's defeated grandson. Achaia was then inhabited by the Ionians, and these Ionians proceeded to fly to Athens as a place of refuge.

The secondary legend also brings Athens into the picture. It concerns Nestor's Pylos, which seems to show up very much in these later times as second only to Agamemnon's Mycenae in importance. The legend tells how Codrus, last king of Athens, saved his city from the Dorians. The oracle had declared that the invaders would be successful if the Athenian king's life was spared. Codrus accordingly saw to it that nothing of the sort should happen, entering the camp of the enemy and getting himself killed. There are two points to the story. The first is that Athens, true to the prophecy, was spared; and this is a historical fact and one of which the Athenians were to be eternally proud, Athens never becoming a Dorian city. The second point is that Codrus was a Neleid, that is to say of the royal house of Pylos, Nestor having been the son, it will be remembered, of Neleus.

Such in fact seems to have been what happened, Athens becoming a refuge for those Mycenaeans who managed to escape from the Dorian invasion, Ionians from Achaia, Neleids from Pylos and no doubt many more. Even Agamemnon's son Orestes ended up, according to one account, in Athens, being tried there for the vengeful killing of his father's murderer and honourably acquitted. There was to follow, as will be related, a further migration from Athens to the 'Ionian' cities of the Asia Minor coast, some of which, says Herodotus, were to elect for themselves kings from the Pylian dynasty. Thus we find the very different world of classical Greece already foreshadowed, and Athens, only a minor Mycenaean city but reinforced by refugees from the major fortresses, already beginning to enter upon its future greatness. . . .

*

So end the Homeric heroes, that is to say the Mycenaean aristo-crats, most of them no doubt dying nobly in the fight but some finding their way to an inviolate Athens.

Of the common people, however, the story must be different. They fled to the hills. Or they were made slaves.

There are some recent archaeological discoveries that are relevant here, though as it were at one remove. In his dig of 1968 at Mycenae Lord William Taylour unearthed some surprising objects.* They are of 'idols', that is to say small votive figures, some of snakes but most of humans. Now, the curious thing about them is that they are naïve and crude and are reminiscent of Minoan votive figures. One can hardly imagine their being made either by or for the Mycenaean aristocratic warriors who, though hardly sophisticated as we under-stand the word, were surely not simple, humble suppliants in their religion nor content with crudity in the things made by hand which they treasured. In other words, here is shown forth, through these humble votive offerings, the common people of Mycenae; and the common people of Mycenae show themselves as different, as still different, from their warrior-caste masters. The finds date to about 1300, a century and a half admittedly before the Dorian invasion but also at least five centuries after Greeks had first arrived in the land. It looks therefore as if the division between the conquerors and conquered persisted; and it must always be remembered that the conquered were of indigenous Mediterranean stock, in other words much like their neighbours in Crete.

And as for their neighbours in Crete, the Minoans: they too were to be invaded by the Dorian Greeks.

* Reported in the *Illustrated London News* of January 4, 1969, and later in *Antiquity*.

Chapter XVI

The Groans of the Cretans

THE MINOANS, it has earlier been suggested, suffered the Dorian invasion as it were at second-hand and through no fault or provocation of their own, whereas the Mycenaeans sought trouble and got it. For that reason the end of the Mycenaeans has been dealt with first, the Minoans having been left in this narrative at the end of their first fifty-year period of occupation by their one-time pupils from the mainland, thus bringing their story to about the year 1400.

The short fifty-year period (the LMII period of Evans and the New Palace Period III of Platon) has been described, from both archaeological and Linear B evidence, as by no means wholly unprosperous, and this in spite of the likelihood that it began with the greatest natural catastrophe the Minoans had suffered, the side-effects or after-effects of the Thera explosion. The Minoans must have been remarkably resilient, just as they were remarkably resistant to foreign influence.

This second quality has already been commented on, with illustrations from such finds as the remarkable painted sarcophagus from Hagia Triada, which showed that in the matters of funeral customs and religious beliefs the Minoans were not only borrowing but intensifying—intensifying at least their search for supernatural comfort. That need for comfort was obviously going to recur.

What must be realized is that after the Mycenaean occupation, although the surrounding towns may have still been flourishing, the great days of the palaces were ending if not already departed. The Minoan aristocracy—proud, sun-tanned men wearing their jewels, and their white-skinned wives and daughters sheltering in their megarons—had disappeared. If they existed at all they existed, one may imagine, as later French or Russian émigrés, rather fantastic people seeking to compensate for loss of importance by increase in bizarre distinctiveness.

Even the Minoan throne, the throne that some Mycenaean has usurped, may have had its day. There is a possibility that Minos— that is to say the second Minos of legend—was not a Minoan but a Mycenaean, dating that is to say to about 1400. It will be remembered that he went in vengeful search of Daedalus and followed him to Sicily. There are, here, pieces of the legend which so far have not been followed. Even Herodotus does not scorn to mention them. They are to the effect that Minos had done very much more than chase a dissident engineer, that he had in effect mounted a highly ambitious expedition against the island of Sicily. What is more significant, the expedition appears to have been a costly failure. A five-year siege of a Sicilian city ends in defeat and the death of the king.

Here, then, is perhaps another example of a Mycenaean warrior exhausting himself and his subjects by an over-ambitious foreign venture, an expedition that may have been worse than the Trojan venture in that it was not even ostensibly successful. In other words, the rot is already setting in, *and in Crete too.* The rest of the story is one of going downhill—gently rather than spectacularly, but inexorably. By the time of Idomeneus, as we have seen, the Minoans were still capable of sending a considerable contingent to the siege of Troy. But when their Mycenaean king came back, the legend says, they turned him out.

*

What were the Minoan people, as distinct from their rulers, doing in all these years? They were, to a certain extent, rebuilding; they were becoming more fervently and humbly religious; they were making pottery less beautiful than they had made for centuries; they were forgetting how to write.

In Hagia Triada they rebuilt. Here was and still is a lovely spot, called in modern Greek 'Paradise', where the 'Old River', Geropotamos, runs down to a bay that looks across to a village now called Hagia Galene or Holy Tranquillity. The Minoan princes at the height of their glory, it will be remembered, built a villa or small palace here, and as there is a paved way between it and Phaistos it has come to be known as the summer palace of Phaistos. Here were found some of the most beautiful and sophisticated examples of Minoan art, the harvester vase and the 'chieftain' and 'athletics' rhytons for instance; here too was found the funeral sarcophagus, described as an early sign of increased piety in Crete under Mycenaean occupation.

But at Hagia Triada there have also been found signs of rebuilding, both by the Mycenaeans and by the Minoans themselves. The Mycenaeans constructed, over the ruins of the original villa, one of their typical great halls, with 'echoing portico' as Homer puts it, which seems to have been the status-symbol of the Mycenaean hero. The Minoans started afresh on a site to the north of the original villa and built themselves a village. It included a market place and a long row of shops.

At Tylissos, some fifteen miles west of Knossos and where no palace ever existed, there have been found signs of building in this late period, with good waterworks and a cistern, together with signs of continued exploitation of one of the best areas for olive growing, in the shape of a great bronze cauldon, used probably for 'drenching' the fruit in hot water before the process of pressing.

The Minoans in fact were getting on, in a practical way, with the business of living. There is nothing grand about it, however: there are no new palaces; there are no new frescoes, not on any walls anywhere.

They are building altars and they are building chapels. They are doing something else with their hands, in a small way but very, very frequently. There is now a truly tremendous increase amongst the archaeological finds of the crude votive offering in the shape of a figure with upraised arms.

This had become the universal benediction. It has some similarity with the 'horns of consecration' which were such a familiar motif in the building of the palaces; indeed that motif could have been a stylization of the blessing gesture rather than the bull's horns. What impresses one, however, on seeing the archaeological finds from this period, is not only the quantity but the quality of this type of figurine. They give an overwhelming impression of a different Minoan Crete: no longer gay, no longer hedonistic, no longer buoyantly artistic, but humble, and anxious, and content with crudity in art.

The other usual and traditional religious motifs appear at this time, the pillar, the dove, the snake. To compare, however, the snake goddess of these times with those found by Evans at Knossos and dating to the sixteenth or seventeenth centuries is to look at two different worlds. Another votive offering shows a goddess—as usual fatuously benign in expression—wearing a cap from which sprout the seed-pods of the poppy. Here is the well-known emblem of sleep and death, hardly the imagery of a people whose working life was very happy. Then there is the figure of a mother with her child, dandling it or worshipping it. This is a subject not new, either in Minoan or Mycenaean art, the mother and child, the Earth Mother and her son, who is the Lord of Creation. But it seems now to be an increasing conception; and it is in some ways a comforting one—certainly this particular dandled child, in spite of or even because of its great crudity, has a human and comforting appeal. Finally, even the votaries themselves have changed, or at any rate the effigies of them. In the times of the palaces two bronze figures were found at Tylissos; they are rigid and tense as they stand saluting the deity. Now, from Gournia, we find a crouched figure which— when one has recovered from the feeling of absurdity that its crudity creates—is not proudly and tensely communing with the godhead but humbly supplicating with it. The raised hand, incidentally, has been interpreted by some as not a salute but rather a shading of the eyes from the divine effulgence; even this the later figure is doing more humbly (if less efficiently).

It is possible to make too much of a few pieces of moulded clay, even though the moulding is by sentient and brain-directed human hands. There is one other aspect of all this which is, however, worth considering. These crude votive figurines of the Minoan decline—of the sub-Minoan era, as it is all too expressively called—have a resemblance to the earliest Minoan counterpart before the palaces were built. They also have some similarity to those figures found recently by Taylour at Mycenae and referred to as being so different from anything likely to have been owned by the Homeric heroes. What we have here, therefore, is surely something belonging not only to the common people but to the *indigenous* people. It seems possible that the aristocrats, whether pleasure-loving Minoans or horse-loving Mycenaeans, had always kept themselves more separate, and the common people of Crete and Greece had always been more alike, than has been usually supposed. By now, in any case, the aristocrats of Crete have gone and the aristocrats of Greece will soon be following them.

There are signs of decadence, or at least of deterioration, in the Minoan ceramics of this time. The potter is still efficient; he is using, apparently, a faster wheel. But he is no longer inspired. He sometimes copies the Mycenaeans, for instance in making a new shape of drinking cup, the *kylix* or 'champagne-glass', many of which were found at the palace of Pylos. Or he indulges in a plethora of stylized pattern, where the trailing limbs of the octopus, for instance, have become no more than a useful medium for filling up space; he has developed a *horror vacui*.

As a final sign of deterioration amongst the Minoans there is the complete loss for a while of the art of writing. As in Greece too, illiteracy descends, until finally in the ninth or eighth century the Phoenician alphabet is adopted and improved and the way is paved for the great classical revival. Perhaps, however, this lapse is really not half so bad as it seems: not to be able to write down such useful but hardly world-shattering statements as 'forty edged cloths of royal type, two hundred measures of wool' is no great loss. For the rest— apart from the cataclysm or cataclysms that had tumbled the palaces into ruin and only partial reoccupation—there is no sign of anything like grinding poverty or conditions of chaos. Liberty had gone, the Minoans were no longer their own masters; glory had gone, and greatness and, within the palaces, gaiety, even though it had been perhaps a rather hectic and artificial gaiety. But there remained at least the ability to earn a living and to continue in the old ways. In his book *Prehistoric Crete* R. W. Hutchinson employs a useful phrase for these times in Crete, a 'provincial obscurity'. It is not exciting to be provincially obscure, as it must have been thrilling to have been an occupant, however humble, of the palaces in the great days; but if not thrilling it is safe. One would be able to tell stories of the old times, one could seek consolation from the everlasting Mother and her infant son, one could hold on stubbornly to one's old Minoan ways. There is a recent excavation at the Phourni hill, east of Mount Juktas and south of Knossos, which dramatically illustrated this last-mentioned ability. A tholos tomb of about 1400 was found, and in it one of those pottery larnakes or sarcophagi such as that found at Hagia Triada, painted with its funeral scenes. This larnax contained the bones of a woman, and with them so much valuable jewellery— seal-stones, gold necklace, little gold rosettes which had been sewn on to an ankle-length dress—that the burial of no one less than a Mycenaean princess could be reasonably assumed. But there was something else. At the entrance to the inner chamber was found the skeleton of a bull. Here in actuality was just such a sacrifice of a bull at a funeral as was depicted on the Hagia Triada sarcophagus. And here, it seems, at the funeral of one of the alien ruling classes, was being performed a custom likely to have been originally Minoan.

*

Such cultural triumphs—assuming the above interpretation to be correct—do not however count for much against the force of arms. The years rolled by, King Idomeneus, whether willingly or with difficulty, made his large contribution to the Trojan war; he returned, like others of his band of heroes, to unpopularity or even revolutionary turmoil, and like others he retired into exile. The Peoples of the Sea came and went, seldom staying but never failing—they or their like—to return. Then the Dorians finally arrived.

The Dorians were armed with iron; and there were many of them. The people fled to the hills, or were enslaved. That is the essence of it.

As for the Mycenaean rulers, they may have already deserted the island in an effort to help on the mainland and prevent the final disintegration of their empire. Or they may have succumbed to superior force and superior weapons as they had already succumbed in Greece. Whatever the exact truth, there is a similarity to the position of the Britons when the Romans left them, in the fifth and sixth centuries A.D., to fight the equally fierce and well-armed Saxons. Then an unavailing appeal for help was sent across to the continent: 'To Aetius, thrice Consul, come the groans of the Britons.'

It is all too easy, in examining the evidence for historical facts when such evidence is very largely archaeological, to let the dry detail stultify one's imagination. It becomes, as it were, bad form to talk of murder and rapine when one is examining only the change of pottery from Sub-Minoan to Early Proto-Geometric; one is stuck in a groove of scientific unemotionalism. It is obviously necessary to get out of that groove.

Because of the evidence that Crete seems to have continued for its three centuries and more of Mycenaean rule in a state of relative prosperity, we may well have underestimated the troubles of the Minoan people after the Thera cataclysm or cataclysms had ended for ever their brilliant centuries of palace civilization. If that is so, then we must not fall into the same error again. Here was the true and final destruction of Knossos, at the hands of the Dorian Greeks; here was the end of the Minoan civilzation. The experience cannot have been anything but terrible.

The site of Karphi shows what happened. The Palace of Knossos, patched and battered Knossos, apologetically half lived in for so long, had been finally abandoned—as in Britain Verulamium with its gateway or Caerleon with its magnificent amphitheatre were abandoned. To the south of Knossos lie the mountains. Some twenty miles to the south-east there rears up a peak, a landmark to sailors along the northern coast, that is nowadays called Karphi or the Nail. One of Crete's many earlier sanctuaries had probably been there, where simple and pious people, living comfortably in the plain, had come up to worship in the caves of the mountains. But now the only help came in the inaccessibility of the site and the protection of the mountains themselves. On the saddle of this mountain, therefore, the Minoans built a town of refuge, an attempt at a market town such as older and near-by Gournia, which was four times as big. The winter weather was bitter; but the Minoans stuck it for a century. And here, besides the private shrines in the houses, was a public shrine. In it were found two of the dove-crowned goddesses, with their thin, distant, fatuous benediction that seems as if it could never have radiated further than their finger-tips.

Other hill villages such as Karphi have been found. Was there perhaps some Arthur, some Mycenaeanized Minoan comparable to a Romanized Briton, to use one of these mountain fastnesses from which to harry the Dorians? Or was the tradition of militarism too weak amongst the Minoans, looking for bravery only in the bull ring? There is as yet no sign of such a heroic saviour.

There is a sign of an importation of religious beliefs. The Hittites and the Egyptians and the Mycenaeans, it will be remembered, were, in their time of empire, exchanging effigies of their gods as prophylactics for each other's kings. Now something of the sort seems to have happened among the common people. Effigies of the Syrian god, who in his place of origin is called Baal, appear. As with the Israelites, there were probably Minoan priests and votaries telling the people not to seek after strange gods. . . .

Chapter XVII

The Aftermath and the World of Iron

WE KNOW little of the Dorian Greeks. These are the Western world's first Dark Ages, as dark in the way of lack of the light of knowledge for the historian as were the second Dark Ages that overtook Europe after the destruction of the Roman Empire.

What is reasonably certain is that the Dorians were the ancestors of the Spartans, or as Herodotus calls them in making this assumption, the Lacedaemons. This should tell us something. The Spartans made themselves into the most tightly bound, efficiently regimented military nation of history, a warrior caste ruthlessly keeping down their conquered indigenous people. They could not have achieved that position, they could not have been the sort of people who wanted to do so, unless the Dorians had had much the same intention. The indigenous people for the Dorians were, in Crete, the dark-white supple little Minoans, and, in Greece, much the same people, only a little changed by not very frequent inter-marriage with the now disappeared Mycenaean aristocracy. The indigenous people were those who made those hopeful, crude votive idols found at Karphi and in the environs of the palace of Mycenae. They become the helots —those, that is to say, who did not become the bandits in the hills.

The conquerors seem to have proceeded slowly. They formed military garrisons which, as with the Romans in Britain, became slowly converted into towns. They favoured a site that included a hill that could be fortified: the Greek *acropolis* had been born. They used iron weapons. They cremated their dead. They wore clothes that needed a buckle or fastening, and soon effigies are showing that this was a single piece of cloth draped round the body. Even some of the later Mycenaean frescoes display something like this. Perhaps the climate was growing colder, as well as drier. At any rate, the classical Greek dress was coming into existence and the tight-waisting of the Minoans was dead, had very likely been dead for a long time.

One other thing the Dorians did. That was to use a pottery known to the modern archaeologist as Geometric. It gradually becomes so through the Proto-Geometric, the process being, as one might expect, less sudden in Crete where there is a much stronger local tradition to overcome. It is a dull form of pottery, shapes being utilitarian and designs a combination of angular lines—the classical Greek key pattern, used in combination with something more lively, may be said to show its fading influence. This pottery, however useful it may be for dating, does not inspire one to much imagining, just as it is itself uninspired. Potters are surely the most conservative creatures on earth. One can imagine a rich Mycenaean or Minoan of the old school, if such still existed, asking for pottery of the old, florid lively style. He would have been told in a shocked voice, no doubt, that it could not be done, the potter adding perhaps, if he were honest as well as conservative, that he would not be able to do it successfully even if he tried. And that would be the truth: the inspiration would not be in him. It was no longer the potter's joy to delight in nature and to copy it, nor would most of his cus-customers have liked it if he had.

That theme, however, had better not be taken too far: we have no right to depict the Dorian Greek as an insensitive utilitarian—his pottery was not so dull as Roman Samian ware. At least it may be said that the Dorian conqueror differed from his Mycenaean pre-decessor in that he does not seem to have recognized the superior merit of the Minoan artist or to have employed him, as the Mycenaeans did, with a pretty fair freedom to do what he liked and continue in his own tradition. That fact may be a considerable pointer to the behaviour of the Dorians in general. Unless, of course, there were by now very few Minoan artists worth employing. . . .

*

From a wider historical viewpoint the aspect of the Dorian Greeks of greatest significance is that they were using iron.

Gordon Childe, inventing one phrase of tremendous insight, 'the Neolithic Revolution', invented another when he talked of the 'democratization' of weapons achieved by iron. Iron is not scarce, it is merely more difficult to smelt, needing a higher temperature than copper. Once, therefore, the method of production has been achieved, the warriors' weapons will no longer be costly and scarce. This change will in the end have far-reaching results.

The Bronze Age, besides being an age of great achievement in the peaceful arts and the art of living—here the Minoans undoubtedly led—was also, and particularly in its later centuries, the age of the warrior-hero. It was also the age of the horse and chariot: we have seen the idea spread, the concern for horses amongst the aristocratic correspondents in the Amarna letters, the care for the chariot in the treasure-house, the proud delineation of the warrior in the chariot controlling his magnificent plumed and prancing horses. All that now ends. There appears instead—on the stele, on the rock-face, on the vase—the marching infantryman. Or rather it is the marching infantry*men*. They march in serried ranks, there are many of them, they are disciplined. The king who has many infantrymen will conquer; and he will never be able to arm his many infantrymen unless he possesses the secret of making iron. Conversely he will not need to be rich, to have like the Pharaohs much gold or like Agamemnon and Menelaus much treasure, to be able to afford his weapons.

The Philistines early possessed the secret of iron, and we see the Israelites (struggling to settle down in the land of Canaan after the exodus from Egypt at the end of the thirteenth century) being for a while kept from a knowledge of that secret. A Hittite king also politely refuses the knowledge to his Egyptian brother. Yet the Hittites do not seem to make much use of their expertise, and succumb to invasion as completely as do the Egyptians. Perhaps they were too conservative-minded. It is the new, poorer nations who come to the fore, the Dorian Greeks, the Phrygians and the Assyrians.

Especially, it is the Assyrians. While the peoples of the lands encircling the Aegean Sea retire into a dark age, the peoples of the fertile crescent return to the limelight of the stage of significant activity. What is the reason for this one may not be able to tell—one cannot expect to be able to interpret in the light of one theory only, the 'democratization' caused by iron, for history is not so simple as that. C. Northcote Parkinson, finding something like another 'law', has suggested a sort of inevitability in a see-saw movement of East against West, and a recurring ascendancy of Oriental and Indo-European, the turn now having arrived again for the Oriental.*

With the Assyrian comes something else, something sinister, an increase in dark, virulent cruelty. To put it like that may be unfair to

* See *East and West* (London and Boston, 1963).

the Semites as a race. Nothing like it, however, had ever appeared in Crete or Greece, and in assessing the legacy of those civilizations it is something to remember. Whether such an increase in calculated cruelty, of cruelty as a weapon in itself, is likely to occur with a change from 'heroic' to 'democratized' warfare it is not possible to say, though it could be so argued. What remains as certain is that, whatever qualities the Assyrians showed, whatever artistic merits they possessed or beneficial administrative efficiency their leaders displayed, they must, and should, go down to history as the cruellest people of the ancient world. 'In the moat I piled them up,' boasts a victorious Assyrian king, 'I dyed the mountains with their blood like red wool. Sidquia, king of Askelon . . . I flayed. I tore out the tongues of those whose slanderous mouths had uttered blasphemies against my god Ashur. I fed their corpses, cut in small pieces, to dogs, pigs, zebu-birds and vultures. I killed the officials and patricians who had committed the crime and hung their bodies on poles surrounding the city. I beat the warriors to death before the gate like lambs . . . From some I cut off hands and fingers, from others noses and ears; I deprived many of sight, I made one pile of the living and another pile of the heads . . . Their young men and maidens have I cast into the fire . . . over the ruins my shadow rested; in gratification of my wrath I find contentment . . . The voice of man, the steps of flocks and herds, the happy shouts of mirth, I put an end to them.' This sort of thing makes the cruelties of Achilles or Odysseus at their worst seem like the explosions of a petulant nursemaid.

At 1100 B.C., at about the time we may reasonably believe the Dorians to be transferring their unwelcome attention from Greece to Crete, the great Tiglath Pileser I was on the Assyrian throne and ruthlessly extending his empire. The great Bronze Age powers of Babylonia, Mitanni, the Land of Hatti, were no more. Further south, that other great power, Egypt, was sliding down into oblivion, was becoming a land that alternated between internal strife and foreign occupation. At 1100 its last truly native dynasty, the Twentieth, whose hero had been the Third Rameses, famous for his victory over the Peoples of the Sea, was ending in civil war and the increasing interference of foreign (Libyan) mercenaries.

Then for something like two centuries, about 1050 to 850 B.C., the whole of the Middle East seems to fall into a time of shadow. The Assyrians cease to flog and flay abroad and, faced with internal unrest, apply their man-made laws: 'If a woman has crushed a seigneur's testicles in a brawl, they shall cut off one finger of hers, and if . . . she crushed the other testicle they shall tear out both her eyes . . . If a woman has had a miscarriage by her own act, when they have prosecuted her and convicted her, they shall impale her on stakes without burying her.' The Hittites, their remnants having been driven south, form their so-called Neo-Hittite empire around Carchemish. But it is a shadow of its old self, produces no literature of its own and comes into written history only as a provider of mercenaries for the Hebrews and concubines for the harem of King Solomon the Great.

As for the Hebrews, having defeated the Philistines—the secret of iron could not be kept for ever—they snatch a time of commercial greatness as the First Millennium begins (Solomon's reign is about 970–930 B.C.). They owe this success largely to the not wholly disinterested friendship of the Phoenicians. Then after their brief spell of glory they retire to their own problem of forging not only a nation but a new and finer conception of Deity.

It is the Phoenicians who are the particular stars of these two centuries. From the time of the first Minoan palaces and the settlement of the Mycenaeans in Greece their trading towns of Byblos and Tyre and Sidon existed; but only with the beginning of Egyptian decline at the end of the thirteenth century (Akhneten's preoccupation and the over-reaching of Rameses II), do they truly expand. Then they become the great traders of the Mediterranean and beyond, the good and honest traders, also the great sailors, the great adventurers, the great colonizers, the great spreaders of both techniques and ideas. As mariners they have taken over from the Minoans, but hardly in any other way, for they seem ever to have been a rather harsh and gloomy race, with no lightness of touch.

All in all, these centuries immediately after the collapse of the Bronze Age seem to be the Semites' great era. There is the commercial success of the Phoenicians, the moral success under adversity of a small nation known as the Hebrews, the military success of the Assyrians. There has arrived, in any case, a very different world.

And things will yet be worse before they are better and before any influence returns from the forgotten world of Minoans and Mycenaeans. The Assyrians revert to their policy of aggression. The land of the Hebrews is affected, so is Egypt, so is Babylonia.

Another couple of centuries of complicated strife pass, in which empires rise and fall and a new Power finally arises, Persia, Indo-

European in origin but Oriental in outlook. That rise will take place
at the same time as the Greek-speaking world, recovering at last
from its dark age, begins to regain its influence.

With the coming of the ninth century Assyria resumed her
aggression, so that soon she was in command of her greatest stretch
of empire, from the Persian Gulf to 'the great sea of the setting sun',
which was the Mediterranean. A biblical character, King Jehu, he
who drove furiously, was one who paid tribute to the all-conquering
power. Then came a respite for the best part of another century
while Assyria again fell into internal strife. Then an army general
usurped the Assyrian throne, gave himself an evocative name,
Tiglath Pileser, and invented a new frightfulness to act as a deterrent
to revolt, the moving of whole populations from their homes. His
successor, calling himself by an even more ancient and evocative
name, Sargon the Second, was the first to meet serious revolt. It
came from south of Babylon, from a people called Chaldeans.
Sennacherib, the next king, met greater trouble, plague in Egypt,
revolt in Babyon itself, where the Chaldeans are now installed,
successful defiance from a people who trust in their god, the
inhabitants of Jerusalem.

We are watching the slow but inevitable crumbling of an empire
based on nothing greater than the power of arms and a policy of
terror. Egypt and the determination to conquer her was Assyria's
final undoing. Esarhaddon and Asur-bani-pal (in Greek Sar-
danapalos) finish the task between them and virtually finish off
their empire in the process. Egypt was to them as Russia was to
Napoleon; it swallowed up their armies. Everywhere the subjected
people began to revolt; Assyria had no friends and she had a new
enemy in the north. In 612 B.C. Assyria's capital, Nineveh, fell to a
combined force of Scythians and Medes. 'How is she become a
desolation,' exulted the Hebrews, 'a place for beasts to lie down in.'

An empire appeared that was meteoric in its rise and in its fall, that
of Chaldean Babylon. Nebuchadnezzar was its great king. He
followed the Assyrian plan of moving people about and shifted to
Babylon most of those Hebrews who had not suffered a similar fate
under the Assyrians. This last of many cities of Babylon was a
magnificent place; it moved the Hebrews only to tears and a
determination to remain a people. Nebuchadnezzar tried to maintain a stable and peaceable empire by methods that were doomed to
failure; he went mad in the attempt.

Four kings in Babylon followed in rapid succession, and the fourth, in his dotage, saw his capital fall to a new coalition of fighting people. These were the Medes, who with the Scythians had sacked Assyrian Nineveh nearly a hundred years earlier and were allied with their neighbours and blood relations, the Persians. Cyrus, grandson of a Median king, was in process of founding the Persian Empire. And before his success at Babylon Cyrus had defeated a coalition which included a country on the Asia Minor coast called Lydia and an important Greek state called Sparta; whilst after his success he was to bubjugate for a while the Ionian Greek cities on the same Asia Minor coast.

The Greeks had in fact at last come into the full flow of history again, and were about to take a major and heroic part. They had by now—the fall of Babylon was in the year 538 B.C.—wholly emerged from their dark ages. It would seem, from reviewing these same ages where history was being enacted, that to have been thus in a backwater was for them not a bad thing. The next and final chapter traces their return into history so far as it is known, and also tries to assess what was the legacy that these Greeks, revived to greatness, owed to the Mycenaeans and Minoans who were their predecessors.

Chapter XVIII

Minoan–Mycenaean: the Legacy for Classical Greece

A SIMPLE SUM in arithmetic presents us with a surprising fact, particularly if we are at all of Arthur Evans's way of thinking. It is this. If, as seems fairly certain, the Mycenaeans took over the administration of Knossos at about 1450 B.C., and if, as also seems fairly certain, the Dorians did not supplant them until 1100 or even a little later, then Knossos is Mycenaean for not less than 350 years. If we work backwards and add these 350 years to the date 1450, we get 1800 B.C. Now, in 1800 Crete had been Minoan for a long time; but we are nevertheless back in the Old Palace period and Minoan civilization had definitely not yet reached its time of greatness. It is therefore possible, and reasonable, to say that Knossos during its centuries of significance, was for a longer period Mycenaean than Minoan.

We must not, however, in a reaction against Evans's constant belittlement of the Mycenaeans, let this discovery carry too much weight. The Minoan civilization, though comparatively short in its flowering, was of supreme importance and of supreme importance too to the Mycenaeans themselves.

All this is something to remember clearly in considering the dark-age centuries under the Dorian Greeks and in trying to assess what in a way of a legacy these Dorians carried across to the Greece of the classical age and to the Western world. The Dorians—other Greeks with other names are distinguished as sweeping south at this time, but to generalize and to speak only of one name is not to falsify history—the Dorians were, it seems likely, harsher conquerors than their predecessors, the Mycenaeans; at any rate they were more numerous. But compared with the Assyrians, from whom they mercifully escaped, with their policies of slaughter, devastation and depopulation, the Dorians were mild. They may have put an end to a twin civilization, but they were not in the least exterminating it.

Rather, one would imagine, like the Saxons in Britain, they were ignoring it, a little nervous of it, and subconsciously attracted by what remained of the thing they had put an end to. Time heals, if given the chance; and slowly, in both Greece and Crete, the enmity between conquered and conquerors would die. The towns of refuge in the hills would be abandoned—as indeed they were—and the two peoples would live in amity more or less, retaining in varying degree their respective individuality but also learning from each other. They would also, together, learn from outside sources, as Minoans had once learnt from Syria and Anatolia and Egypt in the early days.

Pottery begins to show something more than the mere dullness of geometric style. It shows human figures, which is something that Minoan pottery never did. Usually it is the soldier, the ubiquitous serried ranks of spear-carrying infantrymen. Then he rapidly becomes stylized, a curious figure with for a body a very waisted cotton reel or one of those old-fashioned spinning tops called a 'diabolo'. What sort of dress this represents it is hard to imagine; perhaps it had some affinities still with the kilted Minoans, perhaps with the semi-archaic Estvone, the ballet-skirted guard outside the modern Greek palace. That human beings are depicted on pottery for the first time must have some significance, at the least that people were tired of meaningless patternizing. The significance of soldiers is more obvious: those, presumably, were the people who mattered in society and the scheme of things.

The revitalizing evidence in the arts generally in both Crete and Greece came, perhaps inevitably, from abroad. In this one way the Dorian lands were indebted to the Assyrians, in that their conquests must have created hosts of fleeing refugees, and refugees bring their skills and their ideas. There appears often in both Greece and Crete, in metal work or miniature carving, the oriental theme of the god as the 'master of the animals'. This is an idea dating right back to Sumerian times, when the hero Gilgamesh used to be shown doing unpleasant and muscular things to beasts to show his mastery of them. We need not read any more significance into this than that the artists of Crete and Greece were waking up to possibilities and copying, without necessarily taking any notice of their original import, whatever came most often to hand.

Then in the eighth century there appears in Crete what archaeologists have called the Daedalic or Dedalic style, work in stone, clay, bronze and ivory and for the first time (so far as we know) branching out into full-size statuary. In calling this Daedalic the archaeologists are following the historian of the first century B.C., Diodorus Siculus, who, speaking of the statues of this time, credits Daedalus with being the first to give them 'open eyes and parted legs and outstretched arms, for before this time artists made statues with closed eyes and hands hanging down and cleaving to the sides'. Diodorus seems to have got his Daedalus wrong by a millennium or so; but that does not matter very much, and the term Daedalic is useful in suggesting the vital inventiveness of the Cretans, which now seems to appear again and never long to have left them.

There is a real significance in this revival in art and particularly in statuary. It has Assyrian affinities, more plainly Egyptian affinities; it also, in the still rather crude smilingness of the face, is a little reminiscent of Mycenaean and Minoan votive offerings. These statues spread to Greece. In the Athens museums they can be seen in their serried ranks inhumanly smirking down on one, yet impressive and not wholly cold nevertheless, stiff but decreasingly stiff, like so many Galateas beginning to come to life. They are the best sign that there is, in the way of inanimate relics, that the dark ages were over and a new and vital age beginning.

*

Legend and the early historian supply the rest of the evidence for the course of events that followed the final destruction of Knossos and led to the arrival of classical Greece.

It is largely a story of restlessness and expansion, the sort that can only come from vitality, self-assurance, adventurousness, and some modicum at least of prosperity, the kind of prosperity that is yet not keeping pace with growth in population. The result was, in a modern word, colonization; and the Greeks were different from the latter-day Britons in that they did their colonizing at the start of the greatness and not towards the end.

The earliest flow, and the most important historically, was across the Aegean to the opposite, Asia Minor, coasts. Already there were Mycenaean settlements there—we could regard the Trojan war as an unsuccessful attempt at settlement. After the arrival of the Dorians there must have been an intermittent flow for the next four or five hundred years, beginning no doubt as a flight of fugitives rather than a colonization but soon becoming a stream of people looking for new homes by choice. There is a legend that the younger sons of Codrus, that king from Pylos who saved the city of Athens from the Dorians, did just this, crossed the Aegean in search of new homes and new kingdoms.

Athens was in a special postition in this matter. Its citizens always claimed that they were descended from the original, pre-Greek, inhabitants of the land, that they were 'of the soil' or autochthonous. They also claimed that they never succumbed to the Dorians, that they were in fact the leaders of that part of the Greek people who differentiated themselves from the Dorians, calling themselves the Ionians. As time went on, therefore, a band of cities on the Aegean coast, their inhabitants stemming from Athens and the district of Attica, or believing that they did, formed what they called an Ionic Confederacy. They included the already mentioned Miletus; Ephesus, with its famous temple of Artemis or Diana of the Ephesians; and the island city of Samos, which itself sent out colonizers.

It is these Ionian cities, rather than the growing cities of Greece itself, that, curiously enough, constitute an introduction to Greek revival and her classical age. They do so in two ways. Firstly they were very prosperous. Secondly—and no doubt as a result of the prosperity—they incurred the enmity of their neighbours, in particular the great Persian empire, and so were instrumental in bringing about the crucial war between Greece and Persia, the winning of which set Greece on her proud and self-confident century of splendour.

There is really very little more one may say historically without straying too far from the theme of the results of the rise and fall of Knossos. The Greek cities of the Aegean coast had won their wealth, as had their great neighbour Lydia, from the luck of being left alone by the Assyrians (together with the bad luck for the Phoenicians of not being left alone), and from the fact that they were in a good position to act as traders between Europe and Asia. It was Cyrus, founder of the Persian empire, whose deeds set in motion the events that were to prove the great test of the revived Greek nation and from which they emerged so unexpectedly victorious. After defeating King Croesus of Lydia (and only desisting from casting him to the flames, so the legend goes, because he had some interesting philosophizings to utter that were borrowed from the Greek Solon) and before causing Prince Belshazzar of Babylon to see the writing on the wall, Cyrus conquered the Ionian cities. That was only the beginning of their troubles. But the land of their origin came to their rescue.

*

The line of connection between the crucial Ionian cities and the city of Athens that had once been a refuge from the Dorians is an important one. It forms a recognizable link between Mycenae (and so Knossos) and the classical Greeks. There are many other links, however, less easily definable and more tenuous, but real enough.

What must not be done in tracing the connections and seeking to assess the legacy of the Minoan-Mycenaean synthesis, is to claim too much. In particular it must not be assumed that the influence was necessarily all to the good. It probably was not; there is no reason why it should have been.

First, what did that brilliant palace civilization of Knossos pass on to the Mycenaeans? It has been called over-ripe. Perhaps it was by the time it met the Greeks and began to fade away. But it was ripe before it was over-ripe and much more than merely luscious.

We shall never know what Knossos was really like. But it must have been gay and happy and vital, its people growing up in a tradition of friendliness, inquisitiveness and the confident assumption, such as the Elizabethans and the classical Greeks themselves possessed, that anything was possible for them. Though that last is not so easy to recapture, the modern Greeks and Cretans have those other two characteristics, friendliness and inquisitiveness—it is a friendly inquisition that they will always put you to, and in a marked degree.

Too much can hardly be made of the innocent joyousness of Minoan art and the sensitive love of nature and the natural that it shows. It so contrasts with the art of other early civilizations. Look for instance at the tasselled candelabra of sweet corn in flower. How delightfully the Minoans would have made a pattern out of that. To the Aztecs and the Mayas it must have been a highly familiar sight. But they preferred to draw pictures of scowling gods and torture.

The Minoan religion needs some careful handling. Of course the Minoans were religious, because—as was suggested at the beginning of this book—all Bronze Age peoples were religious or, if one likes to use a more critical word, superstitious. It also seems likely that, more lately and in times of adversity, the Minoans had become increasingly religious, more humbly and passionately and supplicatorily so, seeking comfort. In the main, however, they never show themselves as darkly, cruelly religious, not dominated by a priesthood nor indulging often in degrading, reasonless, orgiastic rites. Nevertheless, it *is*, by and large, the Earth Mother religion that leads to such excesses.

Now, the religion of the classical Greeks has been described as a dualism. H. D. F. Kitto, who makes this point in his book, *The Greeks*, continues: 'This is rather surprising in so philosophic a people, and is most easily understood on the assumption that Greek culture is the offspring of two profoundly different ones.' He then goes on to suggest that the Greek Pantheon of the twelve Olympian gods is not so impressively solid as one might imagine. Zeus is married to a lady with a non-Greek name, Hera; and Athena, with her owl as symbol, is another of the same sort, and probably in origin a nature goddess. 'The true Olympian cults,' he continues, 'were based on the ideas of a god who protected the tribe or the state or the family, and took the quest or the suppliant under his care; the god was, in fact, intimately connected with the social organism. He was also a nature god, but only in the sense that he explained certain natural forces.' Into this system, however, something of the Earth Mother religion had undoubtedly been absorbed. 'Cults based on the mysterious life-giving powers of nature existed in Greece side by side with the Olympian cults and in sharp contrast with them; for instance, these mystery cults appealed to the individual, the Olympian concerned the group: these admitted anyone, bond or free, the Olympian admitted only members of the group: these taught doctrines of rebirth, regeneration, immortality; the Olympians taught nothing, but were concerned with the paying of honours due to the immortal and unseen members of the community. They are entirely different conceptions of religion, and it is roughly true to say that the god-conception is European and the goddess-conception Mediterranean; the goddesses come down in straight descent from Minoan Crete.'

It might be said, of course, that the Greek gods did the same as this last, in that the Greeks always held that Zeus was born in Crete. However, when the later Cretans insisted that Zeus also died in their island the Greeks were affronted and held the Cretans to be liars: the Olympian religion, unlike the Earth Goddess religion, did *not* hold with the death (and rebirth) of gods. If Zeus was a Cretan god, then he was no more than the unimportant subsidiary needed to be invented in any system of nature religion, the combined son and husband who did his necessary task of fertilization and then died as a bee or a spider dies. Or else he was the son in that sort of kindly, family trilogy which 'personal' religions always invent, feeling the need for comfort: such a child, whatever his name, appears in the

Late Minoan votives, as also in the much less crude Mycenaean ivory plaque of a baby at the feet of skirted goddesses.

This side of the classical Greek religion may be called part of the less beneficial legacy of the Minoans, at least so far as it was dark, mysterious, orgiastic. And there may have been something of this side in Minoan Crete: the effigies of goddesses or priestesses with snakes writhing about them show something like it. Ariadne on her dancing floor may not have been so innocent, or mundane, as pictures of flying curls suggest; and the legend of her being left by Theseus in the island of Naxos, to be either the bride of Dionysus or or the victim of Artemis, may conceal a truth of strange ritualistic rites.

However, that may be no more than later invention. Comparatively speaking, it must be insisted, Minoan Crete seems to show herself remarkably free of such excesses. As for the more personal and less austere side of so-called mystery religions such as Greece may have inherited from the later, unhappier Minoans, that surely is at least partly beneficial. It seemed necessary in Greece at any rate, as it did in later Rome: the Hebrews may not have been the only people who provided lessons for the Western world out of their adversity.

As for the Olympian gods, these can be called wholly a Mycenaean legacy. It is true that Herodotus wrote that the later Greeks 'knew not their gods until Homer and Hesiod told them who they were'; and it may be true that Achilles and the rest would have hardly recognized the gods of Socrates or Sophocles. Nevertheless the Mycenaeans gave the classical Greeks material to work upon just as Moses and even Abraham gave material on which the poet David and the prophet Isaiah could work. The gods of the Mycenaean heroes were at least healthy and human gods, gentlemen's gods, and as such probably appealed equally to the Dorian warrior.

The one thing for which the Western world must be grateful to the Mycenaeans is that they were willing to learn. And the Dorians too must have possessed at least something of the same magnanimous and open-hearted quality, or the miracle of classical Greece would have been a sheer impossibility. This teachability of the Mycenaeans was all the more praiseworthy in that the Minoan world, when in its heyday they first came in close contact with it, must have been for them such a very different world.

Was that world a feminine, or matriarchal world, such as has been recently claimed?* It is possible to develop that line and to extract much significance from it. But there seems little more than negative evidence that Minoan Crete was a matriarchy in the political sense of the word: claim to the throne may have come from the mother's side, as it did in Egypt and other lands where the Mother Goddess was worshipped, but, as in Egypt, it was, by all the evidence, a king and not a queen who actually ruled. And if no skeleton of a Minos has been found, neither has there of a Pasiphae. As for 'feminine', in a more general way, here is an adjective that can be stretched indefinitely until it becomes somewhat meaningless. It seems more helpful to give Minoan culture such epithets as peacable, artistic, sensitive, unmilitaristic. Whatever the right adjective, however, there must have been much in Minoan culture that Mycenaeans disliked or despised. For, conversely, the adjective 'masculine' does seem to fit the Mycenaean—even better perhaps than 'horsey'. . . .

There is one thing, none the less, which the Mycenaeans must have admired about the Minoans, and that was their athleticism. Particularly that strange, unique exercise, the bull-game, impressed them. They seem, without doubt, to have copied it in their own country for a while. But perhaps, with their less compact, larger and less supple build, they were not naturally so adept—in which case Theseus, if he was really leading a band of enforced trainees for the game, was wise to kill the bull-masked priest-king, or whatever he did do, before he was ineptly gored to the jeers of the populace.

There may be considerable significance in Minoan athleticism. The naked Greek youth contesting at Olympia or Delphi is surely the direct descendant of the boxer and the wrestler on the Rhyton from Hagia Triada. He is also the direct descendant of Ajax and Menelaus and the wily Odysseus at the funeral games at the burial of Patroclus. The two concepts marry.

They marry to produce the last-but-one legacy that we will seek to discover. It is the legacy of competitiveness and individualism and the desire for merit and honour. Again, it may not be a wholly beneficial legacy. For the classical Greeks were to suffer from it, from the reverse side of all their virtues, from their inability to combine rather than compete, from their stubborn refusal to adapt themselves to a world of wider alliances and bigger, less individualized political

* For instance in Leonard Cottrell's *The Lion Gateway* and in particular in Jacquetta Hawkes's *Dawn of the Gods*.

systems. But for all that, it *was* a great legacy to be given, and to accept.

The last legacy must have been almost wholly Mycenaean—and Knossos was as much Mycenaean as Minoan. It may have been partly Dorian, too. It concerns art and it concerns language. It is a matter of humanity and an interest in the activities of man; it is a matter of a regard for orderliness, an intellectual rather than a passionate quality.

There is need again for the help of H. D. F. Kitto in this somewhat difficult concept. Commenting on the fact that in Athens the potter enlivened the dullness of pure 'geometric' patterning by the delineation of human beings, he calls the art of classical Greece not a new creation but a Renaissance. 'The greatness of Greek art,' he continues, 'lies in this, that it completely reconciles two principles which are often opposed: on the one hand control and clarity and fundamental seriousness; on the other, brilliance, imagination and passion. All classical Greek art has to a remarkable degree that intellectual quality which shows itself in the logic and the certainty of its construction. Intellectualism in art suggest to us a certain aridity; but Greek art, whether it be the Parthenon, a play by Aeschylus, a Platonic dialogue, a piece of pottery, the painting on it, or a passage of difficult analysis in Thucydides, has, with all its intellectualism, an energy and a passion which are overwhelming precisely because they so intelligently controlled.'

If, however, he goes on, we turn to Minoan or Aegean art we find a significant difference. 'The best of Minoan art has all the qualities that art can have—except this consuming intellectualism.' A Greek architect, he suggests, could not even under pain of death have produced a building so chaotic in plan as the palace of Knossos. 'Brilliant, sensitive, elegant, gay—these are the adjectives which one instinctively uses of the Minoan—but not "intellectual".'

And whence came, he asks, this power of intellectualism? His answer is, the Greek language. 'In the first place, Greek, like its cousin Latin, is a highly inflected language, with a most elaborate and delicate syntax, and the further back one can go in the history of the language, the more elaborate are the inflexions and (in many ways) the more delicate in the syntax. . . . Consequently, it is the nature of Greek to express with extreme accuracy not only the relation between ideas, but also shades of meaning and emotion.' He then goes on to speak of the 'periodic style' which both Latin and

Greek possess but which only Greek supports naturally, in other words the power to make a long and complicated sentence abundantly clear.

Here there is something in which the tables were turned, the Minoans learning, at least a little, from the Mycenaeans rather than the other and more usual way round. Perhaps it is not for nothing that even in so elementary a matter as the use to which the palace officials put writing, they did not hesitate to change over from the Minoan script to the Mycenaean. Be that as it may, 'with this clarity and constructive power and seriousness,' Kitto concludes, paying a final tribute to the Minoans, 'we shall find a quick sensitiveness and an unfailing elegance. This is the secret of what has been called "the Greek miracle", and the explanation—or an important part of it—lies in the fusion of cultures, if not of peoples too.'

*

That is not quite the end of it. If we seek to define the legacy of a people, or rather a pair of in many ways different peoples, we must turn finally, since peoples are the children of their environment, to the lands in which those people lived.

Here there is not a disparity but a similarity. Both lands, Greece and Crete, are beautiful but both are rugged. Unlike the flat, alluvial lands of Egypt and Sumeria, their fertility, though it is considerable, is not universal, by no means universal, and it has to be worked for. The lands gave their people delight, but it also gave them a challenge. Not every people could have succeeded in either land. But if they did succeed they would be forceful and vital and courageous people. So too the sea around them—a difficult but necessary highway— would breed adventurousness and individuality.

Visit in the imagination for the last time the palaces of Minoan Crete and Mycenaean Greece. Sprawling but commanding Knossos; Mallia between blue sea and green hills, purple-backed with mountains; most evocative of them all, Phaistos, overlooked by the eye of the cave in Mount Ida, where by legend Zeus was born. Or Tiryns, compactly on its small acropolis but commandingly so, with the most cyclopean walls of all, below which the skeletons of one-time defenders have been found; Pylos, of the fortresses most urbane and Minoan in style; Mycenae, boastful, bullying, tremendous. Each trio is different from the other but has much in common with it. All are the product of a great human vitality and imagination. Except for those of Egypt, which are alien to us, except for the megalithic monuments which are difficult to clothe in our imagination with understandable humanity, these Minoan and Mycenaean palaces are the oldest major ruins of the Western world. They existed, and thrived, three thousand years ago, being destroyed after only a few centuries of existence. But their memory, and their influence, remain.

Appendix

*Notes on Some of the more Important Minoan and Mycenaean
Archaeological Excavations*

Knossos

Sir Arthur Evans began in 1900 and continued almost without a
break until 1935. His best-known associates and assistants were D. G.
Hogarth (Director of the British School of Archaeology at Athens),
D. Mackenzie, J. D. S. Pendlebury and Piet de Jong. In the 1950's
and '60's work has continued under J. D. Evans (no relation of Sir
Arthur) particularly on the neolithic era, and under Sinclair Hood
and H. Sackett and M. Popham of the British School: a recent
discovery has been of the so-called Unexplored Mansion, where a
vase was found showing a bull-catching scene reminiscent of the
Vaphio cups.

Mycenae

Heinrich Schliemann began in 1876, followed by the Greek
Ephor, Stamatakis, who had tried to restrain Schliemann's somewhat ruthless methods. Another Greek, Tsountas, had continued
until 1902. There followed the British Professor A. J. B. Wace (who
had several brushes with Arthur Evans) and, in 1952, J. Papadimitriou.
In the 1960's Lord William Taylour has excavated here, as referred
to in the text, as has also G. Nylonas.

Other Sites in Crete

Amnisos S. Marinatos, since about 1930. (This is the port of
   Knossos.)
Arkhanes J. Sakallarikis, in the 1960's.
Dictaean Cave Opened by D. G. Hogarth at the end of the nine-
   teenth century.
Gournia The great finds by Harriet Boyd Hawes have not been
   repeated; the site overlooking the beautiful Merabelou Bay is well
   worth visiting, however.

Hagia Triada   This, with nearby Phaistos, has been mainly an Italian preserve, under Pernier, Halbherr and, later, Dr. Doro Levi.

Kamares Cave   Dawkins in the 1920's

Karphi   Pendlebury in 1938

Khania   Excavations under Sinclair Hood and others, and with other sites in eastern Crete, begin to show that Minoan occupation of this part of the island was not quite so sparse as was once thought.

Mallia   Largely a French preserve, at first under M. Chapontier and still continuing.

Myrtos   Under the British School, with H. Sackett, P. Warren, G. Cadogan. A potter's workshop has recently been discovered there.

Palaikastro   Earlier by R. Bosanquet and R. Dawkins; later by the British School as at Myrtos.

Phaistos   As at Hagia Triada.

Tylissos   Greek and French excavations, under Hazzidakis.

Vasiliki   A site south of Gournia, excavated about 1900 by R. Seager and also in the 'thirties: an Early Minoan house of surprising luxury was found.

Zakro   Some early work by Hogarth and Pendlebury; but the great discovery of another palace was in the 'sixties by N. Platon.

Sites in Greece and the Aegean

Athens   Mycenaean finds have been made, both on the Acropolis and below, by the Germans in the 1920's and the Americans in the 'thirties and 'fifties.

Dendra   This Peloponnesian site, where the suit of armour was found, was excavated by the Americans in the 'twenties and by the Swedes in the late 'fifties.

Enkomi   A site in Cyprus excavated by the French; some of its Minoan-type finds have been shown in the British Museum.

Iasos   A site in Asia Minor recently excavated by Dr. Doro Levi.

Lekadi   A site in Euboea recently excavated by the British School.

Lerna   A site in the Peloponnese, excavated by J. Caskey in the 'fifties.

Orchomenos   A site in Euboea excavated by Schliemann in 1881 and by later Germans in the twentieth century.

Phylakopi   A site in the Island of Melos, first worked by Bosanquet in 1901.

Pylos   The great work here was begun by Carl Blegen in 1935 and continued by other Americans and also Prof. Marinatos, tholos tombs being found.

Smyrna   Excavations near the old town by British and Turkish teams in the 'forties.

Sparta   British excavations from 1906; but Sparta, even up to classical times, boasted little in the way of buildings.

Thebes   Greek-sponsored excavations in the 'sixties, but on sites made difficult by the fact that the modern city is on top of the old: signs of a Mycenaean palace and frescoes of bull-catching.

Thera   S. Marinatos has been doing the main work here; also Mrs. A. Vermeulle and A. Galanopoulos.

Troy   Schliemann in the 1870's, and Carl Blegen in the 1930's.

Tiryns   Schliemann in 1876 and, with his more careful and scientific assistant Prof. Dörpfeld in 1884. Further German work in the 1930's.

Vaphio   The famous cups were found, under the direction of Tsountas, in 1889.

Select Bibliography and Suggestions for Further Reading

A *General Background*
The following are suggested:

Bibby, Geoffrey, *The Testimony of the Spade*, 1957
De Burgh, W. G. *The Legacy of the Ancient World*, 1923, and Penguin Books, 1961
Childe, Gordon, *What Happened in History*, 1942 and Penguin Books, 1946
Hall, H. R., *Ancient History of the Near East*, 1942
Mellersh, H. E. L., *From Ape Man to Homer*, 1962
Parkinson, C. N., *East and West*, 1963
Wells, H. G., *A Short History of the World*, 1922, and Penguin Books, 1952

The above will, in their references or bibliographies, give guidance to more specific or technical books. Three books giving short accounts of the three major early civilizations are:

Aldred, Cyril, *The Egyptians*, 1961
Gurney, O. R., *The Hittites*, 1952
Saggs, H. W. F., *The Greatness That Was Babylon*, 1962

B. *The Early Greeks*
The following are suggested:

Andrewes, A., *The Greeks* (Hutchinson's History of Human Society series), 1967
Blegen, Carl W., *Guide to the Palace of Nestor*, 1962 ·
— *The Trojans*, 1963
Desborough, V. R. d'A., *The Last Mycenaeans and Their Successors*, 1964
Finlay, M. I., *The World of Odysseus*, 1956
Kitto, H. D. F., *The Greeks*, Penguin Books, 1951

Myres, J. L., *Who Were the Greeks?* 1930
Nilsson, M. P., *Homer and Mycenae*, 1935
Rieu, E. V., *The Iliad*, Penguin Books, 1950 (the brilliant prose translation; Robert Graves has done a partly verse translation, and Alexander Pope did one wholly in verse)
— *The Odyssey*, Penguin Books, 1945
Rose, H. J. *Primitive Religion in Greece*, 1925
Vermeule, A. E., *Greece in the Bronze Age*, 1969
Wace, A. J. B., *Mycenae*, 1949

C. *The Minoans*
The following are suggested:
Alexious, S.; Platon, N.; Guanella, H., *Ancient Crete*, 1968 (Informative text by these three experts, around brilliant photographs by Leonard von Matt)
Evans, Arthur, *The Palace of Minos*, five volumes, 1921 to 1935, (major and definitive books, highly illustrated and including Gillérion's reproductions)
Evans, Joan, *Time and Chance, the Story of Arthur Evans and His Forebears*, 1943
Galanopoulos, A., and Bacon, E., *Atlantis*, 1969
Graham, J. W., *The Palaces of Crete*, 1962
Hawes, C. H. & H., *Crete, the Forerunner of Greece*, 1909 (particularly about Gournia)
Hutchinson, R. W., *Prehistoric Crete*, Penguin Books, 1962 (with an exhaustive bibliography)
Pendlebury, J. D. S., *The Archaeology of Crete*, 1939
— *A Handbook of the Palace of Minos at Knossos*, 1933
Platon, N., *Crete*, 1966 (in the Archaeologia Mundi series; highly illustrated and also with a good bibliography)

D. *The Minoans and the Mycenaeans*
The following books are suggested:
Alsop, Jos., *From the Silent Earth*, 1964
Carpenter, Rhys, *Discontinuity in Greek Civilization*, 1966
Cottrell, Leonard, *The Bulls of Minos*, 1951
— *The Lion Gate*, 1963
Glotz, G., *The Aegean Civilization*, 1925
Hawkes, Jacquetta, *The Dawn of the Gods*, 1968
Higgins, C. R., *Minoan and Mycenaean Art*, 1967

Matz, Friedrich, *Crete and Early Greece*, 1962 (beautifully illustrated)

Marinatos, S., *Crete and Mycenae*, 1960 (with brilliant photographs by Max Hirmer)

Palmer, L. R., *Mycenaeans and Minoans*, 1965 (including his views on the Linear B script)

Ventris, M., and Chadwick J., *Documents in Mycenaean Greek*, 1956

Index